All You Want Is Money, All You Need Is Love

Sexuality and Romance in M

Rachel Dwyer

CASSELL
London and New York

For Michael

Like a dear friend, like all one's kin,
Like all desires, like a fortune, like life itself
Is her husband to a woman, and his wedded wife to a man.

Kalidasa, *Malati and Madhava*, VI, 18

Cassell
Wellington House, 125 Strand, London WC2R 0BB
370 Lexington Avenue, New York, NY 10017-6550

First published 2000

© Rachel Dwyer 2000

British Library Cataloguing-in-Publication Data
A catalogue record for this book is available from the British Library.

ISBN 0-304-70320-6 (hardback)
     0-304-70321-4 (paperback)

Library of Congress Cataloging-in-Publication Data
Dwyer, Rachel.
      All you want is money, all you need is love / Rachel Dwyer.
      p. cm.
      Includes bibliographical references and index.
      ISBN 0-304-70320-6 – ISBN 0-304-70321-4 (pbk.)
      1. Indic fiction (English)—History and criticism. 2. Upper class—India
—20th century—Social conditions. 3. Elite (Social sciences)—India—20th
century—History. 4. Love in literature. 5. Love in motion pictures. I. Title.

PR9499.3.D99 A79 2000
8234–dc21

                                                                99-047860

Typeset by BookEns Ltd, Royston, Herts.
Printed and bound in Great Britain by Biddles Ltd, Guildford & King's Lynn

Contents

Foreword

Sexuality and romance in Modern India? But of course. The Ancient India one has been done and written to death. Trust the English to even think of wanting to pick such a topic for research. But Dr Rachel Dwyer's work in *All You Want Is Money, All You Need Is Love* is truly remarkable. As page after page unfolds one cannot but admire the author's acute and painstaking effort at unravelling, with almost scientific precision, what the topic means to her and thereby indeed to all of us.

As a professional actor, what interests me most, of course, is her inclusion of Hindi cinema as one of the subjects of discussion. The Indian cinema from its origin almost one hundred years ago has for most of its life been a medium that has traditionally been looked down upon culturally and referred to as something cheap and frivolous. It is to the credit of the film industry and its resilience that today Hindi cinema has almost become a parallel culture. Its phenomenal reach, not only in India but outside Indian shores as well, has suddenly provoked the so-called elitist and the purist culture-vulture to sit up and take notice. Hindi cinema has now become an integral part of our national existence.

It is extremely creditable, therefore, to find Dr Rachel Dwyer, a Britisher from the School of Oriental and African Studies, London, coming out with a very precise and analytical dissertation on an area totally alien to her. It has the capability of surprising the severest critic.

Issues, events and research that were perhaps hitherto done and looked at almost with casual disdain have been picked up by her and analysed, in so typically Western a manner. As an Indian I would perhaps have overlooked a great deal of what Indian cinema has produced, but the author's clinical manner backed up by severe theory makes you shift rather sheepishly in your chair, with mouth wide open. The only grey areas are the assumptions derived through information that Dwyer has picked up from film glossies. This is unfortunate, since they are not the true representations of many of the happenings that she refers to. That apart, this is incredible documentation, meant for serious notice and not just for posterity.

Amitabh Bachchan
Mumbai, October 1999

Acknowledgements

I should like to acknowledge my thanks to the following:

My friends in India who have provided me with warm hospitality, and sound advice at so many levels: in Bombay, Shaad Ali, Pamela Chopra, Shobha Dé, Imtiaz, Anil and Ayesha Dharker, Reima and Owais Husain, Udita Jhunjhunwala, Aamir and Reena Khan, Maithili Rao, Amrut, Rekhi, Monisha and Sonal Shah; in Delhi, Suzanne Goldenberg, Ashis Nandy, Ranjana Sengupta, Patricia Uberoi and Ravi Vasudevan.

Those who provided materials and other information: the indefatigable Jerry Pinto; Suresh Chabria and the library staff of the National Film and Television Archive, Pune; Ashok Row Kavi of *Bombay Dost*; Khalid Mohamed and the staff of *Filmfare*; and Ashwin Varde and the staff of *Stardust*; Titu Ahluwalia and his colleagues at MARG organization; Roy Singh for his advice on Chapter 3; and the late Iqbal Masud. Thanks to Karan Johar for allowing me to use images from his film *Kuch Kuch Hota Hai* for the cover of the book.

The people who gave me their advice and often extended interviews: Yash, Pamela, Aditya and Uday Chopra, Kiddy and Beena Chadha; the staff of Yashraj Films (especially, Sally Fernandes, Sahdev Ghei, Avtar Panesar and Mr Vakil); Shobha and Dilip Dé; Javed Akhtar, Amitabh Bachchan, Madhuri Dixit, M. F. Husain, Rishi Kapoor, Shashi Kapoor, Aamir Khan, Shahrukh Khan, Khayyam, Dilip Kumar, Rekha, Sadhana and Javed Siddiqui.

SOAS Research Committee for funding most of my fieldwork; the British Academy for the Yash Chopra project.

Those who invited me to present this work at conferences and seminars, for their advice and hospitality: Mihir Bhattacharya, Harsh Dehejia, Theo D'haen, Mark Hobart, Ron Inden, Rohit Khattar, Jim Masselos, Laura Mulvey and Cary Rajinder Sawhney.

My colleagues for their support and encouragement: Faisal Devji, Michael Hutt, Ron Inden, Christophe Jaffrelot, Sudipta Kaviraj, Francesca Orsini, Chris Pinney, Peter Robb and Christopher Shackle.

Two pioneers who introduced me to the study of Indian cinema: Nasreen Munni Kabir and Asha Kasbekar Richards.

Former and present students who have witnessed much of this work in progress, in particular Kaushik Bhaumik, Jessica Hines, Anna Morcom, Kush Varia and Valentina Vitali-West.

My family and other friends, especially *mere hamsafar,* Michael.

Earlier versions of the last three chapters have been published elsewhere:

Chapter 5 'Hindi romantic cinema: Yash Chopra's *Kabhi Kabhie* and *Silsila*', *South Asia* **21**(1), June (1998), Special volume: 'Translatings: Images from India's Half Century': 181–212.

Chapter 6 'Shooting stars: the Indian film magazine *Stardust*', in Rachel Dwyer and Christopher Pinney (eds), *Pleasure and the Nation: The Politics and Consumption of Popular Culture in India.* Delhi: Oxford University Press, forthcoming.

Chapter 7 ' "Starry nights": the novels of Shobha Dé', in Theo D'haen (ed.), *(Un)writing Empire*, Cross/cultures: Readings in the Post/colonial Literatures in English, number 30. Amsterdam and Atlanta: Rodopi, pp. 117–33.

Note for the Reader

Rather than employ a complicated transliteration system which might be confusing for the general reader, I have used a simplified scheme broadly similar to that found in many Indian publications.

All translations are my own unless otherwise noted.

1

Introduction

The idea for this book came to me while I was living among the modern, metropolitan Indian bourgeoisie. As a student of classical Indian culture, my initial reaction to this culture was one of bewilderment. It took much kindness and patience from these people, much work on my part, not least in learning some of their languages, before I began to experience not only the pleasure of their culture, but an understanding of wider aspects of Indian culture and society as a whole.

My basic point of departure is that the modern, metropolitan Indian middle classes are very different from their western equivalents. Given the different historical, social and cultural trajectories of these classes, it may seem a facile point to make, but one must start by underlining such basic facts. While this study is not comparative, some comparisons are inevitable and will recur throughout the book.

Academic research on India has focused on elites or subalterns rather than on the seemingly universally despised middle classes. In this book, I argue that a new middle class, emerging from the lower-middle classes in metropolitan centres such as Bombay, is actively producing and consuming a new public culture. This class has a good deal of economic capital but is regarded as low in cultural capital by the old middle classes, who see its members as vulgar and *nouveau riche*. Since the latter forms a national bourgeoisie which defines cultural legitimacy, their views, expressed in national institutions and the print media, have been taken for fact. This book is the first study to discuss the culture of the new middle class, tracing its roots in a number of Indian and other traditions, and its own distinctive aesthetic style, and looking at why it is becoming the dominant form of popular or public culture in India and yet is denied cultural legitimacy.

Chapter 2 looks at love and romance among the Indian middle classes, as part of the creation of a bourgeois consciousness with new concepts of the person and of individuality. Specific texts are examined for their reinterpretation in different tellings, ranging from Sanskrit prose and poetry to film and television, concentrating on tensions between the family and the individual that revolve around love, romance and marriage.

There has been relatively little serious academic study of love and romance in India, and this book can, at best, only offer preliminary conclusions. Perhaps this absence is because it is regarded as a trivial topic, in the face of social realities, such as violence against women, including rape, bride-burning, female foeticide, infanticide, and domestic violence. But love is important, being one of the central parts of individual and social existence, which can reveal much about the concept of the person, the importance of relationships, sexuality, eroticism and romance. I also stress the centrality of the family, which the new middle classes celebrate as an institution that makes them different from their western counterparts.

I have not written as much about sex as some readers may have expected. Rather, I look at textual representations of eroticism instead of the actualities of sexual encounters. Even these sections on eroticism (pleasure and desire) have been largely subordinated to romantic love. This is because eroticism deals with fantasies which can be fulfilled, rather than ways of thinking about relationships and other people which are always incomplete.

I have made no attempt to define a single Indian sexuality or romantic view but I do suggest some small steps towards looking at histories of textual representations. My work needs to be supplemented by the study of medical books, scientific texts, government legislation, and deviant and criminal sexuality.

In Chapter 3, I look at the middle classes of Bombay. I have chosen to focus on Bombay for several reasons. One is that it is the richest city in India, being its commercial and financial capital. It offers a number of contenders for economic, political, social and cultural dominance, being India's most ethnically mixed city, with no majority population, and has a diversity of languages (including languages not originally from this area – English and Hindi), and religions (a variety of Hindu practices are found along with Shi'ite and Sunni Islam, Zoroastrianism and several denominations of Christianity). Bombayites view their city, which is physically a peninsula, almost as an island in terms of culture. They often regard the rest of India as an undesirable place, apart from a few key locations, and are proud of the modernity of their great city. Bombay is the city in which a great deal of India's public, and often national, culture is produced, notably its Hindi/Urdu film industry. Other metropolitan cities have very different cultural lives: Delhi, as the seat of government, is dominated at some levels by bureaucrats, politicians, journalists and diplomats, at others by Panjabi Jat culture; Calcutta is very much a Bengali rather than a cosmopolitan city; Bangalore has a specific technocratic culture. Research on some of these cities is now under way, while I plan to study small-town middle classes in my forthcoming research. It would be interesting to have comparative material from countries undergoing similar developmental processes such as Brazil, Nigeria, Thailand, Indonesia, Turkey and China, but this all lies in the future.

Bombay became known in English as Mumbai in 1996. Many people have rejected this name because it was introduced as part of the Shiv Sena's 'Marathification' of the city and is a rejection of the English and Hindi names for the city. I am happy to use the term Mumbai when I speak Gujarati, where this has always been its name, but I prefer Bombay in English, just as I call Ireland's capital Dublin, not Baile atha Cliath, in English. Moreover, I find it illogical to use the term Mumbai for the British period and for much of the time since Independence. I cannot deny that this glosses over the politics of the name change, but there is no straightforward solution. The two names seem to be forming their own semantics: Bombay is the old city, which is cosmopolitan and English-speaking; Mumbai is the modern city, which is largely associated with the rise of a politics of religious identity, closely linked with the 1992/3 riots.

The Indian middle classes have been widely discussed by the Indian and international media because they are said to represent a huge potential market (published estimates vary widely from 25 to 100 million people) for consumer goods, both domestic and imported. However, there is little awareness of who these people are, their lifestyles and aspirations. The label seems to cover such a dispersed and diverse group of people that its validity is brought into question. Their exact definition remains problematic. Roland Barthes has argued convincingly why it is so difficult to define this group in non-economic terms, for while the bourgeoisie is 'an economic fact', it

> has obliterated its name in passing from reality to representation, from economic man to mental man. It comes to an agreement with the facts, but does not compromise about values, it makes its status undergo a real *ex-nominating* operation: the bourgeoisie is defined as *the social class which does not want to be named*.[1]

As part of this process of ex-nomination, the bourgeoisie's syncretic processes have allowed it to set itself up as the nation, and as the dominant and anonymous ideology, allowing little room for any cultural contestation:

Everything, in everyday life, is dependent on the representation which the bourgeoisie *has and makes us have* of the relations between man and the world. These 'normalized' forms attract little attention, by the very fact of their extension, in which their origin is easily lost.[2]

Bourgeois culture extends its reach through its anonymous representations in the press, literature and other cultural manifestations, whereby it becomes the norm or the aspiration of the petite bourgeoisie until there is an illusory lack of differentiation between the classes.

The flight from the name 'bourgeois' is not therefore an illusory, accidental, secondary, natural or insignificant phenomenon: it is the bourgeois ideology itself, the process through which the bourgeoisie transforms the reality of the world into an image of the world, History in to Nature. And this image has a remarkable feature: it is upside down. The status of the bourgeoisie is particular, historical: man as represented by it is universal, eternal.[3]

In order to explore this wider bourgeois ideology, I look at their cultural and textual products and questions of 'taste'. I find three major sections of the middle classes in Bombay, namely the old middle classes, who could also be described as a professional or service elite; the lower-middle classes, or petite bourgeoisie, and a group which I label the 'new middle classes'. This last group is visible socially: located at the upper end of the economic spectrum in Bombay, they have non-landed wealth (although many now have wealth from Bombay property inflation), which they use for their patterns of relatively high consumption, they live in western suburbs (the 'right side of the tracks' being easily marked as west of the railway lines), and they speak English as one of their major languages.

The new middle classes would largely reject the term 'middle class', which in Bombay refers more to the lower-middle classes. They refer to themselves as 'upper class'; the professional middle classes call them the 'nouveau riche'. Yet they are located culturally within the middle classes, having largely risen from the lower-middle classes, to create a new space in the middle classes, separate from the grands bourgeoises and the old middle classes. Many would argue that they actually constitute an elite, in terms of economics and because they are mostly drawn from the upper castes, and that they are in no way 'middling'. Yet they are contesting the middle ground, the centre of Indian life. This study is looking at a possible moment of succession, or at least a struggle for succession, being fought between the old and new middle classes, for this middle ground. This is in fact a tussle for hegemony of India's national culture. I argue that the present struggle between the two groups is so bitter, partly because of this ex-nomination of the bourgeoisie, where unnameable ideologies have come into conflict.

In the remaining chapters, I look at three key areas of modern Indian public culture, beginning in Chapter 4 with its dominant form, namely the commercial or popular Hindi cinema. One of the key issues that interest me is the pleasure of the text. Cinema studies have emphasized the importance of sexual desire, and here I examine its manifestations and cultural specificities, in particular situating it in the context of notions of love and romance and the family.

In Chapter 5 I examine two key films of Yash Chopra, a director/ producer whose name in India is almost synonymous with the romantic genre, where he reconciles the romantic couple into a new depiction of the loving bourgeois family. I then look at two cultural products which have developed from the film industry, the film-based gossip magazines (Chapter 6) and popular fiction in English (Chapter 7), which emerged in Bombay in the 1970s and late 1980s respectively. My focus is the interaction between the new middle classes and the creation and consumption of these texts, tracing certain specific cultural features.

It may seem somewhat surprising that I have analysed texts rather than looked at audience studies or reception theories. I should have liked to have had access to these to corroborate my findings. However, the audience's responses are not transparent, they cannot be taken at face value but need to be interpreted themselves as texts,[4] since articulations of desires, love and romance are not a simple matter, as Barthes has shown.[5] Instead, I look at the audience's presence within the texts themselves, at how they are interpellated by these texts, at how they are depicted in the texts and at the reception of these texts by critics. I have tried to link this with what members of the new middle classes and other social groups tell me about them. I also draw attention to differences between the texts' views and depictions and the consumers' views of what the reality is. I also argue that texts are a good source of information, since they are produced by expert players in interpreting the desires of this section of society such as Shobha Dé and Yash Chopra. I consider the extent to which these texts are idiosyncratic and whether they belong to a wider social context.

I have chosen to write about only a small selection of the texts available, because these form a coherent group in their focus on key issues of sex and romance. Cinema is undoubtedly the dominant form of Indian public culture; I have no doubt that the 'Criticism of Omission' will focus on the texts I have not used. These include texts on philosophy, religion and psychology, which I discuss only briefly, giving more attention to literature and film, which are my, and many others', preferred texts of pleasure. I have said nothing about art, which is an important object of collection for these new middle classes and a great marker of taste, although I discuss visual representations in print and in film. There are several media I have not covered at all. I have barely discussed television (on the grounds that its expansion is too recent and too rapid; there is too little audience research; too many inter/multinational channels and showing of western programmes and films; and they have too much coverage of other forms of public culture – film and sport being the two major components);[6] radio (which is not consumed much by this group), newspapers (a valuable source, but largely of the older middle classes, who present news sections as 'fact', although the lifestyle pages, as everywhere, are largely oriented to the social wannabes), pop music, gossip (largely oral, I have discussed only in the context of magazines, to avoid the danger of libel). I could have looked more at advertising, which I mention only very briefly.[7] I have not looked at the forms of public culture which seem to lie outside my topics of sex and romance, such as sport, but which, nevertheless, could be included on ideas of the body.

The use of these texts also allows one to discuss other first-hand accounts that would not be available through ever-changing oral traditions. These are versions of stories which were fixed and codified at some historical juncture when their meaning was particularly representative of some group's cultural narratives. I hope that by using them, by looking at new representations from the end of the second millennium, signs of change will be uncovered.

Working on a new area has its own pleasures and problems. Published research on Indian public culture remains, at the time of writing, extremely scanty. India is not regarded as a major area for research in western universities, and cultural studies is still a relatively new academic discipline in the west and in India. This has led scholars to concentrate on the elites and the oppressed, and so little has been published as yet on India's public culture.[8] There are many studies of Indian cinema, including important critical work published in the last decade by Ashis Nandy, Madhava Prasad, Ashish Rajadhyaksha and Ravi Vasudevan. This, along with the wider thought of Ashis Nandy, forms an essential basis for this book.

I have compiled my own archive for this work, drawing on my time living in Bombay, through observation, interviews, conversations and collecting material from publishers and film producers. I have used a number of archives and published sources including books, newspapers, magazines, films, videos and CDs. The account I present here has its own location and foundation, which has been the time I have spent, and enjoyed, among these metropolitan, middle classes of Bombay. I hope they find something of themselves in this work.

Notes

1. Barthes, 1973: 138.
2. Barthes, 1973: 140.
3. Barthes, 1973: 141.
4. See Ang, 1985, and Radway, 1987.
5. Barthes, 1990.
6. See Merchant, 1996; Mankekar 1993b; Mitra, 1993; and others on Indian television.
7. Rajgopal, 1999; Jeffrey, 1996 and [1999].
8. See Dwyer and Pinney [2000].

2

Tales of Love

Introduction

In this chapter, I examine theories of love and their relation to ideas about sex and romance, most of which have emerged in western traditions. Sex as a biological act is discussed only in its association with the erotic, which, like the romantic, is culturally specific. Looking at certain Indian texts which are of enduring cultural significance, existing simultaneously in high culture and popular discourse, I demonstrate how the privileging of erotic love has severe limitations for the study of Indian popular culture, where other forms of love, notably the familial, are often regarded more highly and are often integral to erotic and romantic relationships. I then suggest how one might trace an Indian language of love.

I use the terms 'western' and 'Indian' as broad, non-essentialist categories covering a spectrum of ideas and attitudes. Given the historical interactions between western and Indian cultures and the plurality of traditions and beliefs drawn on by individuals within them, the terms may seem redundant. But, in common with many academic discourses (Orientalism, post-colonial discourse theory, etc.), I employ them as a useful shorthand.

I first examine love in western traditions, where it has been an object of scrutiny for philosophers, psychologists, creative writers and literary critics. I do not attempt a systematic analysis, which would be reductive; instead I suggest how one might open up this area of enquiry. I have not found Indian equivalents for these studies so I have looked instead at certain key texts for discussions of love across a broad spectrum of ideologies. I do not even begin to give a history of Indian sexuality, but wish to introduce the background to ideas of love and romance in modern India. Little mention is made here of the twentieth century since certain key media and texts are explored in greater detail in the later chapters of this book.

Love is often taken to mean romantic love, namely the love between a couple, including its romantic and erotic aspects. This is the kind of love which is most talked about in the contemporary west, in all cultural production, but perhaps most strikingly in popular culture where it forms the key elements of film, popular music, soap operas, etc. The very predominance of romantic love encourages one to talk more about it, whereas other forms of love, such as the love of country or the love of God, have become restricted discourses. The reasons underlying this current fashion for privileging romantic love need to be explored, looking at discourses on pleasure and sexuality.

History of love

The history of love concerns the nature of love as well as ideas about love. But here I discuss a few key arguments, concentrating on the recent past. Irving Singer's three-volume history of love[1] traces love in western culture, highlighting the tensions between sexual or physical desire and love, from Plato, through the Middle Ages – where there was great ambiguity about the relationship of sexuality and love, in particular in the ideal of courtly love, where sexual desire is a result rather than a cause of love – up to the Romantic ideal. In Romantic love, whose vestiges remain with us today, sexual desire forms an essential part of love, harmonizing human and religious love by accentuating common elements of sexuality. Creativity is seen to arise through eroticism, and the power of love has the ability to transform the lovers.

Western ideas of love and sex changed radically with the rise of the bourgeoisie and the advent of ideologies of modernity. Peter Gay[2] has highlighted the role of the bourgeoisie in redefining the nature of love, as it becomes an intimate and private phenomenon. Drawing on psycho-analytic theories, he looks at tensions in the bourgeoisie between the avant-garde and conservativism. The current preoccupation with seeking individual or personal satisfaction through self-expression draws on the modern idea of sexuality as a key to defining the self, as explored by Michel Foucault.[3] He contended that what we regard as sexuality is the product of the nineteenth-century bourgeois subject. Anthony Giddens[4] argues that this evolutionary change in the way of knowing oneself through relationships of intimacy and sexual relations is central to modernity and the rise of the bourgeoisie.

The women's and Gay Liberation movements have also seen sexuality, albeit along with gender, as a way of defining the self. Yet love, while located in part in the family (marriage, parenthood, childhood in particular), reaches out beyond it to form dense networks of relationships. It is neither a means of self-definition nor an object of legislation like the sexual act and sexuality. Instead, the nature of love has been the major object of discussion for philosophers (including religious philosophers) and creative writers and whose pursuit forms a central part of most people's lives.

For the purposes of the present volume, I look only at writings on modern love, aware of the fact that ideas about the nature of love are deeply rooted in western knowledge systems.

Philosophers on love

There are few restrictions on the object of love. For José Ortega y Gasset 'Love is a pure sentimental activity towards an object, which can be anything.'[5] In contrast, Robert Brown[6] points out that love does not have to be directed at a particular goal. It is not clear whether love is based on judgement or emotion, but the object of love is not necessarily worthy of love and hence love is not a virtue. Singer[7] argues that love requires both appraisal and bestowal and hence an evaluation of the other. It does not have to be reciprocal: one may love without being loved in return.

Loving needs to be distinguished from liking. Brown deftly points out a major difference between the two in that like has synonyms such as 'appreciate', 'be drawn to', and is not necessarily emotional, whereas love relates to one's deepest hopes, wishes and values. Love may be confused with infatuation – an extravagant, foolish, overvaluing of the object of love. It differs from loving care and benevolence, which do not entail loving the object.

The relationship between love and sexual desire is the most entangled and in need of separation. Singer[8] discusses love in its wider manifestations including the love of God, love of one's country, the love of friends, familial love and so on. He subdivides his category of sexual love into the libidinal, erotic, and romantic, three categories which largely coincide with those of Octavio Paz:[9] sexuality, eroticism and love. Libidinal love covers a range of meanings usually discussed under the heading of sexuality. For the purposes of this study, sexuality is the least important of these categories. It touches on all other aspects of sexual love in that all forms of love are biologically driven to some extent.[10] However, as it is an innate, universal, biological function and hence one that is not culturally specific (although its regulation and perceptions are) or even specific to humans as erotic and romantic love, I focus on these latter two terms. We need to try to separate the categories of the erotic and the romantic while recognizing their interdependence. For example, romantic love, while it may diminish sex (libidinal), augments erotic love.

In the view of Ortega y Gasset, desire can be satisfied, whereas love is eternally unsatisfied.[11] Desires may arise and depart rapidly whereas love must be prolonged and continuous. Love affects more parts of personality and in greater depth than desire. Brown defines sexual desire as the wish for contact with another body and the pleasure which that produces. Singer argues that sexual love may be passionate, involving ardent emotions, and sensuous, sensory excitation, but these can exist independently of love. He also argues that sexual desire is likely to change in married love, where there are often no obstacles to extensive and intensive intimacy – hence his categories of romantic passion and marital passion. Love may also exist without sexual desire but still be love. The difference may be partly in focus, in that love is for the benefit of the loved one, desire for pleasure. Love means delight in the presence of the beloved and sadness in their absence. Love, like hate, also involves focus, in that one concentrates on the object of love or hate, whereas desires can be multiple.

Ortega y Gasset argues that love affairs should not be confused with love. Singer suggests that one can differentiate stages of love such as falling in love, being in love, staying in love. These stages may involve a wide range of emotions and attitudes in dealing with others, including, as Singer points out, reciprocity, devotion, value and emotion. The reasons why one should love a particular person, apart from perhaps a member of one's family, remain unclear, despite the evaluation of the loved one. Elements of beauty, fantasy based on choice, opinions, experience, temperament, preferences, distastes are certainly present but hard to assess.

To conclude, we still cannot summarize a theory of love for the west but Singer's remarks 'towards a modern theory of love' come close:

> Love occurs when amorous emotion and sexual desire create so great an attachment to the object of one's choice that self-sacrifices otherwise repellent somehow become acceptable. For the erotic relationship to be worthy of being called love it must include elements of caring and cherishing whether or not it is also possessive and jealous at times.[12]

Psychoanalysis, therapy

In popular as well as medical and other discourses in the west, psychoanalysis has become one of the dominant modes for thinking about the person and about love. Is love, as Freud said, a necessary part of human civilization? Singer shows that Freud's work has love as its central theme in four different aspects: (1) Love as the fusion of sexuality and tenderness; (2) Love as libidinal energy, both aim-inhibited and aim-uninhibited; (3) Love as Eros, the drive or instinct of life which attaches individuals to each other and ultimately unifies mankind; (4) Love as the mixture and dynamic interfusion of Eros with the death-drive which is inseparable from it.[13]

Yet this understanding ultimately reduces love to a sexuality in that all its manifest forms are founded on a single group of instincts. Indeed, as Freud writes in his 'Three essays on the theory of sexuality': 'It may well be that nothing of considerable importance can occur in the organism without contributing some component to the excitation of the sexual instinct.'[14] He sees love (Eros) along with death (Thanatos) as one of two major drives. Love's major goal is reproduction but it is also a basic requirement of civilized society. Freud's reading is essentialist, in that the human libido has a single, fixed and definite goal towards which it drives itself, namely heterosexual coitus. Melanie Klein has extended the biological function to cover the need to love and to be loved.[15]

The psychoanalytic viewpoint has been refined by Freud's more subtle readers such as Adam Phillips,[16] in particular in his essay 'On love',[17] in which he writes that for Freud falling in love is 'a reminder of an impossibility', while for Lacan, 'love is giving something you haven't got to someone who doesn't exist'. He points out that psychoanalysis shows that falling in love is how one gets to know oneself and another person, the consequences of which we shall look at briefly in the section below on postmodern love.

Therapy, much of it deriving with various degrees of looseness from Freud's theories of the mind and the idea of the talking cure, has pervaded much of western public or popular culture appearing overtly in film, television soaps, chat shows, women's magazines, self-help books, etc., mostly in genres disparaged by intellectuals.[18] Its profound impact can be seen in the effect of its technical vocabulary on everyday language ('the libido', 'the unconscious', and the 'ego'). Forms of psychoanalytic discourse have entered western culture so thoroughly that it is almost impossible to discuss people or their emotions without recourse to these and other concepts – 'fetishism', 'narcissism', 'repression' – taken from psychoanalysis.

Julia Kristeva, using psychoanalytic theory, traces love in the western world through the Roman Catholic Church and its saints to Freudian thought. For her love is 'rooted in desire and pleasure ... [it] reigns between the two borders of *narcissism* and *idealization*'.[19] She contends that Freud's thought shows that the psychic space which appeared between the fading of the ancient world and the rising Christian era was destabilized with the rise of humanism, the bourgeois revolution and the 'death of God', leading to the absence of a discourse of love in the (post)modern world. While Freud's 'talking cure', consisting only of words, works through transference love during the analytic experience, psychoanalysis is not an 'amatory code' for 'it asserts the end of codes, but also the permanence of love as a builder of spoken spaces'.[20]

Postmodern love

While Giddens (see above) argued that defining the self through sexuality is a key feature of modernity, Eva Illouz[21] defines postmodern types of love which have emerged in recent years. Her argument is that love and capitalism are bound together by consumption and the mass media. Romance and consumption–leisure–pleasure have become integral to a middle-class lifestyle, created by the mass media. It is the media which have changed culture and social relationships through a wide range of practices including advertising, cinema and photography. A new middle-class utopia has been defined for the enjoyment of love, wealth and equality where the family has become the location for intimacy and sexuality. Much of romance is now located in liminal spaces of leisure, travel/tourism and nature. New social groups have arisen in service sectors – communications (media and advertising), infotech (computing) and international finance – which have educational and economic capital yet lack cultural capital. They are mainstream yet have different aspirations, being obsessed with appearances, identity and the self, which they strive for through a range of consumerist and leisure practices including travel, beauty, fashion, health and fitness. They aspire to certain types of cultural capital but not necessarily those of the former elites. For them the commodity is where they base their aesthetics; their sentiments are expressed in spectacle. Hence commodities and consumption are not opposed to romance but form a key part of it, its preferred romantic situations being sites of consumption whether gastronomic, cultural or touristic.

Illouz finds that romance still operates largely within class restrictions, however these are defined. Most people choose someone of the same 'habitus',[22] in that they prefer a partner with whom they share habits, ideas, etc., and within these class groups certain key trends emerged. The upper classes who opposed the 'commercialization' of romance were the most commodity-centred of all groups in their approach to romance, which they viewed as 'companionate leisure'. Illouz analysed the complaints of lower-class women about their men as showing that to achieve the standard western definition of romance requires middle-class cultural competence and lifestyle.[23] She argues further that modern love comprises three major elements: the sexual, the ritual-consumerist, and the rational-economic. Romance, in her view, is about individualism and self-realization. Love does not arise naturally but needs to be worked at; there is a science of love through a therapeutic ethos. Giddens[24] argued that a relationship is based on authority, rights and obligations; Illouz finds a narrative of emancipation based on self-knowledge, gender equality and communication. All these terms are clearly associated with Enlightenment views which, given the middle-class locus of love, will be examined in later chapters in association with the Indian bourgeoisie.

Love, literature and language

While much, if not the majority of, literature is about love, the study of love has been peripheral to writing about literature. Several literary authors, including Stendhal, Balzac and Paz, have written essays or even books on love, yet it is not a topic which literary theory has often addressed. Perhaps this is because ideas about romance have pejorative connotations concerning 'pulp' novels,[25] magazines and soap operas, and are associated with sentimentality.[26]

Singer discusses several canonical literary figures in his three-volume study of love, so here I mention only two literary and cultural theorists whose ideas about love and language I have found particularly suggestive: Roland Barthes and Julia Kristeva.

Kristeva recognizes the difficulties of a language of love:

> The language of love is impossible, inadequate, immediately allusive when one would like it to be most straightforward; it is a flight of metaphors – it is literature.[27]

Barthes has shown, in his study of the fragments available to lovers,[28] that this most personal of all human experiences is structured and constrained by language:

> throughout any love life, figures occur to the lover without any order, for on each occasion they depend on an (internal or external?) accident ... the amorous subject draws on a reservoir (the thesaurus?) of figures ... the figures are non-syntagmatic, non-narrative.[29]

I shall return to Kristeva when I say more about the film lyric, and expressions of love in India, in Chapters 4 and 5. Love is one of the most ineffable of human affects: its incommunicability emphasized again and again, as it is regarded as a feeling too mysterious and too intimate to be explained. Love and affection are expressed in language, yet these require more than simple translations since emotions are labelled differently in different societies.[30] How can these experiences be communicated? The simple distinction in English between the verbs 'like' and 'love' is not seen even in all other European languages, whereas the French distinction between *plaisir* and *jouissance* is not possible in English. As Richard Howard writes:

> The French have a vocabulary of eroticism, an amorous discourse, which [unlike English] smells neither of the laboratory nor of the sewer.[31]

Yet Barthes points out that the language of love is declining in modern Europe:

> The lover's discourse is today *of an extreme solitude*. This discourse is spoken, perhaps, by thousands of subjects (who knows?) but warranted by no one; it is completely forsaken by the surrounding languages, ignored, disparaged, or derided by them, severed not only from authority but also from the mechanisms of authority (sciences, tehniques, arts).[32]

Love only requires the lovers to reiterate 'I love you', words which are simultaneously meaningless and full of meaning.[33]

Love in Indian sources

These discussions of love provide a fairly slender basis for a study of love in Indian culture. It is clear from the above that love is an emotion, a state. Cultures label emotions differently, by name, norms and symbols.

The rest of the chapter highlights topics that shed light on love in India, some, but not all, of which will be taken up later in this book. One such is recovery of the subaltern voice from history. Given the textual nature of my sources, which are mostly upper-caste, Hindu and male, this goal has not been achieved. While the versions of the texts I discuss here are mostly from elite, male sources they represent simply one telling of the story. The importance of their selection is the fact that the stories are well known to the metropolitan middle classes whose emerging popular culture is my principal object of study. This may well be part of the process of creating a national past for India, the invention of a classical 'Hindu' tradition and a sanitizing of the popular.[34]

In view of the paucity of research on love in Indian culture, I focus on key texts or historical periods in which the discussion of love was foregrounded. I begin by discussing idealized females, women and goddesses, in Sanskrit myth, then mention Sanskrit erotics and their relation to the aesthetic of love in some forms of Sanskrit literature. This is followed by comments on devotional poetry, composed in the 'vernacular' languages, before mention briefly of Indo-Islamic depictions of love. It is worth recalling that such categories are often used loosely: some of the writers of Hindu devotional poetry were Muslims, while the Indo-Islamic traditions are familiar to many non-Muslims. These positions need to be reconsidered further in the new middle-class culture of Hindu nationalism, which is currently engaged in reinterpreting Indian history to silence Muslims, denying the simultaneity of such multiple traditions. These, along with religious and family oral traditions being enjoyed alongside texts studied within a school or academic framework, not to mention the multilingualism of most Indians, are sometimes overlooked in western scholarship. I make no attempt to be comprehensive or even representative in my selection of texts. Most of my sources are drawn from languages I know: English, Sanskrit, Hindi and Gujarati. Those wishing to read more widely will find that much of the published scholarship about the Indian middle classes is about the Bengali *bhadralok* (see below). I have said little about cultures with which I am less familiar, barely mentioning south India, eastern India and other areas. Nor have I said much about India's oral literatures, the folktale, or the story, for example,[35] while performance genres such as folk or urban theatre have not been considered. Instead, I selected my texts on several grounds: their historical significance, especially those stories which have been reworked and adapted over millennia, whose rich developments in contemporary India have surfaced in the most modern of media. The reinterpretations of such narratives have endowed them with the status of myth. While not all of these texts would be known to the consumers of the texts I discuss in later chapters, it seems reasonable to assume that at least one version of these stories would be known to most of these groups. Among the possibilities suggested by these criteria, I have chosen stories which I myself have encountered in different media, different places and different times.

Myths and stories

According to some Hindu traditions, Sanskrit ('polished, refined') is the eternal language of the gods, the vehicle for much of the high culture of early India. It is primarily known as the language of religious texts, including the *Vedas*, the earliest portions of which date back to the second millennium and the Puranas (repositories of Hindu myth). Sanskrit was also the language of early science and technical literature, on topics ranging from grammar to astrology to medical texts. Its use is traditionally restricted to men of the highest castes and Sanskrit was not taught to women or lower-caste men.

The earliest composed texts we have from India are the *Vedas* or 'Knowledges', the oldest sections of which were composed in verse, largely for use at the sacrifices which formed the core practices of the Brahminical religion. (They are still used in many Hindu rituals and ceremonies, notably weddings.) Among them, certain texts relating to love are told, notably the story of Pururavas and Urvashi, the nymph who married a human.[36] However, most of the hymns are eulogies to the Vedic pantheon, and while they contain elements that were later developed in Sanskrit courtly literature, they lie beyond the scope of the present discussion, along with the other Vedic texts (the *Brahmanas*, the *Aranyakas*, and the *Upanishads*), whose focus is on the meaning of the sacrifice and other religio-philosophical enquiries into the nature of the universe.[37]

While known largely for its religious uses, Sanskrit was also the language of collections of fables and folktales (including the *Hitopadesha*, the *Kathasaritsagara*, the *Panchatantra*) and for the two great epics, the *Mahabharata* and the *Ramayana*. While these texts are traditionally attributed to single authors (Vyasa and Valmiki respectively), they are in fact the result of oral composition. As such there is no original text of either, nor one single, correct version but there are many versions of each epic. Their origins are at least non-Brahminical, judging from the names of the characters and given that the *Ramayana* story is first found in Buddhist sources. However, they have been fully incorporated into Hindu religious literature, as key characters are seen as incarnations of gods, the *Mahabharata* now being called the 'fifth Veda'. Although these Sanskrit texts are the oldest extant versions we have of these stories,[38] and are still sources of powerful narratives and imagery,[39] they have no claim to primacy. They should not be read as 'original', because of the plurality of traditions in India, and to avoid myths of origin and authenticity. We should also note that the Sanskrit tradition is predominantly the culture of the male and the high caste while other tellings are found among women, Dalits (formerly known as 'Untouchables') and other subaltern groups. There are still many other tellings of episodes from these epics, whether sung by bards, performed in plays, depicted in comics, made into films and television dramas, or simply told as household tales.

Myth in common speech often means an old, well-known story usually belonging to the supernatural world yet often believed to be true. There are, however, modern myths which can be found in narrative such as those of literature, movies and television; there are also personal mythologies. One of the wittiest explorations of myth in the modern world is Barthes' 'Myth Today'[40] and his updated essay 'Change the object itself: mythology today',[41] where he argues that myth is a socially determined collective representation, which is a reflection but, like other reflections, is inverted as culture appears as nature, which makes it appear to be transparent, as common sense. Myth, importantly, is a type of speech, a form, a mode of signification and as such it is a form of semiology and has a signifier and a signified. He argues that it enters into a higher order of signification than language, where the linguistic sign becomes its signifier, having a new signified and a new sign. Barthes defines myth as 'depoliticized speech'[42] in its avoidance of reality; it is there to allow one to talk about things, make them appear natural, by simplifying and justifying them. One can 'correct' mythology by breaking its message into two systems: the connoted system (whose signified is ideological) and a denoted system (whose apparent literalness makes it look innocent). Barthes points out that semiology's task is:

> no longer to simply *upend* (or *right*) the mythical message, to stand it back on its feet, with denotation at the bottom and connotation at the top, nature on the surface and class interest deep down, but rather to change the object itself, to produce a new object.[43]

Mythological roles for women are found in ancient religious sources and literature, which have been told and retold up to the present. These women's roles are prescriptive as well as descriptive, including Sita-Savitri (selfless, sacrificing), Shakuntala (virtuous, loyal), Durga (avenging), and Draupadi (the woman wronged, whose husbands fail to protect her). Their stories encompass different types of love: romantic and erotic love, love as duty, love for the family; they also concern love's opposite, hate. I have some misgivings about using stories about goddesses in discussing women, partly because no one discusses gods to analyse Indian masculinity[44] and one is at risk of falling into the trap of treating women as some kind of eternal essence of Indian civilization. Yet these stories about women and goddesses, even if we know them mostly from elite male texts in Sanskrit, are still retold in countless versions today across a range of media (film, television, proverbs and tales) and across the social spectrum. They are often juxtaposed with popular songs singing of heroines such as Laila (Persian), Heer (Panjabi) and Juliet (English) in the same verse. Some of these tellings are by women, others are by men but are discussed and analysed by women.

Draupadi – a woman's honour

The episode of the disrobing of Draupadi (*vastraharan*) is found in the *Mahabharata*. Draupadi was not a goddess and her behaviour may seem surprising for that of a role model. In Indian culture, however, women are seen not just as faithful wives or powerful mothers, but also as figures of power: as warriors – goddesses (Durga), queens (such as the Rani of Jhansi[45]), political leaders (Mrs Gandhi[46]), their stories told across a wide range of media. The Draupadi story has been retold for centuries, in many contexts from the Sanskrit epic to contemporary tellings in the television mythological/soap and in feminist discourses. This episode is not primarily about love, although it does concern a woman and her relationship with her five husbands who wrong her, thus leading to a discussion of the importance of a woman's honour and the duties of love. She is rescued by Krishna, who has a brotherly love for her. Its centrality to the current discussion lies in the story of a woman humiliated by men, namely her own husbands who owe her love, and their enemies who hate her. By analysing the discourses this story has we can gain insights into attitudes to women's rights, to violence against women, including rape, and to issues of sexuality, such as the covering of the body, shame and anger.

The core of the *Mahabharata* was composed around the second or third century BC, although some sections are much older. Various episodes, stories and even whole texts (such as the *Bhagavad Gita*) have been interpolated, with it reaching its present form of around 100,000 stanzas sometime around the fourth century AD. The central story is the dispute over the throne between the descendants of King Bharata, the Pandavas and the Kauravas, which ends in a great war.

Draupadi was born as an adult from the fire when her father, the King of Panchala, performed a sacrifice for a son.[47] Arjuna wins her by fulfilling her task of drawing a bow in her *svayamvara* ('self-selection of a husband'), but when he returns home, saying 'Mother see what I've got,' his mother Kunti tells him to share what he has with his four brothers, and Draupadi is obliged to marry all five Pandava princes. The five brothers each live with her for a year in turn. The eldest of them, Yudhishthira, is identified as Dharmaraj, the righteous king. When gambling[48] with his evil Kaurava cousin, Duryodhana, he loses his kingdom and his wife. Duryodhana summons Draupadi to appear before him but her response is somewhat strange. She demands to know whether

Yudhishthira staked himself before her, but receiving no response she appears in front of her father-in-law. She refuses to appear in public because she does not want to be exhibited in front of the elders and she is menstruating. Duhshasana drags her by her hair into the court and begins to disrobe her in public. Karna calls her a prostitute and taunts her, asking what difference a sixth husband would make to her. Seeking neither pity nor respect, Draupadi poses questions about the Law and the orthodoxy of religion, criticizing the assembly where people do not speak out (she is reproached for this many times later during the epic). In the end she is saved from humiliation not by her heroic husbands but by Krishna, who extends the length of her sari. Bhima vows to avenge his wife, an important precipitating factor in the great war, which he ultimately does by opening Duhshasana's chest and drinking his blood.

There are many contemporary versions of this story and I give only a selection of them here. Unfortunately I have not seen Saoli Mitra's influential one-woman dance-drama about Draupadi – *Nathabati-Anathabat* ('Married but a widow'),[49] based on the interpretation of the story by Iravati Karve, which I have also been unable to obtain.[50] In these versions, Draupadi suffers, endures, rebels and asserts herself. She is the opposite of Sita, an indictment of the oppression of war and male power and violence.

Mahasweta Devi's telling of the story[51] is not a reworking of the episode but draws on myth in her telling of the rape and humiliation by the police (the representatives of the Indian state) of a tribal woman, Dopdi Mehjen,[52] a Naxalite from the Santhal tribe. Like Draupadi, Dopdi is tribal; instead of menstrual blood, her genitalia are covered with the blood resulting from police violence, for no gods protect her during her rape. However, she becomes an active agent in this telling, as she refuses to cover herself, rejecting the men's attempt at humiliation, frightening them with her lack of submission.[53] The language in which this is described evokes the bloody image of Kali, as she laughs:

> Draupadi's black body comes even closer. Draupadi shakes with an indomitable laughter that Senanayak simply cannot understand. Her ravaged lips bleed as she begins laughing. Draupadi wipes the blood on her palm and says in a voice that is as terrifying, sky splitting, and sharp as her ululation, What's the use of clothes? You can strip me, but how can you clothe me again? Are you a man?
>
> She looks around and chooses the front of Senanayak's white bush shirt to spit a bloody gob at and says, There isn't a man here that I should be ashamed. I will not let you put my cloth on me. What more can you do?[54]

In a more indirect way, the story of Phoolan Devi, a low-caste woman, beaten, raped and paraded naked, who seeks armed revenge on her humiliaters, has been told in ways evocative of the Draupadi story, notably in *Bandit Queen*, Shekhar Kapur's 1994 film, which is loosely based on Mala Sen's biography.[55] The film generated much controversy over whether it was about the brutalization of a low-caste woman or exhibitionism, exacerbated by the fact that Phoolan herself said the film exploited her. It did focus obsessively on her rape, rather than on other issues of her life.[56] The appeal of this film, which had an international release in India and abroad, may lie in a wide range of discourses including the female vigilante films that almost constitute a sub-genre in Indian cinema.[57] These certainly contain resonances of the story of the goddess Kali.[58] The references to the goddess are clear in *Bandit Queen*, and Draupadi is associated with Kali in folk versions of the story, notably in the Draupadi cult in Gingee (Cenci) in Tamil Nadu, where Alf Hiltebeitel[59] argues she is a folklore goddess who almost prefigures Kali.

The story of the disrobing has produced different gender readings. For example, the Tamil nationalist Subramania Bharati in his poem 'Panchali's vow' wrote that Indian men have taken it as a call to avenge the insults of colonialism, which he likened to the humiliation of the disrobing,[60] while Purushottam Agarwal, in his discussion of the communal discourse of women's status as a symbol of honour and a means of retribution, identifies a fear of Draupadi:

> Draupadi is the mythological archetype of the sexually awakened woman, who affirms herself and is recognised as such. It is such sexually awakened women that the patriarchal cultural discourse is mortally afraid of.[61]

Sunder Rajan argues that the telling of the Draupadi story produces 'shock and sexual frisson'[62] in men, presumably in the form of misogyny rather than voyeurism, while for women, this discourse on their honour arouses the fear of rape and male harassment.[63] One of the most insightful interpretations of the story is given by Purnima Mankekar's study of female viewers of the Draupadi episode in the television version of the *Mahabharata*.[64]

Doordarshan's[65] screening from September 1988 to July 1990 of B.R. Chopra's[66] telling of the *Mahabharata* in over 90 episodes was one of the biggest success stories in television history.[67] This was the second of Indian television's religious soaps or megaserials, following Ramanand Sagar's *Ramayana*.[68] It marked a transition, as India's oldest film genre moved to being firmly established as a television serial,[69] drawing on an eclectic range of tellings of the stories using images from 'calendar art' and film, interwoven with popular music and song, and narratives from the Sanskrit text but developed in a manner similar to soap opera and performative tradition.

Many female viewers took the Draupadi episode[70] to be the key point in the whole narration of the *Mahabharata*. Mankekar examines the reception[71] of this episode among Hindu lower-middle-class and working-class women in New Delhi. She found they enjoyed discussions which allowed them to debate their own family situations and their position in society in general. Their debates on Draupadi as a vulnerable and wronged woman raised wider issues, as she came to stand for the Indian (Hindu) nation, allowing them to discuss issues of sexuality and gender in their own lives, examining their own vulnerability, and questioning the legitimacy of a woman's anger. Cross-generational interpretations emerged as one woman admired Sita's suffering (see below) for her *pativrata dharma* ('wifely duty'), while her daughter criticized her submissiveness, arguing that Draupadi was a role model 'appropriate to contemporary times'.[72] A strange epiphenomenon I have heard reported was that a textile company began to manufacture saris like the one Draupadi wore in the episode and made its connection clear through its advertising. This use of the image of a wronged woman for the pleasure of the consumption of clothing invites its own comment.

Shuddhabrata Sengupta contrasts the literary and other tellings of the episode with their presentation on television as mass media, touching on issues of class at a time at which 'tradition' is being reinterpreted by the Hindu right.[73] The performance of Mitra's (see above) is a questioning of tradition where the sacred becomes profane and is queried, heroes become human, and the gods are diminished. Draupadi eschews an easy appeal to men, but is 'grotesque and comic and serious by turns', thus raising questions of the definitions of femininity and gender identity. Sunder Rajan[74] links the story to a contemporary women's problem, so-called Eve-teasing (harassment of women in public), through the connection of punishment with social sanction and its anxieties about female sexuality.

How do these interpretations of the story relate to one another? They range from the overtly feminist (Mahasweta Devi, and its reinterpretation by Spivak), Mitra[75] and readings which show the limitations of the rights of women, to the conservative, religious readings where television is felt to be truer to 'tradition'. They cannot be reconciled but can co-exist, as O'Flaherty argues:

> Where western thought insists on forcing a compromise or synthesis
> of opposites, Hinduism is content to keep each as it is: in chemical

terms, one might say that the conflicting elements are resolved into a suspension rather than a solution.[76]

Sita: female duty/wifeliness

A colloquial expression for a good wife is to call a woman a Sita-Savitri, a blend of the good qualities of Sita and Savitri. The story of Savitri is found in the *Mahabharata* in the *Pativratamahatmyaparvan* 'The chapter of praise for the faithful wife', which forms part of the *Vanaparvan* 'The forest book', along with the famous *Nalopakhyana*, the story of Nala and his devoted wife, Damayanti. Savitri, the only child of the king of Madra, chose Satyavant, son of the exiled king of the Shalvas, as her husband. He had only one fault: that he had only a year to live. After a year has passed the couple go to the forest to chop wood. Satyavant complains of feeling unwell and falls asleep. Yama, god of death, comes to take him away but Savitri pleads with him, arguing that she must follow her husband. He is impressed with her arguments and grants her a series of boons, restoring her father-in-law's sight and his throne, a hundred sons to her father, a hundred for herself and Satyavant, and finally she is allowed to ask for her husband to be restored to life. She retains her popularity to the present and is still worshipped by women in the hope that she will grant them a long married life and many sons.[77]

The story of Sita, the virtuous wife, is found in tellings of the story of her husband, Lord Rama. In the earliest versions, Rama's divinity seems to have been ambiguous; Sita was always a goddess.[78] Daughter of the king of Mithila, she seems to have origins as a goddess associated with the earth, seen in her name, which means 'furrow'. As Rama comes to be regarded as an incarnation of Vishnu, she is an incarnation of Lakshmi. As such she has all good qualities, in particular those of the ideal wife.

There is no one original story of the story of Rama, the *Ramayana*, there being many tellings in genres ranging from folktales to texts to television serials in India and in South-East Asia, in Hindu traditions and among Buddhists and Jains. There are several key versions, each of which has become the hegemonic version in particular times and places: the Sanskrit *Ramayana* of Valmiki (composed between the second century BC and the second century AD), the Tamil *Iramavataram* of Kampan (ninth century) and the Hindi (Avadhi) *Ramcharitmanas* of Tulsidas (sixteenth century),[79] and the staging of the *Ramlila* which has contributed to making Rama the most popular deity in northern India.[80] The story is roughly the same:

Sita is won by Rama, eldest son of Dasaratha, king of Ayodhya. When the king abdicates he is tricked by his youngest wife into banishing Rama and handing his kingdom to her son. Rama, Sita and his brother Lakshman go into fourteen years of exile in the forest. A demoness, Surpanakha, repulsed by Rama when she tries to seduce him, attacks Sita, provoking Lakshman to mutilate her to punish her for her erotic desire. Her brother Ravana, wishing to avenge his beloved sister and enticed by her tales of the beauty of Sita, carries Sita off to his kingdom of Lanka. Rama's devotee, Hanuman, finds Sita, sets Ravana's city ablaze then brings Rama and his armies to rescue Sita. Rama takes Sita back only after she has undergone a trial of fire to prove that she is pure after living in the house of another man. Rumours persist in Ayodhya and Rama banishes the pregnant Sita from his kingdom. She gives birth to twin boys, Lav and Kush, in a hermitage. She asks the earth to open to allow her to return; Rama ascends into heaven.

Variations in the telling occur as some versions concentrate on Rama and Sita's love and desire for each other, some even describing at length their lovemaking after marriage.[81] Some tell of Sita's heroic deeds such as her slaying Ravana,[82] and while various versions of Sita emerge in Telugu women's songs, the predominant image is of the loving woman, who is caught up in the domestic politics of the joint family, its members presented as realities rather than ideals, their domestic life peppered with loving episodes and various squabbles.[83] All versions present this as a family story, with typical family problems and stock characters, such as the jealous step-mother, who threatens the unity of the entire family, the foolish father who is ensnared by a jealous wife, and the devoted younger brother. While the morality of many of the characters has been debated, the women of the story are presented in negative roles, notably Dasaratha's wives, whose quarrels over seeking preferment for their own sons lead to the exile of Rama, and the humiliating treatment of Surpanakha, a woman who wanders about on her own in the forest, who expresses her desires freely, and is horribly mutilated as a result.[84] However, Sita the heroine is seen as the model of wifely, long-suffering devotion. Even though he is a god, her husband cannot accept that she has remained chaste and so exiles his pregnant wife. This multiple wrong of Rama's, as god, king and husband, does not diminish Sita's devotion to him, and it is her suffering at his hands which has made her such a powerful role model. Although not often discussed, her ultimate rejection of him and her return to her mother, may be a subversive attraction to women.

Rama's harsh treatment of Sita has been justified in many tellings of the story, notably in Bhavabhuti's sixth-century play, *Uttararamacharita*

('The later part of Rama's life'),[85] which deals with this episode in some detail. Here Rama and Sita are presented as two reunited lovers who have suffered terrible grief in separation. The loving couple, looking at wall paintings of their exile, reminds one of a modern couple looking through their holiday photographs. His love for her is deep:

> She is the Lakshmi of this house, a pencil of nectar to my eyes;
> Her touch is like cooling sandalwood paste on my body
> This arm around my neck is cool and smooth like a string of pearls
> What is there about her that is not pleasing – except for separation?
>   (I.38)
> Happy is that fortunate man who obtains the thing (love)
> Which is the same in happiness or sorrow, which adapts to all
>   circumstances
> Where there is rest for the heart, whose essence is unchanged by old
>   age
> Which matures as time uncovers it, into permanent deep reflection
>   (I.39)

Rama is seen to suffer here at the repeated separation, but the happy reunion of the couple brings the play to an end.

The story of Sita remains powerful today not only in proverbs and folk wisdom but also in film. Some of Phalke's earliest films[86] were stories from the *Ramayana*, notably his *Lanka Dahan* ('The burning of Lanka', 1917), and many subsequent films have drawn on these themes. Raj Kapoor's international hit, *Awaara* ('The vagabond', 1951), uses the story of Sita to underline the wrong perpetrated by Judge Raghunath in rejecting his pregnant wife, Leela, after she has been abducted by the bandit Jagga. This is emphasized by the singing of a song about Rama's expulsion of Sita due to his wrongly held beliefs.[87] Leela, unlike Sita, has no mother to rescue her from the ignominious behaviour of her husband and dies in poverty.

The dominant telling of the *Ramayana* in recent years has been the version shown over many weeks on national state television, Doordarshan, in 1988.[88] The influential critic, Iqbal Masud, argues that the Sunday morning slot was given to religious television by the government as a conscious political act, setting up the view of the majority as that of the nation. If anyone – from a different religion or ideology, or caste – objected, it would be seen as treasonable.[89] No one failed to notice the coincidence in the timing of the screening with the rise in popularity of the Hindu nationalist movement, one of whose central campaigns was for the building of a temple at Ayodhya on a site claimed to be Rama's birthplace where a mosque had been built (the Ramjanmabhumi site). The campaign culminated in the demolition of the mosque in December 1992, which was followed by rioting in Bombay and western India during which many people, nearly all Muslims, were killed.[90]

Around this time there was a notable shift in the iconography of Rama. Hitherto, he was usually depicted with Sita, Lakshman and Hanuman in a static or iconic pose. In the Ramjanmabhumi campaign, Rama came to be shown alone, his bow and arrow raised, ready to shoot and with a notable change in his physique as he was increasingly masculinized and muscular.[91] Sita's role seemed to diminish from this point and no mention was made of her in the Ayodhya campaign. Ramu Gandhi's discussion of the shrine, Sita's kitchen, in Ayodhya, reminds us of the importance of her role and the centrality of the nurturing goddess.[92]

The *trivarga*, 'the three goals of human existence'

The *shastras* (authoritative texts) associated with the early formation of Hindu practices are both prescriptive and descriptive texts, which tell us about life as it is and how it should be. The central three *shastras* are guides to the *trivarga*, the main goals of human existence: Vatsayayana's *Kamasutra* on the topic of *kama* ('desire, pleasure, love'), alongside Kautilya's *Arthashastra*[93] on *artha* ('wealth, economy, means of livelihood'), and Manu's *Dharmashastra* ('The Laws of Manu'),[94] on *dharma* ('law'). Much can be learnt about family and other relationships from these works. *The Laws of Manu*, compiled around the first century BC, were central to Brahminical Hinduism, and were used by the British as the basis for the legal system they introduced to India, some of which continues to be in force at present. The significance of this text, intended for the high-castes, is not as applied law, but as an 'encylopaedic organization of human knowledge according to certain ideal goals, a religious world-view'.[95] The work covers a wide range of laws and duties to be observed by high-caste men in areas including caste, class, family, and in particular women, whether wives, mothers, prostitutes, or widows. Manu's low opinion of women is well known:

> Her father guards her in childhood, her husband guards her in youth, and her sons guard her in old age. A woman is not fit for independence. (Manu 9.3)[96]

> Good looks do not matter to them, nor do they care about youth: 'A man!' they say, and enjoy sex with him, whether he is good-looking or ugly. By running after men like whores, by their fickle minds, and

by their natural lack of affection these women are unfaithful to their husbands even when they are zealously guarded here.
(Manu 9.14–15)[97]

However, Manu values the good wife highly and her happiness is part of the duty of the householder:

There is no difference at all between the goddesses of good fortune ... who live in houses and women ... who are the lamps of their houses, worthy of reverence and greatly blessed because of their progeny. (Manu 9.26)[98]

The deities delight in places where women are revered, but where women are not revered all rites are fruitless. Where the women of the family are miserable, the family is soon destroyed, but it always thrives where the women are not miserable ... There is unwavering good fortune in a family where the husband is always satisfied by the wife, and the wife by the husband. (Manu 3.57–8, 60)[99]

The differences between the (inherently wicked) nature of women (*strisvabhava*) and the virtuous behaviour of wives (*stridharma*) are contrasted and discussed in detail in the *Stridharmapaddhati* ('Guide to the religious status and duties of women'), written by Tryambakayajvan, a pandit in the court of Thanjavur (Tanjore) in the eighteenth century. It argues that the family is the centre of a woman's life[100] and her chief duty is obedient service to her husband, which

is not only the most effective religious observance for women; it is the *only* one ... Not only may a woman not worship any god other than her husband, but she is also forbidden to engage in any religious observance other than devotion to him.[101]

The text is concerned only with a woman's duties as a wife – there is nothing about childhood, motherhood or being a mother-in-law or a renouncer, although there is a section on widowhood. The whole focus of these texts is women's function as wives, their foremost role in life.

Vatsyayana's *Kamasutra* (second to fourth centuries AD) is undoubtedly the Sanskrit text best known in the west. Or rather, its title is well known, since its contents have often been cited as primarily concerned with the art of lovemaking. It has been valorized in the west as exemplifying the view of India as the site of European desire. These associations have been reinforced by the name *Kamasutra* being used as a brand name for condoms in India (more associated with pleasure than the Nirodh brand with its image of family planning[102]) and for Mira Nair's

1997 film. However, its scope reaches far wider, as lovemaking is just one element in its descriptions of and prescriptions for the idealized life of the *nagaraka*, the urbane man, the man about town. The text is composed in the typical pedantic style of the *shastras*, in the most unerotic style imaginable with endless catalogues and descriptions.

It is undisputed that *Kamasutra,* the oldest extant theoretical treatise on pleasure, is the pre-eminent text which analyses pleasure in the history of Indian erotic literature.[103] Its relevance to the history of the depiction of the erotic *rasa* (sentiment; see below) in Sanskrit literature has also been examined,[104] yet its wider implications have remained unexplored until recently as a new generation of historians has turned its attention to this text. Daud Ali[105] has argued that *kama* (love) is not sexuality in the Foucauldian sense of the location for individual identity or essence, but is 'pleasure', incorporating romantic love, desire and erotic pleasure, along with other ancillary forms of pleasure including singing, flower arrangement, painting and memorizing dictionaries. He makes the important connection between the courtly pleasure of ornamentation and artifice and new ideas of pleasure in Sanskrit literature (*kavya*, see below), arising through its manipulation of language and convergence of mood.[106] Many similarities are seen between the life of the *nagarika* and the idealized world of *kavya* whose pleasure was deciphered by aesthetes (*rasikas*, see below) who found pleasure in this literature.

Kumkum Roy[107] has looked closely at the form and context of the text, examining in detail the way the text defines desire within an understanding of gender relations. For example, the verses at the end of the prose sections, which she suggests may be or have become part of women's oral traditions, may contradict the prose which contains the expected hegemony of the upper-caste male. The Sanskrit text remains inaccessible to most, while translations of the text, eliding these differences between the verse and prose sections, and omitting certain sections, has led to the normalization of the male and the violence associated with (hetero)sexual intercourse (although, as Roy notes, it warns against the 'excessive use of violence which could and evidently did occasionally result in the death of the woman'[108]).

Representations of love in Sanskrit literature

The *Ramayana* is often called the *adikavya* or 'first *kavya*/poem' because of its relatively poetic use of language within the epic form. The high-form Classical Sanskrit literature is called *kavya*. It is not an oral literature, but is written according to fixed grammatical rules with the aim of presenting convention or conceit in a new way:

> The poet's purpose is not just to say
> The moon is like the lady's face,
> But to express it in a different way,
> And with a certain grace.[109]

Sanskrit literature, which flourished until the twelfth century AD, was divided into three major genres of *kavya*, while prose, which follows many of the conventions of the verse, was rarely highly regarded. These included courtly epics (*mahakavya*), which took their stories from myths and epics; lyrics (*khandakavya* or *subhasita*); and drama (*drishyakavya*), which had its own highly complex rules and structures, to incorporate its many components including prose, song, dance, gestures, the *mise-en-scène*, and even the use of different languages by different characters.[110]

A major function of *kavya* is the ornamentation (*alankara*) of language, whether by sound (rhyme, metre, alliteration) or by meaning (similes, metaphor and other more complicated tropes). Although it is hard to demonstrate these in translation, John Brough comes as near as can be imagined:

> The clear bright flame of man's discernment dies
> When a girl clouds it with her lamp-black eyes.[111]

while sound ornaments are seen in the Sanskrit (translated p. 31):

> iNDīvareṇa nayanaṃ mukha aMBujEna
> kuNDena daNTam adharaṃ navapallavEna:
> aNGāni caMPakadalaiḥ sa vidhaya vEdhāḥ
> kaNTe kathaṄ-Ghaṭitavān upalena cEtaḥ [112]

Most highly regarded, and indeed the hegemonic text of Indian poetics, is a treatise primarily on dramaturgy, Bharata's *Natyashastra* (composed around the second century AD although its form was not fixed until later).[113] It gained a wider status as a key to Indian aesthetics in general, in particular in its sections on the theory of *rasa* or taste, although this is best known from its refinement in the work of Abhinavagupta in the eleventh century.[114] It should be noted that Sanskrit poetics, a theory of aesthetics of Sanskrit literature, is concerned with purposes and form, with aesthetics rather than criticism.[115]

> The *rasa* is a generalized emotion, one from which all elements of particular consciousness are expunged: the time of the artistic event, the preoccupations of the witness (audience), the specific or

29

individuating qualities of the play or novel itself, place and character, and so on.

'Generalization' – of character, of event, of response – is thus the key to understanding the continuing Indian esthetic.[116]

The transcendent *rasa*, generated by the work of art, is apprehended by the *sahridaya* ('man of heart, taste'); in other words, it is the effect a literary work might have on its audience. It is dependent on generalization, which can initially look like stereotyping: there are strict rules about character, place, time, etc., and the use of a certain imagery and symbolism. There are nine *rasas*: the romantic, comic, sorrowful, violent, heroic, terrifying, repulsive, marvellous and (a later addition) peaceful. Each *rasa* has a corresponding *bhava* ('concrete emotion or predominant state'): love, mirth, grief, fury, resoluteness, fear, revulsion, wonder, peace. The *rasa* engenders emotional pleasure in the audience by allowing it to enjoy an emotion in a pure, generalized state, without a personal response.

The romantic *rasa* (*shringara-rasa*) occurs in two main varieties – love in union and love in separation. Each of these was associated with particular events and places (a garden in full flower, the song of a cuckoo, the season of spring, the coming of rains), with particular emotions (anticipation, longing, excitement) leading to trembling, sweating, emaciation and fainting. There is clearly a close relationship between the poetic aesthetic of love and the idealized depiction of pleasure in the *Kamasutra*. Both are concerned with a total sensual and aesthetic experience but for different purposes: *rasa* requires an emotional and aesthetic response whereas the *Kamasutra* is preoccupied with the achievement of physical pleasure.[117]

In the courtly epic, women are usually goddesses and epic heroines and hence approach perfection, while lyric poetry often describes an unnamed heroine. The three major genres of *kavya* share many features in the way they describe the idealized woman and her lover. Indeed the hero (*nayaka*) and heroine (*nayika*) are defined by the *Natyashastra* and the *Kamasutra*. He is modest, handsome, generous, prompt in action, beloved of the people, of a good family, young, intelligent, energetic, skilled in arts; she is a repository of good qualities: she must be young, passionate, beautiful, sweet, brave, dignified, etc. She is the idealized beautiful woman, perfect in every way with the stock descriptions of her lotus-face, lotus-eyes, huge breasts, slim waist, heavy hips, arms like creepers, fingers like shoots, etc. She has all good attributes, she is sheer perfection. As in medieval European courtly literature, the lover can only dedicate himself to such perfection. This is not a creative or enabling love, but worship and a mutual enjoyment of pleasure or a sweet pain:

After God made your eyes of lotus-blue
Took for your teeth white jasmine, shaped the whole
Face as a better lily, chose the hue
And texture of magnolia for your skin,
He then grew tired of soft things, and within
He carved from flint the impenetrable soul.[118]

Kalidasa's *Shakuntala*

Kalidasa's status as the greatest poet in Sanskrit literature has never been questioned. Little is known about him and even his dates are unclear, although the fifth century AD is most widely accepted. His works include the *Meghaduta*, two courtly epics (*Raghuvamsa* and *Kumarasambhava*) and three plays (*Malavikagnimitra, Vikramorvashiya* and *Shakuntala*). While his simple yet sophisticated poetry is admired as the most distinguished of its type, it is his *Shakuntala* which is most highly regarded. Its merits are readily appreciated whether by connoisseurs of the intricacies of Sanskrit poetics or by those who have read it only in translation. The lucidity and elegance of its poetry delight even the undergraduate who not only is untrained in the ornaments of the language but is still struggling with the intricacies of basic *sandhi* ('sound combination') and despairing of ever being able to use the dictionaries in which she has to look up almost every word. The humour is light and amusing, and the playwright is fond of even his most disreputable character, the greedy, foolish Brahmin. It is not surprising that *Shakuntala* has been appreciated for a millennium and a half. When Sir William Jones undertook his study of Sanskrit, which led him to hypothesize a common ancestry between Sanskrit, Latin and Greek, an idea which was later expanded to form the field of comparative Indo-European philology, he was advised by the pandits:

Of literary forms drama is the most pleasing,
And of dramas 'Sakuntala',
And in 'Sakuntala' the Fourth Act
And in that Act four verses.[119]

Jones's translation of the play was one of the first Sanskrit translations into English to be published, appearing in 1789. It proved a great success, and was subsequently translated into German (1791) and French (1803). Goethe's praise for the play is well known:

Wouldst thou the young year's blossoms and the fruits of its decline,
And all by which the soul is charmed, enraptured, feasted, fed,

31

Wouldst thou the earth and heaven itself in one sole name combine?
I name thee, O Shakuntala, and all at once is said.[120]

This coincidence of high praise for the play, but for very different
reasons (in India for the emotional scene when Shakuntala leaves her
parental home; in the west for the romantic nature of the story), merits a
comparative analysis. However, it is to the pandits' praise for the Fourth
Act and the four verses of the play that I now turn. I begin by giving a
brief synopsis of the story.

King Dushyanta, while hunting in the forest, comes to Kanva's
hermitage. He meets Kanva's adopted daughter, Shakuntala, the daughter
of a nymph, and the two fall in love. Soon after they undergo a secret
marriage, Dushyanta is recalled to his capital on urgent business. When
the sage Durvasas visits the hermitage, Shakuntala is so distracted by her
longing that she neglects to offer proper hospitality. The sage curses her,
saying her husband will forget her. Her friends, Priyamvada and Anasuya,
persuade the sage to limit the curse, saying Dushyanta will recognize her
only after seeing a ring which he gave her. Kanva returns to find
Shakuntala pregnant and arranges to send her to her husband. On the
journey she loses the ring in a river and when she reaches the court,
Dushyanta has forgotten her and refuses to accept her. Shakuntala's
mother takes her to live with the nymphs. Meanwhile a fisherman finds
the ring in a fish's stomach and as soon as the king sees it, he remembers
Shakuntala. Returning from defeating demons, Dushyanta meets his son,
Bharata, and Shakuntala, and the family is reunited.

The story of this play was first found in the *Mahabharata*, where its
significance is that Shakuntala is the mother of Bharata, from whom is
descended the dynasty of the Bharatas, from which the name Bharat, the
'Indian' name of India, derives.[121] Kalidasa has skilfully adapted this story
to the strict conventions of Sanskrit drama as laid down in Bharata's
Natyashastra (see above). He has also added the folk-tale element of the
curse and the ring, which allows Dushyanta's behaviour to be excused. It
may seem unlikely that there is much scope for individuality within these
strict conventions, but Kalidasa's Shakuntala is no stock character but an
individual who can also stand in as an archetype. When we first meet her
we, and the king, are struck by her innocence which seems to be at one
with her surroundings.

Yet we are soon reminded we are in an ascetic's hermitage, not in a
pleasure-grove, and, as her more worldly friends, Anasuya and
Priyamvada, point out to the king, she is indeed not really of this
world at all, being the daughter of a sage and a nymph. The description
of her feelings of first love seem almost archetypal, even in her

32

negligence of the sage and the rest of the world. Nonetheless, she has become of this world and the scene of her taking leave of her father is one of the most poignant in Sanskrit drama and it is here we come across the famous four verses mentioned above:[122] the first describing the father's grief at her departure; the second instructing her in the duties of a good wife (obeying elders and her husband, her fellow wives and servants); the third about the joy she will experience when she becomes the mother of a son; and the fourth how she will return to the hermitage with her husband when their son becomes an adult. Here she comes to typify the young bride, taking leave of her parents, her family and friends, setting off for her husband's house. Such scenes have become moments of high melodrama in Hindi film, a time when women of all ages will cry profusely. This is seen as the great achievement of the play, which concerns the woman's relationship to her father, rather than to her husband, giving priority to the father–daughter relationship rather than the husband–wife and showing for a woman that the bond of marriage is also marked by sadness, caused by the rupture with her natal family. These verses must have been selected by the pandits for their emotional rather than their poetic content, given that there are much more linguistically beautiful verses in the play.

Dushyanta does not emerge as an altogether attractive character, even given the device of the ring. Kalidasa is obliged to bring in this folk motif to remove any blame from the king, thus allowing the text to conform to the rules of Sanskrit drama where the hero must be noble and the ending happy. To the modern reader, he is unnecessarily rude to her, saying, 'You will find the female has an untaught cunning.'[123] However, like Rama, it is after seeing his child(ren) that he accepts his wife, now she is the mother of an heir, and Shakuntala's forgiveness of her husband at the end is entirely dependent on the ring device.

We have already mentioned how Kalidasa developed the story of Shakuntala from a much simpler version in the *Mahabharata*. Like that of Draupadi above, we may suppose that the story occurred in many other folk-tales and myths in various regions and times in India. In the nineteenth century, we see reworkings of the story by Abanindranath Tagore,[124] and numerous translations of Kalidasa's play into the vernacular languages. It seems likely that this reawakening of interest was driven by the critical appreciation of the text generated by Jones's translation, at home and abroad. Filtered through the new generation of scholars educated in western literary values, it is not surprising we see Kalidasa labelled as the Shakespeare of India, although this is stretching a comparison too far. Yet Kalidasa's appeal remains strong in the twentieth century, and his Shakuntala has been reworked in cinema,[125] and in mimed dance dramas.[126]

There are also examples of the retelling of the story in new versions: we see the story reclaimed by the women's writing in Vaidehi's story 'An afternoon with Shakuntala'.[127] In this tale there are no magic devices. Dushyanta's refusal to accept the pregnant Shakuntala is that she is just one among many. When he wishes to make her queen in order to appoint their son, Bharata, his heir, Shakuntala declines, choosing to stay living in her ashram.

Religion and love

Erotic traditions of lyric poetry flourished in Sanskrit, such as that of Bilhana, Bhartrihari and Amaru, while Prakrit was used for the famous *Gahasatsai* of Hala (composed between the first and seventh centuries AD). The aesthetic of this poetry is reminiscent of that of the *Kamasutra*, with the same concentration on the visual depiction of the erotic, along with the elements of *shringara-rasa* discussed above. We are fortunate to have some excellent translations of these works, often with helpful introductions.[128] A distinct lyrical tradition is found in south India, which had developed its own early classical literature in Tamil. This *Cankam* (*Sangam*)[129] literature included eight anthologies of lyrics which were compiled during the first three centuries of the first millennium. This poetry was divided thematically into *akam* ('interior') or love poems and *puram* ('exterior, public') poems on kings, war, etc.[130]

A major arena for the depiction of love in Sanskrit literature was in religion. We have already seen the religious centrality of *kama* above. Kama was also the name of the god of love, the Indian Cupid. He is closely associated with Shiva, paradoxically, the erotic ascetic,[131] whose love for Parvati was the subject of much Sanskrit *kavya*, notably Kalidasa's *Kumarasambhava* ('The birth of the prince'). This courtly epic describes at length how the gods, in order to procure the birth of a war-god, sent Kamadeva, accompanied by his wife Rati ('Sexual enjoyment'), and his friend Vasanta ('Spring'), to shoot his arrows of mango blossom to distract Shiva from his meditations in order that he should fall in love with Parvati, the daughter of Himalaya, and beget a son. Shiva was so angry at being disturbed from his meditation, that he turned his third eye on Kamadeva and burnt him to ashes, hence the paradox of the god of erotic love without a body.

Much love poetry from medieval India is associated with the rise in popularity of the cult of Krishna, largely associated with the *bhakti* movement. In the *Bhagavad Gita* (second century BC or later) Krishna told Arjuna of three ways of approaching God: along the path of action (*karmamarga*), or of knowledge (*jnanamarga*) or the path of devotion (*bhaktimarga*). The first is hard to follow since it requires one to act but with detachment, while the second is not open to all. *Bhakti* is seen here as meaning 'sacrifice, discipline and duty'. The word *bhakti* is derived from the Sanskrit root, *bhanj* ('to share') and covers 'attitude, affective reality and ritual practices'[132] concerning contact with God and with other members of the faith and participation in worship. Richard Davis points out that it is not a relationship of equality with God, but a hierarchical relationship involving 'recognition of the god's superiority, devoted attentiveness, and desire to participate in his exalted domain'.[133]

This movement began in the seventh century in the south, where there were two main groups devoted to the north Indian gods Shiva and Vishnu. The former, the Nayanas, were an ascetic group whose means to approaching God included learning, action and asceticism, whereas the Alvars taught that the devotee had to surrender to the grace of Vishnu. *Bhakti* brought about major transformations in Hindu practices. Never a single movement, it spread north from the south, flourishing across the whole subcontinent, generating regional practices and variants. There was never any orthodoxy within the *bhakti* movement itself. The core was a personal approach through devotion to a single chosen deity (*ishtadeva-ta*), usually Shiva or an incarnation of Vishnu: in the south, usually Narayana; in the north, often Krishna or Rama. The gods were often localized, portrayed as having human qualities, often living in families. In the south, pre-Aryan gods were incorporated into the Hindu pantheon, including Murugan, a martial god who comes to be regarded as a son of Shiva. In the north *bhakti* began in the fifteenth century around Vishnu's avatar as Rama, which soon has its major text of Tulsidas' *Ramchar-itmanas*. However, a major division of *bhakti* arose here. In addition to the worship of a personal deity, there evolved a radically different form of *bhakti* only in the 'Hindi'-speaking area,[134] associated with the tradition of saints such as Kabir and Nanak. This was called *nirguna*, where the divine is 'without qualities', to differentiate it from the *saguna* type where the god is 'with qualities'.

Bhakti has often been celebrated as a populist movement, but this has also been exaggerated. It was certainly opposed to Brahminical orthodoxy in its views of caste, gender and ideas of God. The Nayanas and the Alvars included Brahmins, traders, peasants and low-caste washermen, fishermen and even a woman. Nonetheless it was not a folk religion, and soon evolved its own standards of artistic expression. It encouraged the growth of temple worship, generating a whole new institution as temples were sites not only of religious practices but also of education. Brahminical dominance soon asserted itself in many of these temples, in particular with the great Vaishnava teachers who incorporated *bhakti* into Sanskritic practices.[135] They were also culturally important as they became centres of music and dance associated with dancing girls (*devadasis*).

One key legacy of *bhakti* was the development of local languages and literatures. Sanskrit was the language of key texts of these new religious practices, in particular the *Puranas*, the repositories of myths and legends. Until the emergence of *bhakti* all religious composition was in Sanskrit, Prakrits or Pali, learned languages of educated men. Sanskrit continued to be used for philosophical texts on *bhakti* and for some of its liturgies, but was used little for devotional poetry, with the notable exception of one of India's greatest love poems, Jayadeva's twelfth-century *Gitagovinda*.[136] Its combination of eroticism and mysticism became the classical model for much later *bhakti* literature, especially the erotic traditions of Bengali Vaishnavism.

The *bhaktas* – those who follow *bhakti* – composed songs in vernacular languages, expressing their emotional and personal love of God, which even today are still sung. Tamil was the only language that had a literary, written tradition at this time, which clearly gave an impulse to these compositions, the first being a mid-sixth-century poem to Murugan. Compositions in other languages followed: Kannada, in the tenth century, then Marathi (thirteenth century), followed by Gujarati, then by the north Indian languages including the antecedents of Hindi. Devotees developed new popular forms of devotional songs (the *bhajan* and the *kirtan*, hagiographies of the new gurus and saints) in the vernacular languages, leading to restriction of Sanskrit to learned Brahmins and the temples.

The *bhakti* movement brought about significant changes in gender hierarchies with its acceptance of women, most regional movements having at least one woman *bhakta*. It also made maleness an obstacle to reaching God. A woman's love is valued highly, as the love of a mother or a lover (see below), and a man needs to love God as a woman. The *bhakti* movement often challenges the family as it puts a woman in conflict with her family, as she rejects worldly values, giving up her modesty in her love for God. The relationship with God is not one of equals and women treat Him as their husband, thus reinforcing the patriarchy.[137]

The evolution of devotional love as exemplified in the *bhakti* of Krishna can be approached through the writings of Gujarat's greatest

poet, Dayaram (1777–1852).[138] I begin with a brief summary of the life of
Krishna, the episodes of which are the themes of the lyrics and whose
emotions pervade the poetry.

It is only the early part of Krishna's life, which takes place in the
pastoral idyll of Braj, that is really important for the *bhakti* movement.
Wicked King Kams of Mathura imprisoned his sister, Devaki, and her
husband, Vasudeva, because of a prophecy that her seventh child would
kill him. Kams spared their lives on condition that he was to be given each
of her children as they were born. This happened and Kams killed them
one by one. The seventh child was saved by being transplanted as a foetus
to Vasudeva's second wife, who brought him up as Balaram or Balbir.
However, when the eighth was born Vasudeva managed to escape with
him and took him across the River Yamuna to Gokul. Nanda and
Yashoda, king and queen of Gokul, had just had a baby girl, so Vasudeva
swapped the babies, taking the girl back to Mathura. Kams tried to kill
the girl, who turned into a goddess and disappeared.

Nanda and Yashoda raised Krishna in Gokul and in Brindaban in a
pastoral idyll. The idyll was often threatened by demons and demonesses
(the demon nurse Putana, the snake god Kaliya) and the wrath of older
gods (Indra, whose rule was overthrown by Krishna in the episode of
raising Mount Govardhan), but Krishna overcame them all, and spent the
rest of his time grazing cattle, playing the flute, stealing butter and
enchanting the villagers, especially the milkmaids or Gopis.

As he grows older, this attraction becomes sexual. He teases the
women in public, making them hand over their butter and yoghurt, he
hides their clothes when they bathe in the river. They become jealous of
one another and of his flute, which is personified as Murali. However,
they are happy in the full moon nights of autumn, when he invites them to
the banks of the Yamuna to dance the round dance with him alone. In
order to prevent jealousy, Krishna takes on many forms so each Gopi
thinks she is dancing with him. Eventually Krishna is recalled to Mathura
to fulfil the prophecy of killing Kams. He restores the true king –
Ugrasena, Krishna's father – and himself becomes King of Dwarka in
Gujarat.

The *bhakta* or devotee approaches Krishna through practising devotion
to him. In order to do this she needs to adopt a particular *bhaktibhava*
('sentiment of devotion'), usually adopting the role of one of the
characters who participated in Krishna's life in Braj. There are four main
types, the first two being less valued and less practised: *dasya
bhaktibhava* ('a servant's attitude'); *sakhyabhava* ('friendship'); *vatsalya
bhava* ('parental love'), where the devotee acts as if she were the deity's

parent, usually his foster mother, Yashoda; and *madhurya bhava* ('erotic love'), where the devotee imagines herself as one of the Gopis, usually Radha, Krishna's favourite.

Devotees visit temples to worship particular images of Krishna, and some Vaishnava groups follow an elaborate daily ritual performed by Brahmin priests before a temple-based image. The worship is divided into eight periods: the deity is woken, served breakfast, dressed, seen off to his cowherding duties, given his main meal, put to rest, woken, given a snack, served an evening meal, and finally put to sleep for the night. Devotees are permitted to enter the temple only during these periods, when they participate in congregational worship accompanied by music. Most devotees keep an image of Krishna at home, which must be worshipped in a simplified observance of the pattern of public worship, again putting great emphasis on song.

The song lyrics are written to express the emotions of the poet-saint, to please God and to raise the devotion of later singers of the songs. If we look at the songs themselves, we can identify a number of themes and look at how these tie in to the emotions of loving devotion. The subjects of the poems are usually taken from episodes in Krishna's life in Braj.

There are many celebrated *bhakti* poets in Braj Bhasha, the language of the region where Krishna is thought to have lived. These include the greatest of all, Surdas, the master of the expression of parental love, whose songs are sung today. There are also Muslim poets (Rahim and Raskhan) and women poets (including Mira, also claimed by the traditions of Gujarat and Rajasthan).[139] The story of Krishna is told in other media: plays about the life of Krishna, the *Raslila*, which are unique to the Braj area, continue to attract large audiences.[140] The later Braj poets composed poems ostensibly on the love of Radha and Krishna, but 'the beloved seems to be an abstraction, an occasion for a catalogue of the charms of women in general, and, even more, for a rhetorical exercise on rhetoric itself'.[141]

I have chosen to look at a poet from outside this mainstream tradition: Dayaram, considered to be one of the three greatest poets of Gujarati.[142] Dayaram's verses (usually described as *garbis*) are on the same themes as the other poets in the Krishna *bhakti* tradition: the tales of Krishna's life in the pastoral idyll of Braj, his mother's love for the naughty child, his amorous affairs with the milkmaids, and their sadness at separation from him on his return to his kingly duties. Their major theme is love for Krishna, as felt by those who participated in his life and by the poet himself, and for those who listen and sing the songs themselves.

Many of the *garbis* are erotic, describing the Gopis' love for Krishna:

Come to my house for pleasure –
To drink the cup of love's *rasa*, to mount the steed of youth.
Come as night is falling, no one will know.
There are holy men in my street; they mind their own business.
When you leave at dawn, if anyone asks then we'll say you were
    asked to pull the churning vessel.
Forget the rest, but come on time to experience this pleasure.
Krishna's lovely beauty stole my heart, words cannot describe this
    pleasure.[143]

Some describe the maternal love of Krishna's foster mother, Yashoda:

There is a constant flood of joy in the home of Mother Yashoda in
    Gokul,
Hearing the lisping words of her child, she becomes mad.

Infatuation happens automatically when one has seen this form of
    Krishna,
He is obstinate, saying, 'Ma, Ma', he asks for butter.[144]

There are small anklets on his feet, as he walks he makes jingles,
The darling totters on his coloured wooden stick and catches her
    hand.

Such a darling, he walks jingling along.
When the yoghurt is being churned, Govinda seizes the churning
    pot.

He stammers, Krishna becomes childlike, chiming –
'Mother give me some milk' he insists. As he says this he seems dear.

Her milk overflows, giving him a kiss, she embraces his neck,
She smells his head and taking him on her lap she gives him milk.[145]

While many Gujarati Vaishnavas sing these songs of Dayaram in their daily worship, Dayaram's followers keep his tradition alive in Gujarat, where he has joined the canon of Gujarati literature.[146] This incorporation of Krishna poetry by the new literatures of India was widespread, and in the later nineteenth century they were appropriated by nationalists. Bankim Chatterjee (see below) reworked the myth to suit contemporary concerns, making Krishna more masculine and serious than his often androgynous, childlike earlier forms.[147] Similarly, Radha is no longer the desiring female of pre-colonial literature, but has become a pure and chaste archetypal Indian woman or, in the case of Bankim's writing, almost removed. Several early mythological films, such as Phalke's *Krishna janma* ('The birth of Krishna', 1918) and his *Kaliya mardan* ('The taming of Kaliya', 1919), presented episodes from the childhood of Krishna, while in recent years, the television serial *Krishna* achieved high ratings in India and has been screened on international Indian channels.

Other literary representations

This chapter has focused almost exclusively on Hindu notions of love. Religion and ideas about love are often intertwined, and this is true of Islam, especially in the Sufi mystic cults. India's Muslim rulers created a new literature in their courts, originally in Persian but during the sixteenth century in a new language that was later to become known as Urdu. While this was a courtly literature, South Asian Islam also had its own popular traditions. These included the story of the obsessive love of Laila and Majnun, Nizami's Persian epic, retold in the Indian subcontinent. Folk stories about desperate love may be linked to this tradition, including the Panjab's Sohni-Mahiwal and Heer-Ranjha.[148] New genres became popular, such as the tradition of heroic romances and adventures (*dastans* and *qissahs*),[149] which formed pre-novelistic narratives that contributed to the development of the novel in India.

Urdu literature has produced a major literary genre, the *ghazal*, which has become popular in many north Indian languages.[150] It is a much-loved literary form, used by most of the great Urdu poets, although it is disdained by many critics of Urdu literature.[151] The *ghazal* is derived from a Persian literary form, consisting of simple, rhymed couplets mostly using stock imagery of passionate love, full of misery and woe. It often draws on Sufi influences, allowing it to be read as both profane and divine: the *'ashiq* ('the lover', can be the poet and/or a mystic), the *ma'ashooq* ('the beloved', can be human or God), concealed behind the veil. The imagery is that of Persian poetry: the formal garden, the rose, and the nightingale (*bulbul*), quite distinct from the traditional imagery of the poetry mentioned above.

The *ghazal* is a performative genre, usually recited in the poetry gathering (*mushaira*), whether in *tarannum* (semi-melodic chanting), or sung, in *qawwali* or semi-classical style. The performed *ghazal* was an aristocratic genre which became popular in Lucknow in the late 1700s as declining court and feudal landowners (*zamindars*) were replaced by new landlords (*taluqdars*) who favoured light classical forms over traditional classical music. It was sung in a wide range of styles by courtesans, who were trained singers and dancers. Even when they began to give public performances, as concert halls and other venues opened and traditional patronage declined in the twentieth century, the *ghazal* remained an exclusive genre.

The *ghazal* was taken up by film composers right from the beginning, although connoisseurs deplored the popularized style and hybrid music of the cinematic *ghazal*. However, it fell out of favour in film by the end of the 1950s and seemed to be a dying genre, until it was reborn on the audio cassette, whose cheap technology introduced it to a mass market. The first wave of *ghazal* superstars emerged – the Pakistanis, Mehdi Hasan and Ghulam Ali – who sang in a new semi-classical, gentle and sweet style, accompanied by the harmonium and tabla. They were followed in the 1980s by a new generation of popular singers (Anup Jalota, Pankaj Udhas, Jagjit and Chitra Singh), using an even more simplified style, a kind of easy listening that was soothing and sweet but had a classy air. The language was simplified and made more colloquial, to be comprehensible to an audience which knew only Hindi. It became very popular, its soothing, gentle poetry appealing mostly to the middle classes and urban elites.[152] One of the reasons for its success is undoubtedly its classy, easy-listening effect, but the poetry itself remains important as a major medium for sad, romantic love songs which have been largely squeezed out of cinema by upbeat dance numbers.

This *ghazal* is important because it is one of the few public spaces left for Urdu literature in modern India, its aural nature bypassing the script for those who can understand but not read the language. Its influence on the Hindi film lyric is immense, with the whole lyrical language of love being derived from the *ghazal*.

The emergence of new literatures

The nineteenth century is key for this discussion, a period rich in western discourses on the Orient concerning its exoticism, its supposed masculine and effeminate races of Indians, and a time which witnessed the decline of the Indian aristocracy and the emergence of an indigenous bourgeoisie. Among this bourgeoisie, which I discuss in detail in Chapter 3, arose a new literary elite, largely in the Presidency cities – Bombay, Madras, Calcutta – but also in Banaras, Allahabad, Lucknow, Pune and many other towns where they expressed their views in universities, societies and public meetings and opined in newspapers, journals and books.[153]

The new ideas of love and romance which this encounter generated were expressed in poetry, autobiographies, pamphlets and newspapers, but I focus on the rise of *the* art-form of the middle class, the novel. Before

I do so, there are two other genres which should be mentioned, namely romantic poetry and the autobiography. Many students in the new western-style educational institutions studied English romantic poetry. In turn they experimented with poetry in their own languages, which they published, taking advantage of new printing technologies. They were familiar with the medieval poetry of India, often being themselves compilers of new literary canons, hence this new poetry had its roots in both traditions.[154] Bengali literature saw the towering figure of Rabindranath Tagore (1861–1941), the winner of the 1913 Nobel Prize for Literature for his 1912 *Gitanjali* 'Song offerings'. Tagore dominated the literary scene in Bengal and much of India, opening Visva-Bharati University in 1912 in Shantiniketan, to encourage world brotherhood and cultural interchange. The romantic tradition of *riti* poetry continued in Hindi, which later underwent a late romantic revolution after the First World War, notably in the *Chayavad* ('Shadowism') school, which favoured personal and romantic lyrics, before being eclipsed by the 1940s Progressive (*Pragativad*) and 1950s Experimental (*Prayogavad*) schools.

The autobiography was another new literary product of the nineteenth century. Its two best-known exponents were Gandhi and Nehru,[155] but many autobiographies were written by women. These marked the beginning of a flourishing tradition of women writing in India. Partha Chatterjee[156] points out that they constitute their own literary genre, being called *smritikatha* ('memoirs') to distinguish them from men's autobiographies (*atmacharit*). Leading writers included Rassundari Debi (1809–1900),[157] whose subject-matter includes a vivid account of her struggle to learn to read and write, Ramabai Ranade (1862–1924),[158] Laksmibai Tilak (1868–1936),[159] a Brahmin whose husband's conversion to Christianity caused agonizing conflict between love and duty, and Binodini Dasi (1863–1941), an actress who wrote two volumes of autobiography.[160] As Chatterjee points out:

> In the case of the women's autobiographies discussed here, the most striking gesture is the way in which the very theme of disclosure of self remains suppressed under a narrative of changing times, changing manners, and customs, and changing values.[161]

These women's writings are an invaluable source for a study of the private sphere,[162] concerned with mostly the domestic and familial life. As might be expected, they contain little about the erotic, but are invaluable sources for a study of women's beliefs about love. They reveal the inner lives of these women, examining their private feelings, doubts and pleasures, and represent the limits of what could be talked about at that time. Several translations of these autobiographies, which are mostly in Bengali and Marathi, have been published in recent years.

The novel

Before the nineteenth century, prose was written in many Indian languages but rarely used for literary purposes. Sanskrit had some notable exceptions which prove the rule, including pre-novelistic prose narratives such as Dandin's *Dashakumaracarita* (*c.* sixth century) and Bana's *Kadambari* (seventh century). At the beginning of the nineteenth century, the East India Company's language-teaching methods demanded prose texts for educating its newly arrived officers at Fort William College in Calcutta, which led to the publication of the Fort William texts in conjunction with the Serampore Mission Press from 1800 onwards. These were only for the six vernaculars (Hindustani, Bengali, Telugu, Marathi, Tamil and Kannada) which were taught in addition to Arabic, Persian and Sanskrit.

Many scholars cite translations as having stimulated novel-writing in Indian languages, and this time saw translations into the vernaculars from a wide range of sources, including Sanskrit, in particular the drama, western classics such as the *Iliad* and western novels.

The novel emerged in a variety of forms with diverse subjects, in various areas of India at different times. There seems to be no particular pattern, which is supported by the lack of a single Indian word for the genre: in 1862 *upanyas*, the Bengali word for a long prose narrative, is used for the novel in Bengali and then in Hindi; the Marathi *kadambari* is taken up in Kannada; Urdu uses *naval*, while Gujarati opts for *navalkatha*; Tamil, Malayalam and Telugu use 'novel'.[163]

Meenakshi Mukherjee[164] describes three types of novel in nineteenth-century India: novels of purpose, covering social reform and missionary enterprise; historical novels,[165] which drew on indigenous pre-novelistic forms to include supernatural fiction set in remote time;[166] the miraculous novel and political novels; and the novel of contemporary society. The novels drew on a wide range of literary sources, including the European novel, but also incorporated a number of Indian narrative traditions.

The novel, along with the short story, quickly became established in India, with canonical writers such as the Bengali Bankim Chandra Chatterjee (1838–94) to the fore.[167] This is rather surprising, given that some of the major requirements of the novel were not to be found in Indian genres: a sense of realism, the idea of psychologically developing individuals, certain notions of time and space,[168] a language suitable for prose and dialogue, publishing houses and the creation of a reading public. In India the association between the novel and the middle class is complicated by the colonial setting, in which we see the emergence of nationalism, creating dense connections of class, modernity and subjectivity which are woven into the novel.

Tagore's *Ghare baire/Home and the World* (1916)[169] is one of the few Indian novels from this period available in English.[170] It was made into a film in 1984[171] by Satyajit Ray, the internationally acclaimed film-maker and absolute bourgeois. The film is a more successful text than the book, which has overlong monologues and descriptions and is (I am told) poorly served by the translation. Both texts emphasize the interiority of the person, rather than the earlier exteriority and surface descriptions, and depict, with a certain nostalgia, this elegant, fading world of the *bhadralok* (gentlefolk).

Home and the World, the eighth of Tagore's thirteen novels, is a domestic, bourgeois romance set against the rise of the *swadeshi* movement in Bengal in 1905 which sought to boycott British goods. Politics loom large in the narrative, in which Tagore explores through a love-triangle many of the key issues facing the middle classes, discussed by Chatterjee in the context of nationalism;[172] the domains of the home (private) and the world (public), and the places for locating modernity, tradition, women and love.

Bimala, a traditional wife, describes her marriage:

> I had the Prince of my real world enthroned in my heart. I was his queen. I had my seat by his side. But my real joy was, that my true place was at his feet.[173]

Her husband, Nikhil, is a *zamindari* ('landowner'), but a westernized liberal, an idealistic bourgeois,[174] or member of the *bhadralok* – a kind and good man. He believes in progress and modernity and so hires a British governess to teach Bimala English, and other accomplishments, such as playing the piano. When Nikhil's friend, Sandip, who has become a *swadeshi* activist, visits the house, Nikhil decides it is time for Bimala to leave the *zenana* (women's quarters) and meet Sandip. Bimala develops a passion for Sandip as she is won over by his talk of passion, blind to the fact he is a self-centred, opportunist politician, whose real interest is in nationalism. Hearing Sandip's words, Bimala feels she represents the nation:

> Only once, I noticed, his eyes, like stars in fateful Orion, flashed full on my face.
>
> I was utterly unconscious of myself. I was no longer the lady of

the Rajah's house, but the sole representative of Bengal's woman-hood. And he was the champion of Bengal.[175]

When Nikhil discovers her relationship with Sandip, he offers her the choice of staying or leaving, in the spirit of western romanticism, but before her mind is made up, the riots which Sandip has instigated erupt and Nikhil dies in his attempt to quell them.

Although, as Nandy has argued, Bimala represents the nation and the two men two forms of nationalism,[176] of which the Gandhian prevails,[177] it is also about love and romance in the *bhadralok*. Bimala falls in love with both men, but since she has hardly met any others, this makes her seem simply naive and inexperienced. However, there is also the implication that women should not meet men, since the inevitable result is romantic and sexual passion, and that this is merely the first breaking of society's rules. Nikhil's love is very much that of Victorian England, and his passion for Bimala has to be reasoned rather than simply enjoyed. Sandip uses traditional Vaishnava erotic verse in his seduction of Bimala, his Shakti,[178] which celebrates Krishna's adultery, realizing that her love for Nikhil was entirely that of a traditional wife, and that Nikhil cannot get her to love him as a modern wife should. Sandip realizes that an invocation of the traditional imagery of love may make Bimala feel her transgression is not merely sexual. Sandip emerges as a character incapable of love, for his relationship with Amulya, a young boy, and with Nikhil, are entirely exploitative, as is his involvement with Bimala. Adulterous sexual passion is seen as ill-founded, leaving the incompatibility of the traditional and modern wife as the central romantic dilemma. Ironically, it is only Nikhil's progressive idealism which would allow forgiveness, the other women of the house representing the unforgiving face of tradition.

The English novel in India

The *New York Times* heralded Rushdie's 1981 novel as path-breaking:

> The literary map of India is about to be redrawn ... Midnight's Children sounds like a continent finding its voice. An author to welcome to world company.[179]

In fact, there had been much prose writing in English in India since the nineteenth century, beginning with Raja Rammohan Roy (1772–1833),[180] but it is not until the 1930s, a time of political struggle, marked by the rise of the nationalist movement and Gandhian ideals, that three major writers emerge: Mulk Raj Anand (b. 1905), Raja Rao (b. 1909) and R. K. Narayan

(b. 1906). The latter is undoubtedly the most famous of this generation. His first novel was *Swami and Friends* (1935), and he has continued to publish in the 1990s. Famous for their light humour, Narayan's novels are rarely about romantic love but are fascinating for their presentation of a traditional Hindu worldview, in which romantic love and passion play small parts compared to other family bonds. His *The Vendor of Sweets* (1967) concerns Jagan, a sweetshop owner, whose son marries a foreigner and embraces western ways. Jagan's Gandhian beliefs and religiosity are treated ironically by Narayan, but ultimately Jagan chooses a life of renunciation rather than deal with the breakdown in his relationship with his son. V. S. Naipaul famously attacked Narayan's worldview:

> Jagan's is the ultimate retreat, because it is a retreat from a world that is known to have broken down at last. It is a retreat, literally, to a wilderness where the 'edge of reality itself was beginning to blur': not a return to a purer Aryan past, as Jagan might imagine, but a retreat from civilization and creativity, from rebirth and growth, to magic and incantation.[181]

The object of Naipaul's attack is tradition, which he contrasts unfavourably with modernity, for he seems to miss an extraordinary feature of Narayan's literary achievement, namely the latter's ability to incorporate non-modern characters and beliefs in the genre of the novel. Narayan's use of English to convey the very non-English-speaking world of his characters is another part of his seamless and elusive talent.

Narayan's 1965 novel, *Guide*, is somewhat different from his other work, in that the characters' behaviour is scandalous, with a married woman running off with the guide of the title. This novel won the Sahitya Akademi (Literary Academy) Prize and was also made into a highly successful Hindi movie. In the novel Raju, a tourist guide, elopes with Rosie, a married woman, neglected by her archaeologist husband. His village drives them out but Rosie takes up her old vocation of dancing and becomes a major celebrity. As Raju begins to feel neglected by his wife, problems emerge in their relationship. He signs a cheque, forging her signature, for which he is imprisoned. On his release he wanders the countryside, and on a halt in a village is mistaken for a holy man. In a drought, he begins a fast, which becomes a news item. Rosie and his mother come to find him, but it is too late. The film version, starring Dev Anand and Waheeda Rehman (dir. Vijay Anand, 1965), has a different treatment of the story, to suit its visual and narrative conventions (see Chapter 4 below). For example, as Raju dies, the rain arrives, suggesting his asceticism turned him into a holy man, with the power to bring rain.

A further version of the film was made in English at the same time as the Hindi one, but this time with the conventions of Hollywood.

A recent example of literary narratives blending erotic and romantic love is Vikram Chandra's *Love and Longing in Bombay* (1997), a collection of short stories, which is one of the finest products of the recent tide of writing from India in English, in terms of storytelling, style and characterization. The narratives are loosely connected, with an orality which gives a certain freshness and vividness. Visuality is emphasized by Chandra's brilliant observation of a wide range of characters who distill Bombay and Bombayites, and their attitudes to love and romance and their beloved city. The titles of the chapters include *trivarga*, the ends of man mentioned above: *Kama*, *Dharma* and *Artha*, but also *Shakti* ('female power') and *Shanti* ('peace', mentioned as the ninth *rasa*). Although 'Shakti' gives us insights into Bombay's elite society, with its struggle for social dominance of old and new money, its bright style glossing its venom, I look instead at the story 'Kama', and its depictions of modern love in Bombay.

This is a detective story, about a policeman, Sartaj Singh, engaged in a murder inquiry, while examining his personal life, thrown into turmoil by his impending divorce. Sartaj and his former wife, Megha, had a 'love marriage' rather than an arranged marriage and had married each other out of a narcissism *à deux*. This places him half way between the suburban Kaimals, for whom love is automatic in marriage, and Rahul, his former brother-in-law, a college kid with a high turnover of girlfriends – new generation 'too bored with sex to talk about it'.[182] Although Sartaj and Megha have other sexual partners, he regrets his divorce partly because he is still in love with her, but also because he is of a generation where divorce is something which happens to other people. Even though his wife rejects Sartaj, his mother is a more loving person, both to Sartaj himself and to his friend Katekar. Sartaj explores the death of Chetanbhai Patel, finding it linked to his hidden sex life, while also carrying out a postmortem on his own relationship with Megha. The Patels and the Singhs were tied by eroticism, if not by love: Sartaj and Megha end up in bed on their last meeting before the divorce, in an encounter described in terms of love and death. After his own *petit mort*, Sartaj

> watched her walk across the bedroom, past the white wall with its filigree of shadow, and he knew he would remember this image forever, this person, this shimmering body moving away from his life … as he lay on the sheets he was possessed of a certain clarity, and he could hear the world ending. In the huge distances of the red sky,

in the far echoes of the evening he could feel the melancholy of its inevitable death.[183]

The Patels, who seem an exemplary suburban pair, meet couples through contact magazines in seedy Colaba hotels. The Patels' eroticism attempts to find more refinement by references to its Indian traditions: Chetanbhai was fond of Mehdi Hassan *ghazals* and is described as *shaukeen* ('aesthete') by the hotel owner; Sartaj finds a page describing the conduct of the man about town from the *Kamasutra*, now just seen as a risqué book for young girls to giggle at, for others to ignore; the Patels kept a statue of an *apsara* ('nymph') in their flat, which their son, Kshitij, a member of the *Rakshaks* ('Protectors' but homophonous with 'demons'), a nationalistic and militaristic youth organization, throws out after his father's murder, his goddess being Mother India, a de-eroticized figure, the daughter of western and Indian nationalism.[184]

Gandhi

M. K. Gandhi's writings are concerned with a vast range of topics, including sexuality and love. While his theories may not have been practised except by himself, their importance lies in his position as the 'father of the nation', and in playing an important part in his struggle to accommodate 'traditional Indian ideas' into the modern world.

In Gandhi, we see the Indian traditions of asceticism incorporated into his writing, but not with their traditional counterpart, the erotic traditions.[185] Gandhi's views on sexuality are well known: his early sexual passion for his wife is described in his autobiography, then after fathering five children in his mid-thirties he took a lifelong vow of celibacy which he famously tested by sleeping with young, naked women to see if he was in control of his desires. These experiments were often viewed with horror by his followers but, along with his fasts, can be seen as his wish to incorporate part of the Hindu ascetic tradition into his new morality.[186]

Gandhi valued feminine qualities highly, and was the first to welcome women into the public sphere, but he emphasized women's roles only as mothers, never as wives or lovers.[187] Bhikhu Parekh's analysis of Gandhi's incorporation of love into his political philosophy is a neat summary of a complicated process:

> He takes over the Hindu concept of *ahimsa*, finds it passive and negative and turns to the cognate Christian concept of love to help him understand and redefine it. He realises that love is an emotion,

compromises the agent's autonomy and builds up attachments to the world; and so he redefines it in the light of the Hindu concept of *anasakti* or detachment. Gandhi's double conversion, his Hinduisation of the Christianised Hindu concept, yields the fascinating concepts of a non-emotive, serene and detached but positive and active love, and a non-activist life of action.[188]

I now turn briefly to two other important locations of ideas about love and romance in India, namely the family, which is proudly upheld as the pinnacle of 'Indian values' and is the prime site for the location of sexuality and love, and the domain of alternative sexualities, largely outside the family.

The family

As Adam Phillips has pointed out, 'If sex is the way out of the family, falling in love is the route back.'[189] The family remains the key arena for the location of love and the erotic in modern India. It is there we find the de-eroticization of love as it collides with institutions such as those of maternity and patriarchy.

The traditional Hindu family is patriarchal and feudal in that men own property and most of the wealth apart from the women's dowry. They also control the women of the family, whom they can even be said to 'own' to the degree that they give and take dowry.[190] This culture values highly women's sexual purity, virginity before marriage and fidelity afterwards. Although the family is much celebrated in popular discourse and culture (see Chapter 4), this may suggest anxieties about its actual decline and increasingly mythical status, at least to the urban population.

The modern, bourgeois family has largely replaced the traditional extended family in at least the metropolitan centres. Pradip Kumar Bose has examined the new normative discourse on the family which emerged in late-nineteenth-century and early-twentieth-century Bengal.[191] There the family became a private domain, isolated from the kinship system and the world of work, creating new ways of

> distributing powers and pleasures. The discourse generated a radical separation between work and leisure, public life and private life, childhood and adulthood.[192]

The nurturing of the male child showed how the family encouraged the personal development of its members rather than the observation of rules of hierarchy and the upholding of wider social issues. The external world was seen as degraded and loveless, whereas the family is a domain of privacy, the location of 'order, rule, discipline, love and affection'.[193]

This new discourse of the bourgeois family exists often side by side with traditional views, rather than the two being seen as binary opposites. For example, while few urban families live together in the traditional manner, they still acknowledge the kinship networks of the traditional family and spend much of their leisure time reinforcing them. The traditional family is still celebrated as an ideal, although people readily acknowledge that the reality can be less attractive.

In recent years there have been radical shifts in the concept of even the bourgeois family, brought about in part by changing notions of women's roles, partly through the work of India's active feminist and other women's organizations, but also through postmodern or western ideas about the body[194] which are becoming current, at least among some of the elites of Bombay and other major cities. While there is clearly no wholesale acceptance of western ideas about the centrality of the body, several features can be noticed. Ideas of self-realization through intimacy, as suggested by Giddens (see above), are recognized although not often practised. Divorce is becoming more widespread, although still on a small scale, with no indication of the west's current practice of serial monogamy. The wider availability of contraception has led to a decline in the size of middle-class families, whose norm seems to be one or two children, leading to an increase in what Giddens calls 'plastic sexuality', a dissociation of sex and procreation.[195]

There is an increasing cult of the body, whose youth and health represent economic and cultural capital, hence the rise of a dieting and fitness culture, and the fashion and beauty industries. This has led to a perceived decline in the traditionally high status of the elderly, many of whom fear that they will spend their old age in old people's homes rather than with their families. This valuing of the young body has been accompanied by the increasing visibility of the erotic couple,[196] notably in advertising, film and television. The Hindi film has long been preoccupied with negotiating the couple into the wider networks of kinship,[197] which is hardly surprising given the predominance of arranged marriage in India, where for many romantic love is not compatible with marriage.

Discourses on the family have been used for ways of talking about the new nation-state of India. The emergence of a new goddess, Mother India, and her subsequent treatment in nationalist discourse, is discussed in Chapter 4 below. Gandhi was popularly called 'Bapu' ('Father') or the Father of the Nation, while Nehru was referred to as Chacha ('Uncle') Nehru. This may have enabled the Nehru–Gandhi family to become such a political force, whose establishment of a dynastic succession on a hereditary principle was seen most clearly on the swearing-in of Rajiv Gandhi as India's Prime Minister within hours of his mother's assassination. India has also promoted itself as a 'family of nations', which allows it to gloss over ethnic, religious and other cultural differences, a trend seen clearly in the Hindi film *Amar Akbar Anthony*,[198] released just as the Emergency was ending, in which three brothers separated on 15 August (India's Independence day) by a statue of Gandhi, and brought up as Hindu, Muslim and Christian, are eventually reunited with their Hindu parents.

Friendship is often viewed in terms of family, with the saying, 'You are like a brother/sister to me', being the way of acknowledging friendship, while older acquaintances are often addressed using terms for 'older sister' (*didi*), 'auntie' (*Maasi*) and 'uncle' (*Chacha*). There is, significantly, no word for a friend of the opposite gender, the term 'male friend' (*dost*, *mitra*) if used by a woman would mean 'boyfriend', and similarly for 'female friend' (*saheli*, *bahenpani*), showing that language is lagging behind social customs. The high valuation of male–male friendship can be seen in the huge popularity of movies in which *dosti* is a central theme, whether the hero has to choose between his love for his friend and that for the heroine, or as part of a 'buddy movie'.[199]

Alternative sexualities

The examples above have concentrated almost exclusively on hetero-sexual love. Western notions of gay and lesbian culture have found an established place in academia via the school of 'queer theory'. The applicability of such sexual-identity politics to Indian society remains largely unexplored as yet, although Giti Thadani[200] has explored the history of lesbianism in India and Lawrence Cohen has written about the gay scene in Varanasi.[201] The basis of sexual-identity politics is rooted in western notions of the individual's self-definition through sexuality and sexual identity, which suggests its application in India will be problematic since the role of sexuality in defining identity is unclear at present. In India some people enjoy same-sex sexual activity without wishing to claim a gay or lesbian or even bisexual identity; it is simply that they have sex with someone of the same sex but they expect to marry and live in a heterosexual relationship. However, in metropolitan centres, there are increasingly visible, active gay and lesbian organizations and publications, notably Ashok Row Kavi's magazine, *Bombay Dost*, which follow a politics similar to that of western activists. There are also gay clubs and a public gay subculture in many cities, which attract a wide range of social classes and sexual orientations. Gay and lesbian texts are found in highbrow literature, such as that of Vikram Chandra mentioned above, but cinema halls that screened a 'lesbian film', Deepa Mehta's film *Fire* (1997), which had sequences showing sexual pleasure between two sisters-in-law, were attacked by female Shiv Sena activists,[202] who argued that lesbianism is a western, not an Indian practice.

Many texts are open to gay and lesbian readings,[203] in particular the Hindi film. A major preoccupation of these movies, *dostana*, or male friendship,[204] depicts physical affection between men. It has been celebrated as homoerotic by many gay viewers, while lesbian scenes are more overt, notably those in *Razia Sultan*.[205] Many films, notably those of Meena Kumari and the courtesan genre, have been read as camp, and provide inspiration for drag performers, from Bombay's gay parties to London's Club Kali's Chutney Queens.

India has famously had a cultural third gender: the androgyne has long been an important figure in Indian culture, whether divine (Shiva as Ardhaneshwari, half-man, half-woman),[206] or Gandhi's ideal, transcending gender divides,[207] or the modern *hijra*, a category comprising eunuchs, transvestites and transsexuals,[208] represented in Indian cinema from *Pukar* to *Lawaaris* to *Bombay*. Indeed, the prohibition on women performing in India has led to a tradition of male imitators, still seen in many folk traditions and in the earliest Hindi movies, including those of D. G. Phalke.

Concluding remarks

This chapter has traced briefly the salient features of the major Indian discourses on love and romance. The twentieth century has witnessed radical changes in these discourses, brought about by the proliferation of media with the spread of the printed word and increased literacy, the proliferation of visual images through the chromolithograph, photography and magazines (especially advertising and fashion), and the mass circulation of music via radio and the spread of the audio cassette and CD. Perhaps most important of all is the medium where the visual, the spoken word and the lyric have come together: the cinema. The interaction of these media will be explored in later chapters.

The last decades of the twentieth century have seen the proliferation of television in India. The programming has consisted mostly of films, film-related programmes, and a smaller proportion of chat shows, sports and news features. An area opening up which I have not explored is that of the serial, often a prime location for discourses of love and romance.[209] Television is most interesting in its capacity to deal with the local and the regional, whether through state television or through the operations of the cablewallahs.

Many other areas remain to be discussed. We need to consider the role of the body, in particular the emergence of ideas of the body that deserves to be loved, promoted by the beauty and fashion industries for men and women, whose popularity can be seen in the continuation of beauty pageants, such as Miss World. I have not discussed state controls over these areas such as legislation on sexual violence (wife-battering, dowry deaths), fertility control, etc.[210] I have also left prostitution, or sex for sale, until the chapter on cinema when I discuss the 'courtesan film'.

Foucault has argued that discourses on sexuality were produced in the nineteenth century by the bourgeois subject,[211] while Harvie Ferguson contends that bourgeois culture is built on a science of pleasure and a renunciation of fun.[212] Giddens argues that in the west, romantic love and the idealization of the couple originates in the modern intimate world of the bourgeoisie, where it is differentiated from wider kinship ties, the separation of the home and workplace and the limits to family size through birth control.[213] He associates these attitudes with woman's subordination in the home and a detachment from the outside world, the invention of childhood and motherhood, and a sexuality formerly not about identity but about reproduction and the *ars erotica*. He points out the necessity of leisure time for the pursuit of these ideals, showing romance is pursued by the wealthier in society, as Illouz argued (see above).

These views show how much current ideas about sexuality and love and romance in the west were founded in the rise of the bourgeois subject. In the next chapter I turn to the rise of the Indian bourgeoisie, focusing on the middle classes of Bombay. I shall return to the other issues raised here when in the later chapters I examine the cultural texts of the new middle classes.

Notes

1. Singer, 1984a, 1984b and 1987.
2. Gay, 1986.
3. Foucault, 1981, 1985, 1986.
4. Giddens, 1992.
5. Ortega y Gasset, 1959: 38.
6. Brown, R., 1987.
7. Singer, 1987 and 1994.
8. Singer, 1994.
9. Paz, 1996.
10. See below.
11. Ortega y Gasset, 1959: 11.
12. Singer, 1987: 375.
13. Singer, 1987: 100.
14. Freud, 1953.
15. Singer, 1994: 3.
16. e.g. Phillips, 1993 and 1994.

17. Phillips, 1994: 39–41.
18. In recent years these have been incorporated into academia in cultural studies, itself often disparaged. Works by Ien Ang on *Dallas* (Ang, 1985) and Janice Radway on romantic fiction (Radway, 1987) have become classic studies. Popular understandings of love in western culture lie beyond the scope of this book. There has not yet been a study of aspects of love in western popular culture ranging from popular song lyrics to women's magazines to Hollywood movies.
19. Kristeva, 1987: 6.
20. *Ibid*. 381–2.
21. Illouz, 1997.
22. Bourdieu, 1977.
23. Illouz, 1997: 285.
24. Giddens, 1992: 206.
25. See Chapter 7 below.
26. See, for example, Anderson and Mullen, 1998.
27. Kristeva, 1987: 1.
28. Barthes, 1990.
29. Barthes, 1990: 6–7.
30. See V. Geetha, 1998, on the language of violence and terror used against women.
31. Barthes, 1975: v.
32. Barthes, 1977: 1.
33. Barthes, 1990: 147–53. This may well be part of the decline of the *ars erotica* in modern Europe, which has been discarded in favour of a *scientia sexualis*, which has produced its own pleasures, namely the production of 'the truth about sex' (Foucault, 1981: 67 and 71).
34. Chatterjee, 1993: 73.
35. See the work of A. K. Ramanujan and Stuart Blackburn in the bibliography.
36. *Rigveda* X.95. Translated with notes in O'Flaherty, 1981: 252–6. See Thadani, 1996: 38–45, for a gendered reading of this text.
37. See Brockington, 1981.
38. The core parts of the *Mahabharata* were composed around the second century BC, although there are older portions. Other texts, such as the *Bhagavad Gita*, were interpolated until it reached its present form of over a hundred thousand stanzas (*shlokas*),well into the first millennium AD.
39. Wendy Doniger, aka Wendy Doniger O'Flaherty, has made many excellent studies of early Indian mythology (see bibliography). She gives an early 'positioning' on her understanding of myth in O'Flaherty, 1973.
40. Barthes, 1973.
41. Barthes, 1977: 165–69.
42. Barthes, 1973: 143.
43. Barthes, 1977: 169.
44. Although Hindi films often refer to the husband being the wife's *parameshwar* or living god.
45. See Lebra-Chapman 1986.
46. Sunder Rajan, 1993: 103–28, Chapter 5, 'Gender, leadership and representation: the "case" of Indira Gandhi', where she demonstrates Gandhi used mythology in her political manoeuvres.
47. The sacrifice for a son may suggest she has some 'masculine' qualities. Draupadi's darkness and the practice of polyandry suggest her possible non-Aryan origins.
48. Gambling, far from being frowned on in ancient India, was often a sacred obligation. The consecrated playground was established by ritual and the final outcome of the game is in the hands of the gods. The world itself was conceived as a game of dice which Shiva plays with his queen. Nonetheless addiction to dicing was known to be dangerous, as can be seen in 'The gambler's lament' (*Rig Veda* X.34, O'Flaherty, 1981: 239–42).
49. Produced in New Delhi in December 1991.
50. These two versions are discussed by Sunder Rajan, 1993 and 1999, from whom I have taken the critical argument.
51. Devi, 1988.
52. Dopdi is a variant of Draupadi.
53. The stripping of women to humiliate them still occurs. A famous case when Dalit women were made to parade naked in Sirasgaon, Maharashtra, in 1963 is discussed in A. Rao, 1999.
54. Spivak, 1987: 196.
55. Sen, 1991.
56. See Gopal, 1999.
57. Gopalan, 1997.
58. Devi, the goddess, is the *shakti* or power of her consort, Shiva. She appears in a number of forms: in benign form as the devoted wife, Parvati, mother of Ganesh and Skanda; as Durga, the warrior who vanquishes demons, such as the Buffalo Demon (Mahishasura); and in her terrifying form as Kali, where she is garlanded with skulls and girded with human hands, her tongue hanging out. As Shiva is an ambivalent god, as Wendy

Doniger has aptly called him, 'The erotic ascetic', so his consort is likewise a complex, composite goddess.

59. Hiltebeitel, 1988 and 1991.
60. Cited in Mankekar, 1993a: 485.
61. Purushottam Agarwal, 1995: 54–5.
62. Sunder Rajan, 1999: 344.
63. As indeed occurred in times of communal violence, notably the Partition.
64. Mankekar, 1993a.
65. Indian state-owned television.
66. B. R. Chopra is the older brother of Yash Chopra, whose work is discussed in Chapter 5.
67. Mitra, 1993.
68. Lutgendorf, 1995. On *Chanakya*, see U. Chakravarti, 1998.
69. The first film ever made entirely by Indians, D. G. Phalke's *Raja Harischandra* (1913), was a story from the *Mahabharata*; in 1923, 70 per cent of films were mythologicals, according to Derné, 1995b: 197. Apart from 1975's famous exception *Jai Santoshi Maa* (see Kurtz, 1992), mythologicals are now infrequent, but religious invocations at the beginning set the context, characters often have names of these mythological characters (Karun Arjun); and many characters are clearly derived from myth. See the discussion of Sita in *Awaara* below.
70. Mankekar, 1993a: 473–6, gives a detailed account of the televised narrative.
71. Mankekar, 1993a: 476–8, also looks at the producer's beliefs about the episode.
72. Mankekar, 1993b: 552–3.
73. Cited in Sunder Rajan, 1993: 142.
74. Sunder Rajan, 1999.
75. See also others given in Sunder Rajan, 1999.
76. O'Flaherty, 1973: 318.
77. Babb, 1975: 142–3.
78. O'Flaherty, 1973: 79.
79. See Lutgendorf, 1991a, on the performance traditions of this version.
80. Kapur, 1993: 85.
81. Lutgendorf, 1991a.
82. Richman, 1991a: 14.
83. Narayana Rao, 1991.
84. See Erndl, 1991.
85. Kale, 1934. I have modified his translation of the following verses.
86. See Chapter 4.
87. See Vasudevan, 1998, for a discussion of these issues.
88. See Lutgendorf, 1995.
89. U. Chakravarti, 1998: 245.

90. See Chapter 3 below.
91. Bharucha, 1995, and Kapur, 1993.
92. R. Gandhi, 1992.
93. Kautilya, [1992].
94. Manu, [1991].
95. Doniger in Manu, [1991]: lxi.
96. Manu, [1991]: 197.
97. Manu, [1991]: 198.
98. Manu, [1991]: 200.
99. Manu, [1991]: 48–9.
100. Leslie, 1989: 171.
101. Leslie, 1989: 259.
102. John, 1998.
103. See De, 1959, and Bhattacharyya, 1975.
104. De, 1959: 18.
105. Ali, 1996.
106. Ali, 1996: 21.
107. K. Roy, 1998.
108. K. Roy, 1998: 63.
109. Brough, 1968: 38.
110. Only high-caste men speak Sanskrit in the drama. The other characters speak varieties of Prakrit ('natural' language) apart from the Brahmin clown who speaks the same Shauraseni dialect of Prakrit as the high-caste women. Lower-class characters speak a variety of Prakrits while all Prakrit lyrics are sung in Maharashtrian Prakrit.
111. Brough, 1968: 56.
112. Brough, 1968: 45. See translation, p. 31. 'After God made ...'.
113. Other key works on Sanskrit poetics are the *Dasharupa* of Dhanamjaya (tenth century AD), which summarizes much of the *Natyashastra* and the *Sahityadarpana* by Vishvanatha Kaviraja, a general treatise on poetics from the fourteenth century AD. Later treatises include the *Dhvanyaloka* (*c*.850), which expounds the theory of *dhvani* ('tone or suggestion'), a complicated theory of how literature evokes the mood.
114. Gerow, 1974, is a useful introduction to classical aesthetics.
115. I have not discussed the theory of *dhvani* ('suggestion'), whose complexities lie beyond the scope of the present discussion.
116. Gerow, 1974: 216–17.
117. This requires further elaboration, including an examination of language used to describe these pleasures. See Ali, 1996; Ali plans to develop this for the publication of this thesis.
118. Brough, 1968: 57.
119. Trans. Coulson, in his introduction; 1981: 31.

120. Trans. Eastwich, cited in Coulson, 1981: 33.
121. See Khoroche, 1992, for a translation of this version.
122. Coulson, 1981: 32 gives these as Act IV vs 8, 21, 22, 23, but the first lines and numbers do not match the text.
123. Coulson, 1981: 114–15.
124. Radice, 1992.
125. The first Tamil talkie, made in 1931, was *Kalidas*, the story of the life of the author. Rajadhyaksha and Willemen, 1994: 551, list 13 films called *Shakuntala*, and a further two with *Shakuntala* in the title.
126. For example, a version by Vishnukumar Vyas of Mumbai which was taken on a successful world tour in the early 1990s.
127. Vaidehi, [1995].
128. Brough, 1968, and Miller, 1990; and Mehrotra, 1991.
129. 'learned assemblies of Brahmins'.
130. See Ramanujan, 1994.
131. O'Flaherty, 1973.
132. Ali, 1996: 84.
133. Davis, 1991: 7.
134. Hindi (*Khari Boli*) does not emerge as a distinct language until the nineteenth century.
135. Ramanuja (d. 1137), Madhva (1197–1276), Nimbarka (thirteenth century) and Vallabha (1479–1531).
136. Siegel, 1978, and Miller, 1984.
137. Sangari, 1990.
138. See Dwyer, 1999, for a study of Dayaram in the history of Gujarati literature.
139. Hawley and Juergensmayer, 1988, give elegant translations of the poems of six of the most famous poets of medieval India – Ravidas, Kabir, Nanak, Surdas, Tulsidas and Mirabai. Each poet is introduced with his/her pseudo-history and hagiography and the present use of their works. Kumkum Sangari examines issues of gender in Mira's lyrics, while Parita Mukta looks at the emotions and meanings of her work today in western India. See Sangari, 1990, and Mukta, 1997. On gender and *bhakti* see also *Manushi*, special issue, January–June 1989, Numbers 50–52 'Women Bhakta poets'.
140. Hein, 1972; Hawley, 1981 and 1991. Hawley, 1981, gives a lively account of the setting of the plays and relates the drama to the religious and emotional world of the viewers and of the performers.
141. Rubin, 1998: 7.
142. See Dwyer, 1999.
143. Translated from Raval, 1953: Garbi 40.
144. The imagery of milk occurs frequently in these stories of Krishna's life as a cowherd. While O'Flaherty, 1980: 17–61, demonstrates symbolic sexual links between milk products and sexual fluids in her analysis of Vedic and Puranic texts, milk is a function and archetypal symbol of maternity and so may be seen in the context of the Krishna story as a metaphor of love, as indeed are other forms of food in other aspects of this cult. (See Toomey, 1990, 1992.) As a concentrated form of milk, butter may thus be seen to be a more concentrated form of love. Hawley, 1983, Part IV, explores interpretations of the motif of butter, the motivation for Krishna's stealing, the complaints made by the Gopis, his excuses and how these link to maternal and erotic love. He argues that a god who steals provides an image of inversion and becomes one who transgresses boundaries, while the accusations and excuses form a 'dialect of the language of love' (Hawley, 1983: 278). Hawley explores the connections made by O'Flaherty between sexual and maternal aspects in the symbolism of milk and finds that the boundary between the two *bhavas* becomes even fuzzier.
145. Translated from Raval, 1953: Garbi 62.
146. See Dwyer, 1999, for a discussion of Dayaram's incorporation into the canon of Gujarati literature.
147. Nandy, 1988: 23–4, and Kaviraj, 1995: 72–106.
148. See Kakar and Ross, 1986: 43–73.
149. Pritchett, 1991.
150. Sadiq, 1995; Matthews *et al.*, 1985.
151. Muhammad Sadiq, in his widely read history of Urdu literature, is deeply ambivalent about the form (Sadiq, 1995), which Frances Pritchett attributes to the influence of the new poetics created by Azad and Hali in the nineteenth century.
152. This recent history of the *ghazal* as a song lyric has been traced by Peter Manuel in Manuel, 1991.
153. Dalmia, 1997, on Banaras; and Orsini, 1996 and 2000, on later developments.
154. See Dwyer, 1999, on Gujarati poetry.
155. Nehru, [1989] and M. K. Gandhi, [1982].
156. Chatterjee, 1994: 138–9.
157. Tharu and Lalita, 1995a: 190–202.

158. Tharu and Lalita, 1995a: 281–8.
159. Tilak, 1998.
160. Dasi, 1998.
161. Chatterjee, 1994: 138.
162. See Karlekar, 1991, and Chatterjee, 1994: 135–57.
163. Mukherjee, 1985: 11–13.
164. Mukherjee, 1985: 16.
165. There seems to be no study of the historical novel in India, but a number of features of the genre explain its popularity in India.
166. E.g. Devakinandan Khatri's 1891 bestseller *Chandrakanta*.
167. Kaviraj, 1995.
168. Most famously theorized by Mikhail Bakhtin, in his generic chronotope (Bakhtin, 1981). The relationship between the chronotope and the change in the concept of time from 'simultaneity' to 'meanwhile', required for nationalism (Anderson, 1991), remains unexplored.
169. Tagore, 1985.
170. The greatest Gujarati novel, Govardhanram Tripathi's *Saraswatichandra*, published in 4 volumes from 1887 to 1901, has not been translated into English even after a century.
171. See Dirks, 1995.
172. Chatterjee, 1994.
173. Tagore, 1985: 19.
174. It was largely for its political views that the book was angrily trashed by George Lukacs (1978).
175. Tagore, 1985: 31.
176. Nandy, 1994: 12–3.
177. Nandy, 1994: 19.
178. Tagore, 1985: 97.
179. Rushdie, 1982: front cover.
180. There had been much prose writing in English in the nineteenth century – Swami Vivekananda (1862–1902), Rabindranath Tagore (1861–1941), Aurobindo (1872–1950), Radhakrishnan (1888–1975), and Nehru (1889–1964) – and some poetry was written in English – Toru Dutt (1857–77), Sarojini Naidu (1879–1947) – but although the earliest novels in English date from the beginning of the twentieth century, these are mostly obscure.
181. Naipaul, 1977: 43.
182. Chandra, 1997: 93.
183. Chandra, 1997: 123.
184. See Chapter 4 for a discussion of the film *Mother India*.
185. See O'Flaherty, 1973, for a discussion of the seeming paradox of Shiva as the erotic ascetic.
186. See van der Veer, 1994: 96–7, and Parekh, 1989b: 189–95.
187. Parekh, 1989a: 210.
188. Parekh, 1989a: 195.
189. Phillips, 1994: 39.
190. See Uberoi, 1993, for recent work on the Indian family.
191. Bose, 1995. He draws on the *Santaner caritra gathan*, first published in 1912, still in print in 1989.
192. Bose, 1995: 118.
193. Bose, 1995: 124.
194. Turner, 1996, gives a good summary of these concepts. India, of course, has its own ways of understanding the body, many of them based in indigenous systems of medicine such as Ayurveda. See Wujastyk, 1998, and Alter, 1997.
195. Giddens, 1992.
196. John, 1998.
197. Uberoi, [2000]
198. Dir. Manmohan Desai.
199. Such as *Sangam* ('Union', dir. Raj Kapoor, 1964), *Zanjeer* ('The chain', dir. Prakash Mehra, 1973) and *Sholay* ('Embers', dir. Ramesh Sippy, 1975); some actors have regularly appeared together as 'buddies' or brothers, including Amitabh Bachchan and Shashi Kapoor in the 1970s, and Akshay Kumar and Saif Ali Khan in the 1990s.
200. Thadani, 1996.
201. Cohen, 1995.
202. See Chapter 3 below on the Shiv Sena.
203. See Chapter 6 below on gay readings of *Stardust*.
204. See above.
205. Varia, 1999, discusses *dostana* (Buddies in chuddies), lesbians (Lesbians behind the purdah and action girls), cross-dressing (Rampaging ranis) and camp (Camp classics: saris and sequins).
206. See O'Flaherty, 1980, for an extended discussion of the androgyne in ancient India.
207. Nandy, 1988: 7–8, 52–3.
208. See Cohen, 1995.
209. See Ang, 1985, for a discussion of the international success of the American soap *Dallas*.
210. Uberoi, 1996; Geetha, 1998; John and Nair, 1998 provide good discussions of these and other topics.
211. Foucault, 1981.
212. Ferguson, 1990.
213. Giddens, 1992: 26–7.

3

The Rise of the Middle Classes
of Bombay

Popular discourse in India refers frequently to the nation's 'middle classes', yet scholars have failed to identify accurately who the middle classes are, to analyse their origins, or even define their membership. This is hardly surprising given the lack of any serious social history of India since Independence – surely a gap which requires its own commentary – and the fact that most recent academic research on India has focused on the elites and the oppressed. There seems to be universal distaste for the middle classes, which is ironic given the social origins of most academics.[1] The only two monographs I found which had 'middle class' and 'India' in their title find the term impossible to define.[2] Given my own background in the humanities, I do not pretend to offer a fresh definition of this group using precise economic, political and sociological (among other) analyses. Instead I begin by looking at the background to the use of this term, and other possible ways of describing this social group through other cultural practices, and finally explain why I use the term 'middle class' even though I am not making a class-based study.

The term 'middle class' emerges in England in the later eighteenth century although references to people of 'middling sorts' and of 'middle station' are found frequently in the late seventeenth century.[3] Here also the term is elusive and used to define what people are not. They are to be distinguished from the upper classes, the gentry and aristocracy, those who had independent means, usually landowners, and hence did not need to work, and from the working class or labourers. The middle class described those who worked but did not get their hands dirty, usually commercial or industrial capitalists with money from gift, inheritance or loan with which they increased their capital. They employed those without money and who depended on others for their livelihoods. So they were economically in the middle, but had their own particular lifestyle and often shared a liberal individualism.[4]

This general description highlights some key elements of the middle class. It is a post-feudal group, which has wide economic opportunities; it emerges around the same time as the ideology of modernism, which has long been associated with the middle class; and it is a very wide group in terms of wealth, income, education, occupation and status and hence has often to be defined in negative terms, against what it is not. A further complication is added in that the terms 'bourgeois' and 'middle class' are often used to cover the same social groups, although they are sometimes contrasted – the first being used as an entirely economic description, meaning the owners of capital, according to Marx, with no account being made of status or wider cultural features. In popular usage, both terms are used interchangeably for congeries of individuals who share a certain ideology of modernity, of secularism and of rationality. In East and South-east Asia, the term 'new rich' has been coined to describe a new group, which has emerged in the last twenty to thirty years, who do not share this middle-class ideology.[5] This 'new rich' group seems to be quite different from that of India in terms of its world importance, although many Indians see it as one to emulate (see below).

For the present I shall stick to the term 'middle class', accepting its incoherence as a category, covering a wide variety of economic, occupational, political, ideological and cultural positions. I use it to cover a class ranging from the professionals, the public and private bureaucrats, and small businessmen, to the capitalists, the big business-men in the industrial, commercial and financial sectors. In India, many of those I call 'middle class' would regard themselves as belonging to the category of the 'elite', while the term 'middle class' is reserved for the lower economic strata of the groups I define as 'middle class'. This is further complicated by questions of caste, given that most of this class belong to the upper castes. I use the wider range of meaning in my analysis of the emergence of the Indian middle class, concentrating on its cultural aspects. I then identify sub-groups within this class before devoting the next four chapters to the middle-class culture of Mumbai.

The beginnings of the Indian middle classes

The Mughal revenue system was based on land as the primary unit of value and so landowners formed the dominant social group after the king and his courtiers, most of the landed aristocracy being Muslim. The Permanent Settlement, allowing the landowners (*zamindars*) to continue collecting their revenue as capitalist landlords, also enabled the emergence of a more independent gentry from which much of the higher bourgeoisie was to emerge.[6] Trade was not seen as a high-status occupation despite the fact that a number of merchants from the traditional mercantile (*bania*) communities amassed considerable wealth in these pre-capitalist economies. This incipient bourgeoisie, based in trade and later also in industry, certainly had its origins in these old business communities.[7] It was strengthened by the abolition of the East India Company's trading monopoly in 1813, which released capital and stimulated production. Lata Mani defines them deftly:

> [They] were the middlemen of the East India Company's revenue and commercial transactions, the classic comprador class, benefiting from opportunities afforded by colonial rule, but ultimately constrained by the conditions of colonial subjugation. The economic and political context of colonialism meant that their empowerment as landlords did not enable their emulation of the improving English gentry as East Indian Company officials had hoped. On the contrary, they were to become a rentier social class divorced from the productive economic functions that had characterized their English counterparts. This was partly because the rise of these landed elites turned not on technological innovations, but proceeded on the backs of a peasantry made vulnerable both by the loss of their customary rights in land and by new laws which strengthened landlord control over peasant labor. At the same time, land continued to attract those whose fortunes were made through trading or money lending but who had relatively few avenues for productive investment in the commercial sector.[8]

Published research on nineteenth-century India has focused on the politico-economic or the religious and literary aspects of its social transformations.[9] This period also sees the rise of a new Indian professional, educated middle class. This group was largely a creation of the new system of western-style education, introduced during the early part of the nineteenth century and intended to create a new class of Indian administrators, undoubtedly one of the goals of Macaulay's infamous Minute (1835). I return to this below.

What little research there has been on the middle classes in the nineteenth century has been concerned mostly with Calcutta,[10] perhaps because it was the first city to witness the emergence of a new urban elite, who called themselves the *bhadralok* ('gentlefolk'),[11] and also because many intellectuals are themselves members of this Bengali class. However, since my focus in later chapters is the new middle classes of Bombay, I shall concentrate on the origins of the city's middle classes.

The city of Bombay

In the 1991 Census of India, Bombay's population was reckoned to be
12.57 million. It is hard to believe that only three hundred years ago, this
city of tropical Gothic architecture and modern skyscrapers was seven
islands sparsely inhabited by Koli fisher families. Bombay has been
created from the Arabian Sea by a series of land reclamations, so that now
it forms a peninsula although it is often referred to colloquially as an
island, perhaps in a metaphorical sense, as Bombay has become the centre
of India's economic modernization.

Although it is a relatively new city, Bombay lies near some of the
world's most ancient trade routes, those of the Indian Ocean. Merchants
and traders have been active in western India since prehistoric times, as
seen from excavations at the Harappan port of Lothal in Ahmadabad
district of Gujarat. A number of migrant traders came to settle in the
principal cities of western India from the ninth century onwards, the
majority coming from the Persian Gulf.

The Portuguese were the first Europeans in western India and had
gained control of the islands of Bombay by the seventeenth century, and in
1661 the islands were transferred to the English king, Charles II, as part of
the dowry brought by his bride, Catherine of Braganza. In 1668 the islands
were leased to the East India Company for an annual fee of £10 sterling in
gold. At that time the islands seemed of minor importance: the English
were based in Surat (in modern Gujarat) where a factory or trading post
had been established in 1612, Surat having been the centre of internal and
external trade routes under the Mughals and its port for the Hajj pilgrims.
Mughal exactions and corruptions, attacks by the Marathas, along with
the silting of the River Tapi and other economic problems,[12] prompted the
British to decide they were safer in Bombay, which they made their
commercial headquarters in western India. They became the dominant
power in the area after defeating the last Maratha Peshwa in 1818,
consolidating their rule in 1858 and from then present-day Gujarat and
Maharashtra were ruled as part of the Bombay Presidency with British
Residents in the many princely states.

The physical construction of Bombay

Until the British moved their capital from Calcutta to Delhi in 1911, the
port cities of Bombay, Calcutta and Madras, all founded by the British,
were their bridgeheads in India. These three Presidency cities developed
very different cultures. As the centre of British interest in India, Calcutta
had a larger British expatriate community, and was the centre for western

education. Its indigenous elite consisted largely of absentee landlords or *zamindars*, many of whom began to study at these new educational institutions. This elite, and a less wealthy middle class, formed the *bhadralok* ('gentlefolk') who were the originators of the 'Bengal renaissance', where issues of English and Indian literature, Hindu reform and other intellectual ideas were debated. Although several great indigenous capitalists such as Dwarkanath Tagore rose to prominence in the early nineteenth century, the colonial situation in Calcutta did not encourage the development of Indian capitalism and only saw a 'caricature' of bourgeois modernity.[13] Madras, with its traditional Brahminical elite and greater agricultural revenue, had a much lower level of British–Indian interaction, while Bombay developed differently as a largely commercial centre.

Indigenous cities such as Delhi, Ahmadabad and Lucknow remained strong regional centres, with British cantonments added outside the city walls.[14] Very different from these were the cantonment cities of India, of which there were more than 150. The most important of these was Bangalore, one of India's most middle-class cities. Its original hill-station character may have diminished, but its airy feel remains even though it is now the centre of high technology in India, especially for defence, communication and computing. These industries have in turn created a new middle class of highly paid professionals who participate in global employment networks. The British hill stations developed as places of escape from the cities in the hot weather, whether for the British families living in India, the wealthier Indians, or, in the case of Simla, for the entire bureaucracy.

Although Gerald Aungier, the Governor of Bombay 1672–77, established Courts of Justice and the Company militia – hence his British name 'the father of Bombay' – the Company was almost exclusively interested in trade and ways of making money.[15] Bombay had relatively few British inhabitants but there was a large indigenous business community which interacted with intellectuals to form an urban middle class who were active in municipal politics and journalism and who, although not creating a renaissance on the scale of that in Bengal, generated a new intelligentsia and public culture. The communities lived separately, the British first living in the Fort area. Then after a fire in 1803, they built a new town with wider streets. When the Company's monopoly on trade was abolished in 1813, Bombay flourished; migrants from all over the country moved to the city and by 1864 the population was 816,000. Industry developed rapidly, the city's great wealth originally being built on the textile industry. The first mill was established in 1854, and by 1885 there were nearly fifty, employing over 30,000 workers.[16] In the 1860s the blockade of Confederate ports in the American Civil War allowed India to become the main supplier of cotton to Britain. Bombay became the world's third greatest centre of the cotton trade, after New York and Liverpool, and this was run largely by Indian enterprise.[17] Fortunes were made as prices soared, accompanied by a stockmarket boom, until the crash in 1865, when the American war ended.

Bombay's principal economic advantage has been its excellent communications, first by sea to the Middle East, Europe and the Far East, then inland after trade was opened into the hinterland with the building of the first railway line in India – in fact, the first railway line East of Suez – from Bombay to Thane, in 1853/4, which was soon followed by lines into the hinterland of the Deccan. This railway development led to the creation of some of the most significant buildings in Bombay, including Stevenson's Victoria Terminus. Much of the building took place under Sir Bartle Frere, Governor 1862–7, including most of the great Victorian Gothic, and ambitious land reclamation began. Although trade with China remained important, the opening of the Suez Canal in 1870 and the development of steam navigation allowed Bombay to trade more easily with European markets. Bombay thus gained pre-eminence over Calcutta by the end of the First World War, aided by its mercantile adaptability,[18] establishing itself as India's major port, and its major commercial and financial centre.

These new Indian capitalists began to move out of their traditional *wadis, pols* and *mohallas* (caste-based residential areas) in the Black Town on the edges of the British Fort. Along with the richer British, they began to build villas (known locally as bungalows) on Malabar and Cumballa Hills, while others moved to Cuffe Parade in the south. Many of these have been demolished to make way for aesthetically challenged high-rise buildings, all of which are of little architectural merit and which are for the most part poorly maintained. In between these smart residential areas and the Fort lay the great piles of nineteenth-century fantasies of Gothic and Indo-Saracenic architecture of the British public buildings, including the university and the lawcourts, while the Cooperage and the other greens reached the sea. This was changed dramatically by the great reclamations of Bombay in the 1930s, creating the vast sweep of Marine Drive, an area of striking Art Deco architecture, followed by further reclamations in the 1960s, which led to the building of the skyscrapers for commercial premises on Nariman Point and the mixed commercial and residential Cuffe Parade, now mirrored by an outburst of skyscrapers on Malabar Hill. While the elites have remained in these preferred residential areas, there has been a steady drift north of the middle classes, with the railway line dividing the wealthier west, near the Arabian Sea, from the poorer and more industrialized eastern suburbs. Like Malabar and Cumballa Hills, the rich first built bungalows in small areas, followed by a mushrooming of apartment blocks, heading north through Worli, Bandra's Pali Hill, Juhu and Versova. The less-well-off middle classes have filled in the gaps between these areas, creating their own heartlands, including Parsi colonies at Dadar and Andheri; Maharashtrians at Shivaji Park and Dadar (W); Gujaratis at Santa Cruz and Andheri. This drift has been helped by the relatively successful urban transport of Bombay, while business has remained in the south of the island, around the Fort, leaving the inner city, the former home of the rich, now largely for the lower-middle classes. There has been little urban planning of these later developments and although there is some open space – greens, parks, sportsgrounds – there is little in the way of public squares and 'other open space'.

Bombay has become a victim of its own success and its population continues to grow at an alarming rate, the island with an area of around 600 sq. km. and a population of over 12 million now supporting a population density of over 17,000 per sq. km. The city's chawls and slums are home to around 5 to 6 million people. These are not the very poor, but a lower-middle or working class, while an unknown number of people sleep on the streets. These slum and pavement dwellers account for more than 50 per cent of the population, but occupy only 8 per cent of the city's land;[19] Bombay has the largest slum in Asia, Dharavi, where around 300,000 people are estimated to live in an area of 175 hectares. This pressure on space has led to high prices of real estate: at its peak in the early 1990s they were higher than in Manhattan, in a city where a good middle-class wage is around £100 a month. Many people live far from their work, commuting over four hours a day, and the public transport system has to deal with millions of passengers a day. There have been attempts to develop a new planned town, New Bombay, across Thana Creek on the mainland, but this has not been a successful project as the city still exerts its attractions.

So if Bombay is so crowded, why are people still coming? One factor is educational, in that Bombay is the leading intellectual centre in western India, but the major factor is its economic pulling power. Although Bombay may look poor to a westerner, it has the highest per capita income in India, paying one-third of the country's income tax, and is India's financial, industrial, commercial and trading centre. There is always some work available and there are many good things in Bombay such as rapid transport, the advantages of a modern city and its glamour. Bombay is India's city of possibility, where many of its wealthy people are those who have made their fortunes in one or two generations.

The elites of Bombay

The early migrants to Bombay interacted with the British to give Bombay its unique character. Here I look at the elite groups, who were drawn from a limited number of castes which formed political and social organizations in nineteenth-century Bombay and shaped its cultural history.[20] There are two main groups: merchants and rulers, mostly Parsis, Gujarati merchant classes (Hindu and Jain Banias, Muslim traders) and intellectuals (some Gujarati Nagar Brahmins, but mostly Maharashtrian Brahmins).[21] It was from these groups that most of the commercial and intellectual leaders emerged who shaped the cultural life of the city. The majority of people to profit from these new opportunities was from the upper castes and the Parsis, and was, of course, mostly men.[22] These groups were very heterogeneous and included the mercantile and industrial bourgeoisie who formed the beginnings of the middle class; later they came to represent only a small part of this middle class, of which by the end of the nineteenth century the majority was professional, consisting of government servants, lawyers, college teachers and doctors. These two groups, namely the industrial and mercantile bourgeoisie and the intellectual middle classes, were not discrete and mutually exclusive categories. The bourgeoisie was not a single community, but included a wide spectrum of castes and also of social class from the small shopkeeper to the rich merchant, who might aspire to the highest social status and could certainly dominate the commercial, and to some extent the political, life of the city. It interacted with the middle classes not only in the political arena, but also in spheres of education, where even if the wealthy merchant himself did not study he may well have sent his son to the new educational institutions. Many of the middle classes were to emerge from the same communities and castes as the bourgeoisie. Both these groups knew that to enter into the highest society in the nineteenth century, they needed to be educated, not least to learn the language of the predominant and only truly elite group in their society, namely English, 'the classical language of India'.[23] The use of English was further encouraged by the diversity of Bombay's communities, with their variety of languages, again providing a striking contrast to Calcutta, where Bengali was the only other major language along with English.[24]

Ironically, many of the British elite were actually from the British middle classes, but were able to live a lifestyle in India that was closer to that of the upper classes at home. This group was often the model which the Indian groups sought to emulate in various degrees, not only in the public sphere, but also in dress, furniture, leisure and entertainment. Nevertheless, the British presence in Bombay was much less obtrusive than in Calcutta and, apart from the Parsi community, there were far fewer Anglicized Indians.

The new mercantile bourgeoisie

Social unrest and political upheaval in western India during the late eighteenth century precipitated large-scale migration to Bombay, which was perceived as a safe haven. At that time, the bulk of the population consisted of Maratha labourers, Koli fishermen, various Muslim communities, Goans and a small number of Europeans, all of whom had their own specific cultures. Hindu and Jain Banias (merchant castes), Parsis and several Muslim communities from Gujarat soon came to dominate the commercial life of the city in association with the East India Company, leading to Gujarati becoming the *lingua franca* of Bombay, while the other major communities, the speakers of Marathi and Konkani, formed a service elite, through their roles in government and adminis-tration. These groups were not from the castes that formed the major trading and banking networks of pre-colonial India, but a new elite which emerged only in colonial Bombay.[25] By the end of the nineteenth century, new classes of intellectuals, many of whom emerged from these traditional elite communities, challenged the leadership of these dominant groups, through their knowledge of English and of British political traditions. Elite leadership was shared among a number of religious and regional communities that responded to colonial demands for municipal leadership and participation in civic society out of their need to evolve their own public roles.[26]

The most successful of all Bombay's communities were the Parsis (Zoroastrians), migrants from Iran who became agriculturalists in Navsari, Gujarat, then migrated to Bombay from the late eighteenth century, where they served as agents, contractors and middlemen to the British, eventually becoming shipbuilders and traders. In the nineteenth century they were easily the wealthiest group in Bombay, where they made their fortunes from trade with China. Although only 6 per cent of the population at that time, they controlled an enormous proportion of its wealth: in 1851, one Parsi, Dadabhai Pestonji Wadia, owned about a quarter of the island.[27] The Parsis have always been very distinctive, being the most Anglicized of all the communities, and they mixed more with the British than any other Indians did. Parsis played important roles in the intelligentsia, in law, publishing, social reform and philanthropy. They have remained prominent in independent India in spite of constant worries within the community about their demographic decline.[28] Statues of Parsi worthies can be seen all over Bombay. Streets and institutions bear the names of some notable families including the Wadias, the Camas and the Petits and, most famous of all, Jamshetji Jeejeebhoy (1783–1859), the first Indian to be made a baronet. The most famous family in present-day India is the Tatas, who have huge interests in iron and steel, shipping, and motor industries.

Unlike the Parsis, the other mercantile communities tended towards a social conservatism often associated with such business groups, and, apart from some key individuals, few of their members joined the reform movements discussed below. The Hindu and Jain Bania[29] castes are from the Vaishya class. In Gujarat, at a politico-economic level the Vaishyas are dominant over the Kshatriyas and even in terms of ritual hierarchy, the nominal superiority of the Kshatriyas is questioned by many Vaishya. Since traders and financiers are more socially prominent than administrators, landowners and chiefs, it is not surprising that business acumen is more highly valued and respected in Gujarat than in any other part of India. Indeed Gujarati and Marwari Banias (the latter come from the adjacent area of Rajasthan) are commonly stereotyped as *the* businessmen of India, both in the subcontinent and beyond.

The Gujarati Banias (apart from the considerable number of Jains[30]) are mostly Vaishnavas, and many are followers of the Pushtimarg sect; as a group they also have a reputation for adhering to ritual purity, and for being strictly vegetarian. While only those Vaishya groups with a very long history of mercantile activity behind them are regarded as 'true' Banias, several prominent trading castes which are not of Bania origin have to all intents and purposes acquired Bania status by adopting these forms of behaviour. For example, the Bhatias were originally Rajputs, but having become very successful traders in Saurashtra and Kutch, they adopted Vaishnavism and vegetarianism during the fifteenth century. Their prosperity increased further when they migrated to Bombay from the early nineteenth century, where they were soon involved in the Middle-Eastern trade. Few now question their status as fully incorporated Banias.

Two further closely connected castes, the Lohanas and the Bhansalis, have similar origins, and have followed similar paths. They too achieved considerable economic success in nineteenth-century Bombay; the Lohanas as grain-dealers and shopkeepers and the Bhansalis as general traders. Most members of these castes are enthusiastic Vaishnavas, and besides their involvement in Pushtimarg, many are also devotees of the Lohana saint Jalaram.[31]

By no means all of Gujarat's merchant communities are Hindu, however, for a significant minority converted to Islam, in both the Sunni and the Shi'a traditions, with the latter being divided into numerous sectarian sub-groups. The schism between Shi'as and Sunnis over the succession to the leadership arose soon after the Prophet's death, the former believing that his authority as Imam was passed on to his family. In turn various Shi'a sub-sects emerged because of disputes over the nature of the succession, and hence over the identity of the Imam himself. Among the merchants, the most important Muslim groups are the Shi'ite Bohras and the Khojas (who include the Aga Khanis and Isna Asharis) and the Hanafite Sunni Memons.

As elsewhere, conversion to Islam usually occurred among entire social groups, rather than individuals. In striking contrast to north India, where upper-class Muslims often claim descent from Afghan, Turkish or Persian invaders, most Gujarati Muslims freely acknowledge their Hindu origins. Thus the Khojas acknowledge that they were originally Lohanas (peasant-farmers) by caste: their name is a Gujarati form of Persian *khwaja* 'lord', itself a translation of the Lohana caste title, *thakur*. Among the Khojas the largest and best-known group are the Nizari Ismailis,[32] who trace the succession back to the seventh Imam, Ismail, and recognize the authority of a living and visible Imam, H. H. the Aga Khan. As hereditary Imam, the Aga Khan has absolute authority over his followers in religious and social matters; under his guidance they have adopted practices which are regarded as highly unorthodox by most other Muslims, for they are no longer required to perform *namaz* (daily prayers), to observe the Ramadan fast, or even to undertake the *haj* (pilgrimage to Mecca).

Late in the eighteenth century, some two thousand Ismailis, then known only as Khojas, migrated from Kutch and Saurashtra to Bombay, where as merchants and shipowners they soon became wealthy, well educated and highly influential. Prior to the Aga Khan's arrival in Bombay from Iran in 1843, the Khojas had acted outwardly as Sunnis (*taqiyya*), but when a lengthy dispute in the British-run courts was resolved in 1882, most agreed to accept the authority of the Aga Khan. The Khojas who refused to do this defected to the closely related Isna Asharia sect. This latter group are 'Twelvers', who assert that when the twelfth Imam disappeared in AD 873 he simply went into hiding, and that he will remain concealed until he reappears to herald the Day of Judgement.

By contrast the Mustalian Ismailis, more commonly known as Bohras,[33] believe that although God's messenger remains hidden he is to be found on earth at all times, where he lives and dies as an ordinary man and names his own successor. The Bohras include several sub-groups, including the Daudis, the Suleimanis, the Alavis and the Atba-e-Malik. The Memons, who are Sunnis rather than Shi'as and were also Lohanas before their conversion, came from Sindh and Kutch, but they were among the first groups to move to the new European trading centres of Surat and then, later, Bombay.

Other smaller mercantile groups in Bombay included Konkani Muslims, shipowners, merchants and government clerks; two groups of Jews – the Bene Israel Jews from Arabia who moved from the mid-eighteenth century to Bombay, where they were mostly small traders; and the Baghdadi Jews from the Ottoman Empire, who controlled the retail trade. Among the Maharashtrians, Sonars (goldsmiths) and Kasars (workers of copper and jewellers) were the only group of significance. While Pune remained the cultural capital of Maharashtra, the intellectuals and professional Maharashtrians have played a key role in the cultural and intellectual life of Bombay. Nevertheless, the Maharashtrians' absence from the mercantile and trading classes is important in that they were largely insignificant in the major concern of Bombay, notably commerce, which was controlled by the British and mostly Gujarati-speaking groups. While this has undoubtedly given Bombay its cosmopolitan air, it has also been a major factor in the Maharashtrian feeling of being a minority in this city which they regard as historically and culturally part of their homeland, the political consequences of which became increasingly apparent in the rise of the Shiv Sena from the 1960s and 1970s.

The intellectual and professional middle classes

Bombay's intellectual and professional middle classes were, by and large, separate from this mercantile bourgeoisie. They came more from the traditional learned castes of western India, the Gujarati, Maharashtrian and Konkani Brahmins. Among Gujaratis, the Nagar Brahmins, the most prestigious of all Brahmins, have always dominated intellectual life and served as bureaucrats and administrators at least since Mughal times. They were the first to take advantage of western education and to this day they have maintained this status, but they have never had much political or economic clout. The Maharashtrian castes (Chitpavan Brahmins, Saraswat Brahmins and the Kayasth Prabhus) had worked for the East

India Company and, in the case of the Prabhus, even for the Portuguese in Bombay, but the majority of Brahmins who had administered Poona's government during the time of the Maratha empire, came to Bombay after the Peshwa was finally defeated in 1818, using their experience and training to dominate the bureaucracy of Bombay. They were joined by further migration of Saraswats and Chitpavans from the Konkan.

Many members of these castes profited from the new British educational system, which had been intended to create an intermediary class between themselves and the Indian population.[34] Western-style vernacular school education began in 1820 in Bombay and soon spread all over the province. In 1825 the first English school opened in Bombay, and 1834 saw the founding of the Elphinstone Institution for teaching English and the arts, sciences and literatures of Europe. In 1856 it was divided into Elphinstone High School and Elphinstone College, with degrees awarded by Bombay University. Bombay University had only three colleges when it was founded in 1857, but by 1903/4 it had sixteen. Elementary arts colleges were opened in the princely states, including Vadodara (Baroda College, 1882) and Bhavnagar (Shamaldas College, 1885). Since the medium of instruction was English, and given that the literature, politics and history of Europe were the major subjects, and the teaching was highly critical of Indian life and society, it is hardly surprising that this education had a major impact on the Indian students. Nevertheless the students were not brainwashed into accepting western values but decided according to personal preference and social opportunity which elements they wished to adapt to their own lifestyle. This can be seen clearly in the case of literature, where, despite the high esteem in which English Romantic poetry was held, the new group of writers chose mostly to write a new poetry in their own languages, adapting these new themes and structures to varying degrees.[35] (It has been argued that the discipline of English literature was formed in Indian universities and it was from here that the discipline returned to England.[36]) These colleges also provided Indian students with training in how to function in a British institution. They began to form learned societies that trained them in debate and activism and published journals through which they made their opinions known to a wider audience. These activities would prove an essential part of acting as intermediaries and spokespersons in Bombay's municipal government and legislative councils.

While European literature, politics and history dominated the new curriculum, other vocational options became available at this time, notably medicine and law. Grant Medical College opened in 1845, taking mostly Parsi and Goan and Maharashtrian Brahmin students, including

Bhau Daji Lad, who also collected Indian historical materials.[37] Government law colleges were set up in the 1850s, and eventually a Law School was founded at Elphinstone, awarding the first LLBs in 1865. Nevertheless Indians still had to read for the Bar in England, but the rich, realizing the benefits a legal training might bring to the business world, sent their sons to England to train as lawyers from the 1860s, including many who would use their new education to argue for Indian political rights, including Pherozeshah Mehta.

As intended by the colonizers, the products of this new education mediated between the British rulers and the local population, creating a new public sphere. Unlike the merchants, they bridged the ethnic divide, coming, as most of them did, from a range of religious and caste backgrounds, though nearly all from socially elite groups such as Brahmins and Parsis. Haynes[38] reminds us that this elite remained apart from other sections of society, with the majority excluded from the new public sphere. The elites often had to develop two forms of politics, one to talk to the British institutions and another to talk to the city dwellers on more traditional grounds.[39] They used models of British municipal and parliamentary politics, and concepts of colonial discourse (progress, public good), to create new institutions (associations, educational societies, and the press[40]) to make themselves heard by the government as they raised questions of social reform, often centred on the 'women's question' (see below), and on religious reform.

Middle-class women

Women as agents barely feature in the social history of Bombay at this time. The 'women's question' (issues concerning women's roles including the topics of *sati*, the age of consent, widow remarriage) was often grounds for debating wider social issues in the early and mid-nineteenth century.[41] However, it had disappeared during the later nineteenth century from the time when nationalist politics was dominant. Partha Chatterjee argues that anti-colonial nationalism

> creates its own domain of sovereignty within colonial society ... by dividing the world of social institutions and practices into two domains – the material and the spiritual. The material is the domain of the 'outside,' of the economy and of statecraft, science and technology ... The spiritual ... is an 'inner' domain bearing the 'essential' marks of cultural identity.[42]

While the nationalist struggle focused on the state and political power, nationalism located women's issues in the sphere of culture, the inner domain of tradition.[43] Traditional myths and stories about women were reworked as part of this cultural shift and, whatever their origins, versions of these stories became part of Indian national culture (see Chapter 2 above).

Women were not silenced by this largely male-led nationalism. Recent research, notably the publication of *Women Writing in India*,[44] reveals that this was the time when women's writing increased, often for purposes of political or social reform. Their writing included some of the earliest Indian autobiographies,[45] which give us a unique insight into the private world of the middle classes. The authors included figures such as Pandita Ramabai Sarasawati (1858–1922), who was initially trained by her father as a Sanskrit scholar, but later became a social reformer and converted to Christianity. She was the first Indian woman to support herself through writing, earning enough to travel to Europe and the USA. Most other early women writers studied privately, with varying experiences of support or obstruction from their families, including Ramabai Ranade (1862–1924), who was educated in English and Marathi by her husband, M. G. Ranade, the first LLB graduate of the Law College. The first girls' schools were opened in 1849 by the Parsi community, but there was much opposition to the education of women in other communities. The first female graduate of Bombay University (in 1887) was Cornelia Sorabji (1866–1954), 25 years after the first male graduate. It is noteworthy that the next woman to graduate took her degree in 1911. Some women were able to study overseas, notably Sorabji herself, who studied law at Oxford and was finally called to the Bar in 1923. Anandibai Joshi, Pandita Ramabai's cousin, trained in the USA to become India's first woman doctor.

The middle classes and the independence movement

A new period of Indian history is often said to have begun in 1885 when the Indian National Congress was founded in Bombay.[46] For the first forty years the majority of Congress leaders and supporters were from Bombay and Poona.[47] They were rarely drawn from the rich bourgeoisie, who remained loyal to British rule at least until the 1920s, but comprised the new middle classes, the educated rather than the rich or socially powerful, mostly lawyers, journalists, teachers and doctors, all products of the new education system. This domination of the Indian independence movement by the middle classes became the norm. Most nationalist leaders came from elite and upper-caste backgrounds, although these varied widely in economic and cultural terms, and their lives took very different courses. It is striking how many of them were lawyers, having studied usually in Britain and often been called to the Bar in London.[48] They included Mohandas Karamchand Gandhi (1869–1948), a Gujarati Bania from Porbandar, who studied law in London, practised as a barrister in South Africa, then returned to India where he came to dominate the Indian National Congress; Jawaharlal Nehru (1889–1964), the son of a very wealthy Allahabadi Brahmin lawyer, who was educated at Harrow, Cambridge and Inner Temple, and became India's first Prime Minister; and Mohammad Ali Jinnah (1875–1948), the son of a Gujarati Bohra trader, who trained as a lawyer in London, working in Bombay and London before becoming leader of the Muslim League in 1935 and the first Governor-General of Pakistan.

These three great leaders were undoubtedly shaped by the new-middle-class ideologies emerging in the late nineteenth century, although their backgrounds were so different in terms of community, region and upbringing. All three had to reconcile their 'Indianness' with their 'westernness', which they documented through writing autobiographies in which they analysed themselves in fascinating detail, inventing and creating their public images as they were also creating their ideas about the new nations. They also manifested these in their changing sartorial styles, which varied from formal western dress to various regional and traditional styles.[49] While Nehru and Jinnah remained firmly within their elite and professional spheres, changing the middle class itself, Gandhi reached out to a wider, non-elite audience, creating a whole new concept of society by bringing indigenous concepts of religion and morality to politics.[50] However, as communal politics arose in the 1920s, the middle-class liberals took the upper hand in Congress, a lead that they never lost.

Bombay's middle classes in the twentieth century

The composition of the middle-class communities of Bombay has changed during the twentieth century, largely due to further migration to the city. Iranian Shias arrived at the beginning of the century, but by far the largest migration was during Partition in 1947 when some 200,000 migrants arrived, mostly refugees from Sind (including the Sindhi business community which has become one of the most dominant in Bombay over the last fifty years), while many of the Muslim elite left Bombay for Pakistan. Although the number of Panjabis who came at Partition was small they have taken a significant role in several industries, notably automobile sales and servicing, and the film industry. Further mercantile communities have migrated, attracted by the commercial opportunities, in particular the Marwaris, whose main commercial centre has traditionally been Calcutta. More recent arrivals included Tamils during the 1960s, often taking clerical work, where their knowledge of English has been an advantage. Lower-class men, from Gujarat and Maharashtra, have continued to migrate for mostly menial work as factory workers, artisans and servants, along with men from Uttar Pradesh, who are mostly taxi drivers, thus keeping a high lower-class male population.

There has been a significant shift in the balance of political power in Bombay since Independence. Unfortunately it cannot be said that these communities have always lived together peacefully. Intercommunal riots have always been a feature of life in Bombay, the worst being those between Hindus and Muslims. Prolonged language riots in the 1950s led in 1960 to the division of Bombay State (capital: Bombay) on linguistic lines into Gujarat (capital: Ahmadabad; since 1970, Gandhinagar) and Maharashtra (capital: Bombay). Maharashtrians are in a minority in Bombay, where they form around 40 per cent of the population, and the largest other minority is that of Gujaratis, who continue to dominate the city's commercial life. Gujarati remains one of the official languages of Bombay (along with Marathi and Hindi), but is starting to come under pressure in recent legislation in favour of Marathi.

Bombay's most traumatic events in decades were the riots and killings that occurred between December 1992 and the bomb blasts of March 1993 after the destruction of the mosque in Ayodhya. Although there were local specific causes for these disturbances, these need to be put into a national perspective by looking at the middle classes since Independence.

The Indian middle classes after Independence

As India's first Prime Minister, Nehru continued in office for Congress, the ruling party, until his death in 1964. Although many of his government's policies were aimed at improving the lot of the poor, it was by and large a middle-class rule and is looked back to as a golden age for the professional and intellectual middle classes, a time of high morality, ending with the defeat by China in 1962.[51] Nehru's daughter, Indira Gandhi, introduced a style of personal politics which was seen to be to India's advantage after the success of the division and defeat of Pakistan in 1971 and India's entrance to the nuclear world with the testing of a nuclear device in 1974.

The 1960s saw a number of developments that were key to the economic growth of the middle class, including the nationalization of the banks in 1969, government support for small-scale enterprises and the emergence of a rural middle class, with Charan Singh as its spokesperson, aided by the Green revolution.[52] The explosion of the 'black' economy, reckoned to be around 50 per cent of the 'white' economy,[53] far larger than that of similarly developing countries, led to a perceived increase in corruption, which was one of the complaints of the professional middle classes. Their salaries were not increasing in tandem with the private sector, where a new middle class with more money, evolving a new lifestyle, was emerging. A real-estate boom led to increases in the black economy as tax was avoided and to anxieties among those wishing to get on the property ladder. These new middle classes were unable to participate fully in a consumer society, however much advertising was expanding during this period, given state controls and economic protectionism, which increased in 1974 when restrictions were placed on foreign exchange and the multinationals were reduced in power by the banning of majority foreign ownership of companies in India. Nevertheless these years were crucial to the emergence of a new middlebrow, middle class, as the socialist rhetoric of Congress became subservient to a new authoritarian populism.

As Congress began to decline and fragment in the 1960s, Mrs Gandhi began to fall back on her family. There was a scandal when her younger son and heir apparent, Sanjay, was awarded the Maruti licence for building a new small car, which was to make car ownership more widespread among the middle classes,[54] and his plans for urban 'beautification' (which meant demolishing slums and enforcing family planning), led to the feeling that the Gandhis were creating a hereditary dictatorship, a sentiment given credence by the imposition of a national 'emergency' in 1975–7. Although Sanjay died in 1980 before inheriting his mother's mantle, her elder son Rajiv was sworn in as Prime Minister within hours of her assassination in 1984. Although politically unskilled, Rajiv was felt to be a young, modern technocrat and pro-middle-class, and his speeches referred frequently to opening up the closed economy, welcoming foreign investment and encouraging technological progress.

The middle classes gained in numbers and in strength during these years as the landed aristocracy's decline became terminal, partly as a result of their failure to ally themselves to this group. They remained largely free of foreign capital, with their own indigenous industry, mainly owned by Indians, leading to its being labelled a 'dependent capitalist country' and 'the most self-reliant and insulated capitalist economy in the third world'.[55] Yet wide divisions were opening up within this group –

economic, cultural and political. I discuss the last of these now, returning to the others at the end of this chapter.

Political realignments in the 1980s and 1990s

The early 1980s saw the Bharatiya Jan Sangh reform as the Bharatiya Janata Party (BJP), espousing a revised form of *Hindutva* or Hindu nationalism.[56] In its new incarnation, it began to reach beyond the traditional Brahminical membership of the Hindu right to the middle castes and classes, a position it achieved through its anti-secularist stance, arguing that although Hindu culture had long been sidelined, now was the time to reclaim a Hindu identity with pride. Its new definition of modernity and the modern state, with an emphasis on family values and religion, had great appeal. The BJP and its allies were able to harness the media in the form of television religious soap operas,[57] use of popular visuals[58] and technology such as the music cassette[59] to get its message across. Middle-class women have played key roles in the BJP, claiming public spaces and new political identities around leaders like Sadhvi Rithambara and Uma Bharti.[60]

The BJP has been opposed not only by Congress but also by lower-caste movements. The latter began to gain more political power as they withdrew their traditional support from Congress, as a result of Prime Minister V.P. Singh's decision to implement the report of the Mandal Commission to reserve jobs for 'Backward' classes. This led to widespread demonstrations by the middle classes, the self-immolations of a few high-caste students attracting the most media attention. In the populous northern state of Uttar Pradesh and Bihar, low-caste, 'un-Anglicized' politicians such as Mayawati and Laloo Prasad Yadav came to power, on an OBC (Other Backward Classes), anti-middle-class platform, opposing the BJP.[61]

Bombay has also been a centre for the Maharashtrian Dalit movement, the term Dalit 'oppressed' being the name the so-called 'Untouchables' use for themselves.

The Shiv Sena and the 1992/3 Bombay riots

While the BJP has grown in popularity in north and parts of north-western India, Maharashtra has seen the rise of the Shiv Sena, 'the army of Shivaji', a Maharashtrian nationalist party named after the seventeenth-century Maratha leader who posed a threat to the Mughal Empire.[62] The Shiv Sena was founded in 1966 with the slogan 'Bombay for the

Maharashtrians', as even after the creation of the state of Maharashtra with Bombay as its capital, Marathi-speakers still felt themselves under threat from migrants to the city: in 1971, over 60 per cent of Bombay's population had arrived within the last thirty years. Its politics are staunchly pro-Maharashtrian, aimed at the 40 per cent of the population of Bombay from that community, the vast majority being lower-middle class. To a large extent it is a communal or nativist party. Initially it targeted the Tamil population who threatened Maharashtrian dominance of clerical and lower-class occupations, then it became a party of beautification, which can be read as favouring the demolition of the slums, many of which are inhabited by migrants. Its membership dropped in the 1970s but has grown ever since the 1980s when it formed an alliance with the BJP and targeted the Muslim population of Maharashtra. This was seen most clearly after the Shah Bano case, when Hindu parties began to press for a uniform civil code, and after the destruction of the Babri Masjid in 1992. Shiv Sena supporters are overwhelmingly male and from a variety of backgrounds across the lower end of the social scale, mostly lower-middle to working class, together with unemployed youths. Its attractions to these classes are its efficient organizational networks, which mobilize participatory spectacles to reclaim public space, ranging from events such as public *pujas* (religious ceremonies),[63] to motorbike and scooter processions promoting its cult of *dadagiri* or urban toughs. This emphasis on participation is in contrast to the spectatorship offered by mass culture, such as watching cinema, television and sport. Its spectacles draw on culture and symbols of religion and Maharashtrian nationalism (the image of Shivaji is now found among chromolithographs along with other leaders and gods[64]), its provision of public services to its supporters, including basic facilities to slum-dwellers, and so on.[65] The Shiv Sena has been supported by elites, in particular the film industry, although many attribute this to fear of the Shiv Sena toughs. Nonetheless, clear links between the Marathi and Hindi cinema industries and the Shiv Sena can be seen in the populist or mobilizing roles played by actors who are known Shiv Sena supporters, notably Nana Patekar. These roles are clearly appreciated by the Shiv Sena cadres who vociferously cheer Patekar's rousing partisan dialogues.

The Shiv Sena's power is said to have been most clearly demonstrated in some of the worst riots in the history of independent India, which occurred in Bombay in December and January 1992/3, marking the end of Bombay's traditional and celebrated cosmopolitanism.[66] No one thought these riots could ever happen; now everyone pretends they did not. Many journalists attributed the deaths of hundreds of Muslims to a Shiv Sena pogrom, while the largely Maharashtrian Hindu police were said to have colluded with the attackers.[67] The riots were certainly limited to specific areas, mostly in the new suburbs in areas of middle-class housing and slums, in Muslim locations such as Bombay Central, around Mohammed Ali Road and in some mixed areas of South Bombay. The causes of the riots are various: *The Times of India* summed up the political background to the riots by looking at Bombay in the 1980s. The paper identified three contributory political developments: the collapse of the textile strike and subsequent decline of industrial trade unions, the 1985 Shiv Sena victory in the municipal corporation elections and the 1989 BJP–SS alliance.[68] Another factor was the criminal nexus between the underworld,[69] politicians,[70] real-estate developers and the film industry.[71] The election of the Shiv Sena to the Vidhan Sabha in 1993 seemed to mark the triumph of the lower-middle class over the higher bourgeoisie. The shift towards regional nationalism was enforced when the name of the city was changed from the English Bombay/Hindi Bambai to the Marathi (and Gujarati) Mumbai.

The middle classes of India at the end of the twentieth century

India's middle class is by no means entirely metropolitan.[72] India now has over two hundred cities with populations of over one hundred thousand.[73] These small towns have become richer through the increase in agricultural productivity brought about by the Green Revolution, and from remittances from migrant labourers, notably the Gulf money sent to Kerala and money sent to Panjab by its diaspora.[74] Although these small towns have little in the way of infrastructure and civic amenities, their middle classes have developed a lifestyle of consumption, purchasing cars and luxury goods and enjoying new leisure facilities such as sports and eating out. They participate to some degree in the same culture of the metropolitan middle classes, through their consumption of print and other media including viewing satellite and cable television, and the use of the Internet and vastly improved telecommunications. It was these small towns which the BJP leader, L. K. Advani, sought to unite in his 10,000-km. *rathyatra* ('journey by chariot') of 1990, as he progressed across India, with communal riots following in its wake. Khilnani has noted the stark contrast between this *yatra* ('journey, pilgrimage') and Mahatma Gandhi's *padyatra* ('journey on foot') when he sought to unite India's villages.[75] Advani was astute enough to know the BJP votebanks were to be found in these small towns.

Delhi, Calcutta and many other metropolitan cities in India now have middle classes similar to those of Bombay in the broadest terms, although Delhi has many more professional bureaucrats and, along with Calcutta, a higher number of intellectuals and journalists. Although many of the most wealthy members of the bourgeoisie live in Bombay, they commute regularly between the metropolitan cities, taking advantage of better consumer opportunities in the different cities, such as shopping in Delhi and restaurants and night life in Bombay. Many of them also retain important links with their rural roots or small-town origins. However, Bombay's political situation is very different from these other cities. As mentioned above, there is no majority population in Bombay, which partly explains the rise of the Shiv Sena and Maharashtrian regionalism.

Consumerism and the middle classes

At the end of the twentieth century, the middle classes are said to be hegemonic in India.[76] They are undoubtedly a powerful force if only in terms of their size, which is said to be as great as 100 million or 10 per cent of the total population, but is more probably 4 million households or 25 million people.[77] They have also become far more visible as the result of a series of government policies in the 1990s. This decade undoubtedly saw the most visible changes in consumer lifestyle choices and spending patterns. In 1991, Prime Minister Narasimha Rao and his finance minister Manmohan Singh implemented a series of economic reforms, lifting state controls on the economy, and liberalizing trade by opening India to world markets. These reforms, which replaced planning as the major economic discourse, were instigated by middle-class pressure after a foreign-exchange crisis in 1991.[78] Cities like Bombay seem to have been transformed by a media invasion (satellite and cable television since 1991[79]), a communications revolution (the mobile phone and the Internet), and a flooding of western brand-names in the Indian market. Although growth has been robust in recent years, reaching around 7 per cent by the mid-1990s, there are still an estimated 400 million people who live in dire poverty: gender inequalities, hunger and illiteracy remain enormous problems.

India had hoped to see the emergence of a 'new rich' as in South-east and East Asia. On the surface this seems to have happened during the 1990s as imported cars, mobile phones, cybercafés and other signs of conspicuous consumption and global (largely American) popular culture are now in evidence throughout the country. Yet, while they can enjoy many benefits of being middle class, they are still the middle class of a poor country and remain economically fragile not only at the lower end of the economic scale but in the face of the ever downward slide of the rupee on the global markets. Even though shaken by the 1992/3 riots, foreign investors continued to put money into India. Given low labour costs, foreign companies were initially happy to invest, but now many have found the markets for their products to be smaller than expected. Sanctions imposed after the nuclear tests in 1998 have led to further reductions in foreign investment and the shock-waves of the collapse of the East Asian economies are still being felt.

Liberalization led to an explosion of consumer goods in the Indian market, but in recent years several of these have been withdrawn, suggesting the boom may be short-lived. This failure is significant in that it shows that a number of wrong assumptions were made about the lifestyle of the middle class. This, I would venture, was largely based on an overestimation of their economic power and a misidentification of their lifestyle aspirations with their western equivalents. The consumption patterns of this new class depend on three major variables: their economic power, their lifestyle and their cultural capital, which I now look at in turn.

Economic power

At the beginning of India's economic liberalization, there was a widespread belief that the Indian middle classes were increasing in number and in wealth. Whether 25 or 100 million, this represented an enormous market ready for an influx of goods. However, India is becoming richer and income is rising overall, but distribution of income is more disparate. Liberalization is not yet having the 'trickle down' effect that was anticipated. While the Indian middle classes may be perceived as enjoying a high standard of living, they are worried about inflation and the devaluation of the rupee, and very few among them are rich by international standards. One only has to compare the average annual incomes of the USA and India ($32,000 and $350) and the annual GDPs of the two countries compared to their populations (India's 950 million people with $300 billion to the USA's 270 million people with $8.6 trillion).[80] Thus India's consumer spending power is only a thirtieth of that of the USA, that is the size of one small American state. Such low purchasing power can also be illustrated by the price of a car. The cheapest car in India, the quintessentially middle-class Maruti, costs around $5,000, where a good middle-class income is $1,800 p.a., only the very rich earning $1,200 p.c.m.

It seems surprising that so many people get this simple economic assessment of the Indian middle classes so wrong. However, straightforward numerical conversion of currency can be misleading in that although the rupee may be low in terms of exchange, its purchasing power in India is higher, especially given the cost of labour. For example, in the USA only the super-rich have servants other than perhaps cleaners and gardeners, who are hired on an hourly basis, whereas in India, even the lower-middle classes would have someone to clean and wash clothes, with the richer middle classes having whole teams of servants (cooks, cleaners, drivers, gardeners, nannies, etc.).

The major confusion seems to have been at the cultural level, which was largely caused by an over-identification with the western middle classes, from which the Indian middle classes differ significantly. Consumer goods in the west are regarded as basic necessities, and it was expected that Indians would aspire to this level of consumption, whereas in India there are many local products which are preferred, with many consumer goods being regarded as expensive luxuries.

Lifestyle and consumerism

The study of consumption has received increasing academic attention in recent years, as there is a shift away from the study of production to one of consumption. Daniel Miller points out that modern consumption

> is an attempt by people to extract their own humanity through the use of consumption as the creation of a specificity, which is generally held to negate the generality and alienatory scale of the institutions from which they receive goods and services.[81]

While no one could deny that India, or at least parts of Indian society, has become increasingly consumerist, no study of the social implications of this trend has been made.

Before liberalization, during the so-called 'Permit Raj', there was a lack of consumerist opportunity for the middle classes. This was epitomized by the lack of choice in consumer goods reflected in the availability of only three cars, two brands of toothpaste and washing powder and the ubiquitous green paint. Luxury items were radios, fridges, water heaters, fans and 'mixies' (electric mixers). With the advent of liberalization, the basket of goods available changed radically. Advertisers and their big-business clients assumed that people would automatically become more brand-aware and select premium rather than economy brands. However, the restrictions of these times and an almost Gandhian ethos of frugality have often resulted in a marked preference for local goods, especially for food. This can be seen clearly in the failure of Kellogg's breakfast cereals and Pepsi foodstuffs to establish a significant market share. Fast food outlets (such as McDonald's) – widely regarded as luxury food in India – have succeeded, albeit by breaking the code of universality with the absence of beef and the introduction of 'Macimli' (tamarind) sauce.[82] Fast-moving consumer goods such as toothpaste and washing powder have fared better, with many more varieties coming on the market, but the virtues of thrift and economy, along with economic necessity, have allowed economy brands to retain their hold on the market. Luxury goods have always been purchased overseas, and this remains the case today, with the wealthier sections of the middle class making shopping trips to Dubai, Singapore and, increasingly, the USA. The underlying idea is that money should be spent on very visible signs of consumption, such as designer-labelled clothes, mobile phones and cars, whereas frugality is still observed for hidden consumption of everyday items, in particular because these are often handled by servants.

These different patterns of consumption can also be traced to the attitude to money which the middle classes share, especially those with roots in India's mercantile communities. Money is often regarded as belonging not to the individual but to the whole family. India has also had a long-established culture of saving, traditionally in gold and jewellery but now increasingly in banks and unit trusts, with little saving in pension funds and life insurance. India has only just begun to develop a credit culture, as credit cards and mortgages are beginning to become middle-class items with increasing middle-class property-ownership.

A particularly fruitful arena for analysing consumerist culture in Bombay is advertising, as a study of consumerist texts produced by and for the middle classes. Advertising has a long history in India, first in the print media, then more recently on television. The advertising industry grew in the protected national economy, dominated by advertisements taken out by the government and by multinationals (after the 1974 Foreign Exchange and Regulation Act, by the companies in which multinationals had minority shares, such as Hindustan Lever).

Advertising really took off in India from 1976,[83] stimulated by opening markets and a rise in consumer awareness from NRI (non-resident Indian) connections. The advertising industry is now worth US$1 billion,[84] and is estimated to reach Rs10,000 crore by 2000.[85] Market research in India has shown that although globalization has increased the reach of markets, and information about these newly available products is available, local patterns of consumption have remained strong.[86] Multinationals have to produce images in their advertisements which are suitable to the local market, to portray their intimacies, in their local languages. By 1980, India's largest advertiser, Hindustan Lever, increased its spending on advertising in vernacular languages to around half its budget, on the grounds that there was now a market for its products among a new middle class that was emerging outside the cities. It was estimated that among this group there were 160 million literate people who could be targeted by such advertising.[87] Since the recent return of Coke and Pepsi, the archetypal advertisers' products, I have seen their advertisements painted on village walls in rural Karnataka and Andhra Pradesh, where not only could local people not afford to buy these drinks, they were not even on sale. Brand awareness is everything; many advertisements are seen as providing educational information.[88]

Arvind Rajgopal has argued that Indian television has portrayed the upper-class, upper-caste Hindu as the norm, not only through its programmes but also through its advertisements.[89] Advertisements have reinforced the links between money, desire and beauty, often connected with loving images. I return to this in discussing the advertisements in the magazine *Stardust*, in Chapter 6 below.

Cultural capital

Bourdieu's analysis of taste in French society[90] presents certain problems in the Indian context, for, unlike France which has a clearly defined 'French culture' created by the bourgeoisie, India has a plurality of cultures, further complicated by postcolonialism and the relationship to western culture. However, the national bourgeoisie has created one hegemonic version of Indian culture, perpetuated through government organizations (academies, universities, museums, etc.), which, I argue, has attacked the new middle classes largely on the grounds of taste.

Bourdieu argues that taste is part of a struggle for social recognition or status, in which lifestyle plays a key part, emphasizing cultural consumption rather than production. Taste is defined by the dominant class, the bourgeoisie, who have economic capital (in terms of income, employment status, etc.). They impose their taste in order to establish their cultural legitimacy, to 'define the legitimate principles of domination, between economic, educational or social capital'.[91] Thus the bourgeois aesthetic becomes cultural capital, seen as being inherent in the bourgeoisie rather than learnt or acquired. The bourgeoisie define what is legitimate culture, and other sections of the population are seen to be lacking in taste, liking what is middlebrow or popular. In Bourdieu's terms, members of the petite bourgeoisie have to strive to differentiate themselves from those who are below them in the social hierarchy, but they may lack the education to acquire the cultural capital of the bourgeoisie. I wish to emphasize that I do not regard the idea of cultural legitimacy as totally arbitrary and beyond any aesthetic definition, but I see it as a useful working model in a social rather than purely textual analysis.

The *bhadralok* and its descendants have defined India's legitimate culture in terms of writing, music, painting and theatre through their institutions such as universities, academies and museums. They have also dealt with a category which in Bourdieu's terms is 'legitimizable', namely cinema, by incorporating certain film-makers such as Satyajit Ray and later Shyam Benegal and others into the canon of taste, and have, albeit to a limited degree, granted some institutional support through government bodies such as the National Film Development Corporation and Film Festivals. However, they have not legitimized India's commercial cinema and the cultural products associated with it, for reasons I return to in Chapter 4.

Language as educational and cultural capital

Before looking at the middle-class culture which has been regarded as a legitimate source of cultural capital, the language of this culture deserves comment. It would be easy at a first glance or hearing to think that the majority language of Bombay is English. Visual manifestations of language are nearly all in English – road signs, shop names, cinema hoardings, etc. English is used by a small minority in Bombay as a major language even in the home, and is used as a link language and a language of culture by many, but this is only among the highest elite. Many use a form of colloquial Hindu-Urdu, known as 'Bambaiyya', as their major public language, while speaking a regional language at home. During the nineteenth century Bombay was undoubtedly the cultural capital of Gujarat[92] and for much of Maharashtra, although Poona played a more significant role for Marathi culture than Ahmadabad did for Gujarati. This remains true to a large extent now, although the political separation of Gujarat and Bombay has undoubtedly had some effect on a shift towards Gujarat, as local politics move towards making Bombay more of a Marathi-speaking city. The major regional languages are Marathi and Gujarati, with Urdu and Tamil spoken by sizeable minorities. English remains of great cultural importance as the language of corporate business, of much high culture, a knowledge of it still speaking of educational and cultural capital. It is seen to transcend regionalism and is associated with the secular, old middle classes. The new middle classes use more Hindi and more 'Hinglish' and code-switch happily between English and Hindi.

This multilingual situation is seen at many levels, both in print (newspapers, magazines, advertising and books) and the spoken word (broadcast media, theatrical performances). The cinema industry in Bombay makes nearly all its films in Hindi, but uses English for communication, advertising and trade. Popular music produced in Bombay is also multilingual. Many offices function in a mixture of these languages, with English and Hindi mandatory. Knowing English remains an essential part of being middle class in Bombay, and is an important vehicle for middle-class culture.

Bombay's educationally and culturally sanctioned middle-class culture

Bombay has been a literary centre since the nineteenth century.[93] The writings of the new intelligentsia of the Presidency cities can be said to mark the beginnings of modern Indian literature. These writers introduced new literary forms into Indian languages, including the novel and the short story, and western poetical forms such as the sonnet. They wrote on topics that had not been considered appropriate to literature, such as social reform and nationalism. Instructed in the values of English literature, they brought these to their new critical studies of indigenous literature. The sphere of production also changed as they no longer sought patrons but printed and sold their work, often while pursuing professional careers in the British administration for which their education had prepared them. The reading public for these literatures was small, given the low rate of literacy, and they were produced and consumed by the intelligentsia.[94] While Marathi and Gujarati, along with English, literatures have formed the major part of Bombay's literary output, Bombay has been an important centre for Urdu literature, not least through the economic support provided by the film industry.[95]

India's best-known cultural product internationally at the end of the twentieth century is undoubtedly the Indian novel in English,[96] which is often studied either as part of English literature or under a variety of categories such as Commonwealth literature or postcolonial literatures. However, the first Indian novels in English were written only in the early part of the century, fifty years after the first novels were written in other Indian languages, and the novel in India needs to be discussed in its historical context both as part of Indian writing in English[97] and as part of

Indian literature,[98] as the art form of the middle class, and 'the celebrated artifice of the nationalist imagination'[99] and its specific Indian forms.[100]

The category of literature has been queried in recent decades, and is now taken to include a wider number of genres than have often been considered. In the Indian context, there is a great need to examine the wider category of print culture, to include such genres as autobiography, journalism and diaries,[101] along with oral and traditional 'literatures'. The coexistence of these written forms has not been discussed in the context of Bombay. Non-elite forms of literature, such as the writing of the Dalit communities, of women and of Muslims, have been largely ignored until recent years.[102] The arenas in which this literature is written, read, published, debated and translated have barely been mentioned.

There is little information on the print culture of Bombay that is produced by the middle classes, although it is read by a wider social group.[103] Even though newspapers have been published in Bombay for almost two centuries, and are seen as one of the necessary cultural products for imagining the nation,[104] we know little about their owners, their incomes, contents, distribution and reading communities. There have been no studies of Indian magazines,[105] some of which have been read nationally by the middle class, including the recently deceased *Illustrated Weekly of India*. These new publications need to be examined: What do they tell people to think about, to admire? Recent years have seen a publishing boom in magazines and books, probably a result of technological improvement such as computer typesetting, but also responding to a demand. While much of this output has been fiction, there has also been much non-fiction, in particular books about self-help and diet and fitness. The changes in this whole range of publications could provide us with a much clearer picture of how these middle classes see themselves and the world and how others see them. We need to know more about the different languages used and what they tell us about their different readerships.

Bombay's public culture

The study of the public culture of Bombay is still in its infancy. Scholars are addressing this gap, although few are working on the earlier periods,[106] and most research has concentrated on the cinema. To date there is nothing to compare to the work on nineteenth-century Calcutta.[107] We know very little of how Bombay's middle classes spent and enjoyed their riches, in the absence of analysis of autobiography, diaries, private papers and public sources such as contemporary comment, law and government papers, and of course literature. One of Bombay's major forms of public culture has always been its theatre, whether the nineteenth-century Parsi theatre,[108] the Marathi *tamasha* (spectacle), the Gujarati popular drama, or the Hindi and English theatre.[109] Their different audiences, their texts, their financial and commercial operations and state sponsorship have barely been discussed. Even less information is available about the locations and spaces given to public culture in Bombay in the past and today – cinemas, theatres, libraries, restaurants,[110] pubs, clubs, sports centres,[111] shopping centres, beauty parlours. Recent years have seen bowling alleys and fashionable restaurants opening in the former mills in Parel, which are going to change radically the urban geography of Bombay and its public culture. There has been little work on the history of cultural sponsorship and institutions.

At present there are many public cultures[112] in Bombay, ranging from those that are accessible only to the rich and leisured classes, to those which can be enjoyed by those with only some free time. Bombay's geography enforces proximity on its citizens, with its high population density and its restricted choice of commuting options. This allows everyone to witness the lifestyle opportunities that are available, given the economic requirements. Given Bombay's commercial mentality, these lifestyles are aspired to by many who begin to adopt elements of them, however restricted they are by finance or cultural considerations.

Although Bombay has long supported a consumerist class, in recent years this has become far more visible. How this lifestyle is depicted in various cultural texts, I discuss in subsequent chapters, but first I outline briefly some of the key locations of this new public culture.

No single use of leisure time predominates, with patterns differing widely across age, gender and income groups, but some key trends can be seen. Sunday is the most important day for leisure, it being the only full non-working day in Bombay. It is largely spent by the middle classes at home or at friends' homes or in a private club, in contrast to the lower classes, who spend it in the few public spaces such as Chowpatty beach, Juhu beach and the scarce parks. Maintenance of the body is an increasingly important component of leisure and shows lifestyle choices. Sports and fitness may be practised at home as yoga or on fitness machines but more usually in clubs, which have only western sports – tennis, golf, swimming – and are beginning to build gyms. The oldest clubs, some with British origins (the Bombay Gymkhana and the Willingdon), are now almost impossible to join because of their waiting lists and vastly inflated prices and remain the haunts of the professional middle classes and new corporate memberships. Membership of one of these clubs is almost a shibboleth of the old middle classes, their hostility to the *nouveau riche* being seen in their banning of mobile phones, the trophy of this class. There have been chains of fitness centres/gyms, such as Tavalkars, which has opened branches throughout the middle-class suburbs. American ten-pin bowling is regarded as highly fashionable and the first bowling alley has just opened. Such activities are contrasted with lower-class indigenous games and wrestling in traditional gymnasia (*akharas*),[113] and playing cricket on the public *maidans* (open spaces) or on the streets. The beauty parlour is part of the middle-class woman's life, encompassing all aspects of grooming from hairdressing to manicures and pedicures and a whole range of depilatory activities unknown in the west.

The middle classes inhabit many cultural spaces: cinemas, theatres, concert halls, the museums being largely visited, it seems, by tourists. One of the major lifestyle changes has been the increasing number of restaurants, which range from the cheapest cafés to those costing thousands of rupees.[114] These are often regional restaurants or specialize in a particular type of food such as Gujarati *thali* (set-meal), vegetarian (Rajdhani being the most fashionable), or seafood, encompassing a variety of styles such as Mangalorean (Trishna), Maharashtrian (Viva Paschim), Goan (Goa Portuguesa), Bengali (Only Fish). International choices include Italian (Trattoria), Thai (Thai Pavilion), Mexican (Casa Mexicana), Chinese, which remains ever popular (China Garden), and the icon of globalization, the inevitable McDonald's. Their importance is that Bombay now presents a variety of national and international cuisines, which is probably one of the greatest manifestations of its cosmopolitan nature. They offer great opportunities for the consumer to manifest a particular identity through the choice of restaurant, which provides grounds to display wealth, taste and style, and insider knowledge of where to eat and to be seen.[115]

Youth culture has its own locations, although many of these spaces are also used by older people, division by age being prevalent in the Bombay fashion. They include restaurants such as the Fashion Bistro, and an ever increasing number of nightclubs, from the suburban to the downtown, including those with exclusive memberships, such as the Piano Bar and the Taj Hotel's 1900s. Bars are increasingly popular, with notable successes in the Latin American themed Copa Cabana and the strangely named Ghetto. These are regarded as haunts of the elite, and the Shiv Sena's policy of early closure, supervised by the police, reveals the class and cultural tensions generated by these places.

The five-star hotels, so long the only location of luxury culture, are not used by Bombayites as accommodation, although they hire the public rooms for parties and other functions, such as weddings, and patronize their restaurants, beauty parlours and shops on a more regular basis. The Oberoi shopping arcade in downtown Bombay has a mixed range of shops and is used extensively by the urban rich for many of their shopping expeditions.

A major lifestyle activity is shopping for clothes, as designer boutiques expand with their astronomical prices, wedding outfits costing as much as a small car. There are several western clothing shops, mostly the western high-street brands such as Benetton, with few of the big designers available. Interior decor is becoming increasingly popular, although there are still few shops for interior decoration, mostly soft furnishings, several of which have overseas branches (Shyam Ahuja, Anokhi), or material is bought by the yard to be made up by tailors. There are an increasing number of shops offering expensive designer household items – modern ethnic or imported – such as Good Earth and Bombay Store, Tresor and Beautiful Boulevard. Antiques have become fashionable items, available from Philips to Chor Bazaar, antique silver from Chandni Bazaar, while more functional household goods (chatai mats, pots and pans) from Crawford Market (Mahatma Jyotiba Phule Market). Most of the furniture shops are seen as in poor taste, so antique ethnic furniture is becoming fashionable along with fake antiques from the suburb of Oshiwada or designs from magazines commissioned from local carpenters.

Cosmetics and perfumes are among the luxury items where foreign remains best. The Oberoi boasts a shop where one can smell foreign perfumes but not buy them, but indigenous upmarket ranges such as the Ayurvedic Biotique range, similar to Body Shop, are available. Laboratoires Garnier have started manufacturing an identical range to that in the UK, and similarly with shampoos and conditioners; Maybelline have just come on the market.

Foreign goods have retained their high status, formerly largely as gifts from NRI family members, now with an increase in foreign travel and import duties dropped. Western designer labels, which are heavily promoted in the media, encourage a fashion for young sportswear (Gap, DKNY and Tommy Hilfiger) which still has to be imported, while Swiss watches can be bought from Marks.

Even at the other end of the market, that of fast-moving consumer goods such as toothpaste, washing powder, etc., important choices are made as the choice is not only thrift and efficiency but between indigenous products and multinational goods. Even among the latter, a distinction exists between Hindustan Lever, which is regarded as almost Indian, and more recently arrived multinational brands. Lifestyle images at this end of the market can be seen from the fact that these are the products which dominate advertising even now.

Books and magazines are for sale all over Bombay – at its thriving bookshops (Strand, Crosswords, Nalanda for English books; while whole streets of shops selling books in regional and other languages are found, such as Princess Street's Gujarati bookshops or the Urdu and Arabic bookshops in Mohammed Ali Road), from pavement stalls and from vendors at traffic lights. Recorded music is similarly available from well-stocked shops (dominated by Rhythm House, which has been on the same premises for around fifty years and the new funky shops like Groove) and pavement vendors.

The explosion of cable and satellite television that first came to India in 1991 has been phenomenal.[116] Many channels are now available, both international (BBC, CNN, MTV) and locally made programmes uplinked from Singapore or Hong Kong (STAR, Zee, [V]). The latter channels are very much in tune with the culture of the new middle classes, with their mixture of serials, film-based programmes, films, chat-shows and news. The programmes are mostly in Hindi but also in English with Hindi subtitles, and regional language channels have increased rapidly. Many of the serials endorse the modern nuclear family, finding the feudal patriarchal family and its traditions oppressive.[117]

The last decade has also seen the rapid spread of other new media, such as the Internet, electronic mail and mobile telephones. While these have changed access to information and provided new levels of communication, we do not know much about their reach or their cultural impact.

Defining the middle classes

Bourdieu's concepts of cultural capital and cultural legitimacy allow us to define more clearly divisions within Bombay's middle classes other than purely economic or political factors. The middle classes remain in the middle of society, between the 'aristocrats' of Bombay, themselves originating in the grande bourgeoisie, who have acquired vast amounts of economic, educational and cultural capital (the Godrejs and Tatas being the prime examples); and Bombay's working class, its urban proletariat, its slum and pavement dwellers who are denied access to these forms of capital.

The middle classes can be divided into three main groups: the old middle classes, the new middle classes and the emerging petite bourgeoisie.

The old middle classes are mostly professionals, who do not have large amounts of economic capital and are reliant on earned income, but have high stocks of educational (degrees and qualifications) and cultural capital. They work in the administration and bureaucracy, in education, medicine and journalism. They have a bourgeois mentality, being mostly democratic, secular and nationalist; they are English-speaking although they may use another language at home and read another language, mainly Marathi and Hindi. In alliance with their peers in Delhi and other metropolitan cities, they control India's cultural values, legitimating them through the institutions they control – government organizations, educational institutions, museums and other cultural venues, print culture, and some of the modern media, at least in the form of censorship, thus forming part of a national bourgeoisie. They participate in Bombay's public culture to varying degrees, but maintain a deep ambivalence towards it, deploring its increasing vulgarity and commercial nature. I call them the 'old middle classes'.

A small but significant group is Bombay's rich, whose wealth is based in business, property development and the media, especially the commercial cinema. They know English, which is the major language they read, but speak a mixture of Hindi and English and their own language (mostly Sindhi, Gujarati, Marwari, Panjabi or Marathi). They have economic capital but not cultural capital as defined by the old middle classes. Ashis Nandy has argued that India's upper-middle class (bourgeoisie?) is by and large a lower-middle class (petite bourgeoisie?) with more money.[118] This group rejects the label 'middle class', referring to itself as 'upper class'. I call them the 'new middle classes' and they are the focus of the following chapters. Not only are they generating much of India's public culture, they are now also setting their own definitions of what is culturally legitimate, contesting the values of the old middle classes. This cultural conflict has led to the almost hysterical rejection of the culture of the new middle classes that I describe in the subsequent chapters.

The emerging petite bourgeoisie, mostly Maharashtrian or Gujarati, has smaller resources of educational, economic and cultural capital but aspires to increase these, through a combination of self-help, education, acquisition of English, saving and consumer choices. They are often the consumers of the texts produced by the new middle classes and the professionals, and their significance to the commercial viability of these products is considerable. This is the group from which the new middle classes must distinguish themselves to avoid what Ashis Nandy has identified as the terror of the slum.[119]

A gap in lifestyle between the generations is opening up. A new generation, reminiscent of London's 1980s 'yuppies', is working for multinationals, whether banks or media (television, advertising, etc.), earning starting salaries which are vastly over-inflated by local standards. Former middle-class jobs in public service (the Indian Administrative Service, education, and the armed forces) offer salaries which are tiny in comparison, notwithstanding their considerable perks. This new metropolitan elite forms a distinctive consumer group, distinguished from others not only by its economic power but also by its lifestyle. They are often foreign-educated, wear western clothes and pursue a more western style of leisure activities (such as bowling alleys, nightclubs, eating out). However, it seems they remain socially conservative when it comes to living with their parents, having arranged marriages, etc. They may not have large amounts of cultural capital in the sense of high culture, but they follow a lifestyle culture of designer labels, foreign holidays, etc. This metropolitan elite has begun to feature with increasing regularity in the films, magazines and novels I look at in subsequent chapters, being largely associated with film and not with television, which has concentrated on a more middle-class group.

Concluding remarks on Bombay's middle classes

In this chapter I have traced the origins of Bombay's middle classes and defined the three separate elements which they comprise. None of these three elements constitutes a homogenous class *per se*, so I have kept the plural 'classes' to mark their diversity. This diversity was also a feature of the earlier groups which I included in this study of the middle classes (the Bania bourgeoisie and the intellectual elites of the nineteenth century).

On the political side, I have suggested that many of the new middle classes are supporters of the Hindu nationalists,[120] not liberal secularists as the term 'middle class' suggests in a western context, where there has been a bourgeois culture of rationality and secularism. Bombay's new middle classes share many non-modern values, such as caste observance (at least with regard to marriage), and pay respect to feudal values of honour and status, while often challenging the claims of law, individual rights and merit. This raises the question of whether secularism and liberalism are middle-class values at all or are just western values or even western mythologies.[121] It may be that India is sharing in a worldwide phenomenon of xenophobic nationalism and religious fundamentalism or revivalism. India may be finding its own ways of enjoying materialism and consumption within the family unit which it upholds as core to its values.

It seems that Bombay and the rest of India are evolving a populist new middle class with different ideologies from a secular, international bourgeoisie. In order to examine this suggestion further, I turn to some of the most important cultural texts of this middle class, whether made by them, depicting them, or consumed by them. Their discussions of social power, gender, the family, the state and the nation give us some of the greatest insights available into this new social group.

Notes

1. See later in this chapter for a discussion of 'taste'.
2. Misra, 1961; Varma, 1998.
3. Earle, 1989: 3.
4. See Earle, 1989, for an historical analysis of this group. Also Cannadine, 1998, for an analysis of class relations in Britain.
5. This can be seen in the first of a series describing the 'new rich' of Asia. Robison and Goodman, 1996.
6. Raja Rammohan Roy being a good example. See Joshi, 1975.
7. Bayly, 1983.
8. Mani, 1998: 44.
9. Including Kopf, 1969; Kaviraj, 1995; S. Chandra, 1994.
10. See, for example, Chaudhuri, 1990; Banerjee, 1989.
11. Chatterjee, 1993: 35, reminds us this is the name they called themselves.
12. See Haynes, 1991, on the decline of Surat.
13. Ray, 1975: 17–19.
14. Khilnani, 1997: 107–49, is an elegant essay comparing several Indian cities. Calcutta has been well served by Chaudhuri, 1990; see also Gillion, 1968, on Ahmadabad; Oldenburg, 1989, on Lucknow.
15. There are several good studies of the evolution of Bombay city. Gillian Tindall's (Tindall, 1982) is a 'biography' of Bombay, an elegant and lively study of the history of British Bombay, while Dwivedi and Mehrotra, 1995, is a lavishly illustrated history of the city. Several books deal with the architecture of Bombay, notably Evenson, 1989.
16. Chandavarkar, 1994.
17. Chandavarkar, 1994: 4.
18. Markovits, 1995.
19. Patel, 1995: xxii.
20. For a more detailed analysis of caste migration and occupation in Bombay see Dobbin, 1972: 3–8.

21. Dobbin, 1972, describes the urban elites of Bombay in a social and political context.
22. Sarkar, 1983: 65–70, reminds us of the wide disparities in these groups in that they were not all by any means 'elite'.
23. Marshman, 1853, quoted by Chatterjee, 1995: 9. Literacy in English increased rapidly, especially in Bengal (*Census of India*, 1921, Vol. V, pt. I: 298, 394); while literacy in Bengal was low, at 18 per cent, 3.4 per cent were literate in English.
24. Chatterjee, 1993: 7, discusses the emergence of the bilingual elite in Calcutta.
25. Chandavarkar, 1994: 66.
26. See Dobbin, 1972, on leadership in Bombay, and Haynes, 1991, on the creation of the public sphere in Surat.
27. Dobbin, 1972: 12.
28. See Luhrmann, 1996.
29. In Gujarati the term for a merchant is *vaniya*, but since the same word is pronounced Bania both in Hindi and in Indian English, that is the spelling I will use here.
30. See Dundas, 1992, on Jainism.
31. Dwyer, 1991.
32. For a brief outline see the introduction to Shackle and Moir, 1992.
33. Engineer, 1980.
34. The success of this policy is seen most clearly in Calcutta, where in 1918 Calcutta University had 27,000 students, making it the largest in the world at that time.
35. See Dwyer, 1999: Chapter 3, on the impact of western education on Gujarati literature.
36. Viswanathan, 1989.
37. The Victoria and Albert Museum of Bombay has been renamed the Bhau Daji Lad Museum.

38. Haynes, 1991.
39. While this book is concerned with the middle classes, it is notable that alternative ideologies were offered by movements such as Jotirao Phule's low-caste movement in modern Maharashtra (O'Hanlon, 1985), and the adivasi movement in Gujarat (Hardiman, 1987).
40. The sheer volume of the press is seen in the fact that printing was the second-largest industry in Bengal in 1911, despite the low rate of literacy (Roy, 1995: 30).
41. Mani, 1998, argues that the issue of *sati* was really a debate about the nature of Indian society and Hindu tradition.
42. Chatterjee, 1993: 6.
43. Chatterjee, 1993: 116–34.
44. Tharu and Lalita, 1995a, b.
45. For a discussion of these in the context of nationalism see Chatterjee, 1993: 134–57.
46. See for example Sarkar, 1983, entitled *Modern India, 1885–1947*.
47. Johnson, 1973: 2.
48. Even those whose origins were not middle class, such as Bhim Rao Ambedkar (1891–1956), seemed to enter into a similar trajectory. Born an 'untouchable' Mahar from Maharashtra, he took doctorates from the universities of Colombia and London, became a barrister and drafted the Indian constitution.
49. Tarlo, 1996, traces the evolution of Gandhi's dress.
50. Amin, 1984, shows how Gandhi's actions were open to highly divergent analyses.
51. Naipaul, 1977: 137.
52. Bardhan, 1988, calls these 'the proprietary classes', comprising industrial capitalists, rich farmers, white-collar workers and professionals.
53. Vanaik, 1990: 36.
54. Varma, 1998: 85–6.
55. Vanaik, 1990: 8.
56. See Jaffrelot, 1996.
57. See Chapter 2 above; also Lutgendorf, 1995; Mitra, 1993.
58. Kapur, 1993.
59. Sadhvi Rithambhara's speeches are widely distributed on cassette tape, thus bypassing the need for a literate audience.
60. Jaffrelot, 1996: 426. Jaffrelot cites Basu: 'the ideal woman from the Hindu nationalists' point of view is not only maternal and discreet, but also resolute in her dedication to the cause. In this context male Hindu nationalist cadres seem to be prepared to recognise a public role for women' (Jaffrelot, 1996: 428).
61. Jaffrelot, [2000].
62. See Heuzé, 1995, and T. Hansen, 1998, on the rise of the Shiv Sena.
63. These can be seen as a continuation of Tilak's political mobilization of the Ganpati festival in 1893 and the Shivaji festival of 1895.
64. See Pinney, 1997, on the uses of chromolithographs.
65. Naipaul, 1990, for an analysis of the appeal of the Shiv Sena to these classes.
66. See K. Sharma, 1995.
67. Padgaonkar, 1993 is a collection of the coverage of the riots in Bombay's most prestigious newspaper, *The Times of India*.
68. Padgaonkar, 1993: Chapter 7, 'The great betrayal'.
69. The black economy of Bombay is said to have generated a huge underworld, largely Muslim-dominated, its current leader, Dawood Ibrahim, being resident in the Gulf. The Muslim underworld is said to run all manner of rackets in Bombay, to finance the film industry, and to have organized the bomb blasts in March 1993 in retaliation for the massacres of Muslims in the December–January riots.
70. Padgaonkar, 1993: 184–5 and *passim*.
71. Mohamed, 1993.
72. The metropolitan cities of India are Delhi, Bombay, Calcutta, Madras and Bangalore.
73. Stern, 1993, studies the rise of the small-town middle classes.
74. P. Mishra, 1995, is a journalistic travelogue through some of these small towns.
75. Khilnani, 1997.
76. See Chapter 1 above on the 'ex-nomination' of the bourgeoisie.
77. Figure from the *Economic Times of India*, quoted by Rajgopal, 1999: 91.
78. Nonetheless these people voted for the more protectionist BJP in 1996 and 1998.
79. Merchant, 1996.
80. Comparative figures for the two countries' middle classes would be more useful but are not available.
81. D. Miller, 1995: 31.
82. Meanwhile the UK McDonald's have started making Indian-style burgers.
83. Jeffrey, [1999].
84. Jeffrey, 1996.

85. Rajgopal, 1999: 78.
86. This was emphasized heavily during my interviews with Titu Ahluwalia and his colleagues at MARG, one of India's major market research bureaux.
87. *India Today*, Dec. 1980: 115.
88. Monteiro, 1998: 199.
89. Rajgopal, 1999.
90. Bourdieu, 1984.
91. Bourdieu, 1984: 254.
92. Mallison, 1995.
93. See also Chapter 2 above.
94. Few of the literatures which were produced in Bombay, mainly Gujarati and Marathi, but also Hindi and Urdu among others, have been translated into English. Even the great novels of these literatures, for example, Govardhanram Tripathi's (1855–1907) four-volume novel *Sarasvaticandra* (1887–1901), whose eponymous hero was a Bombay-educated man, although canonically regarded as the greatest Gujarati novel, has not yet been translated into English.
95. Many of the Progressive Writers' Movement worked in the film industry, mostly as lyricists but also as dialogue writers. See Chapter 4 below for further details.
96. Bombay's writers in English include Salman Rushdie, Rohinton Mistry, Firdaus Kanga, Vikram Chandra and Shashi Deshpande. Although many Bombay poets write in English, the only ones to come to international attention are Arun Kolatkar and Imtiaz Dharker.
97. See Chapter 2 above.
98. Dharwadkar, 1993, traces the orientalist category of Indian literature from the mid-eighteenth to the mid-twentieth century.
99. Chatterjee, 1995: 8, discusses Anderson, 1991, on the role of print-capitalism in the rise of nationalism, in the context of Bengali literature.
100. Mukherjee, 1985, remains the best introduction to the Indian novel.
101. Chatterjee, 1993: 135–57, on autobiography, and Banerjee, 1989, on Bengali popular culture. Much of the writing in Tharu and Lalita, 1995, is from autobiographies and journals.
102. See Dwyer, 1999, on histories of Gujarati literature.
103. But see Jeffrey [1999].
104. Anderson, 1991.
105. See Chapter 6 below on film magazines and the role of gossip.
106. See Hansen [2000].
107. Banerjee, 1989; Guha Thakurta, 1992a and b.
108. K. Hansen [2000].
109. See Gokhale, 1995.
110. See Conlon, 1995.
111. Although see Nandy, 1989, and Appadurai, 1995, on cricket.
112. See Pinney [2000] for a discussion of this term.
113. Alter, also portrayed in Chandra, 1997.
114. Conlon, 1995, on the history of eating out in Bombay and its relationship to wider cultural 'taste'.
115. See also Appadurai, 1988, on the creation of a national cuisine.
116. Merchant, 1996.
117. Monteiro, 1998: 184.
118. Nandy, 1998: 5.
119. Nandy, 1998.
120. The majority of these new middle classes are Hindu, although there is a significant, though small, Muslim sector.
121. Robison and Goodman, 1996.

4

Industry of Desire: The Hindi Cinema

Cinema's status as cultural capital is uncertain, its legitimacy never assured.[1] This can be seen clearly in India, where some cinemas are legitimized, while others are not. Tracing these cinemas back to a popular middle-class culture, I focus on the one whose legitimacy has been most vigorously contested, the Hindi cinema of Bombay, India's national, popular cinema. Although many of the grounds for this contestation are to do with wider social issues, namely denying legitimacy to the culture of the new middle classes and lower classes, they are usually presented as being inherent to the film text, including distinctive features such as its deployment of genre, and its use of language and music.

One of the most striking features of the Hindi cinema is the operation of a star system, where the star emerges as a text, the focus for discourses on sexuality, desire and the body, love and the family. These discourses come together in the 1990s in a new genre of films that shows the rising cultural confidence of the new middle classes, as they depict their cultural aspirations in the high-budget romantic films which have been the super-hits of the last decade. These films depict the nature of sex, romance and the family in the context of the super-rich and set the pace for India's upwardly mobile.

Indian cinemas

The cinema is one of India's most vibrant cultural products and a major industry:[2] now nearly 100 years old, it makes the largest number of films in the world, at its peak estimated at around 800 a year, that is, a quarter of the total number made worldwide. India's 13,000 cinema halls have a daily audience of around 15 million,[3] and many of these films are hugely popular overseas, in Europe and North America, not only among the South Asian diaspora, but also loved by much of the rest of the world. However, the industry's budgets are small in comparison with Hollywood, but in the sheer volume of employment and taxation which it generates, its economic importance is considerable. India has not one but several cinemas which can be distinguished in terms of film-making (methods of production and distribution), the film text (technical and stylistic features, language) and by the film's reception (by the audience and by critics). These categories are not entirely discrete, but may be placed on a continuum, with clusters of defining features forming at certain points. The separation of these categories during the 1970s is connected with wider issues of social change and political ideology, including the emergence of new middle classes.

Cinema in India began on 7 July 1896 with a screening of the Lumiere Brothers' Cinematograph films in Bombay. The first entirely Indian-made film, *Raja Harischandra*, produced and directed by D. G. Phalke, was released in 1913. This film drew on a wide range of Indian popular or middlebrow culture, including the visual regime established in the nineteenth century by Ravi Verma's painting, and developed in the new technologies of chromolithography ('calendar art') and photography;[4] the use of mythological narratives (this film was based on an episode from the *Mahabharata*), the narrative on the silent screen elaborated by story-tellers, in a manner similar to that used for telling folk stories from scroll paintings; and musical accompaniment in a popular style.

During its first few decades, Indian cinema remained within this wider sphere of Indian popular culture. The early days of Indian cinema are known as 'the studio period', a time when all persons involved in making a film, from the spotboys to the stars, were contracted to studios, in a setup similar to that of Hollywood's studio period.[5] These people, and the cinema's audience, were from a wide range of social backgrounds, from the elites to the lower classes. Nevertheless, cinema continued to struggle with its dubious status, which must be contextualized in the wider association in India of the performing arts with prostitution and the low castes. The cinema continued to evolve its own genres (including the mythological, the devotional, the stunt, the historical and the social concern film, and the social) and techniques, mixing indigenous aesthetics with the codes of classical Hollywood.[6]

Even after the rise of the independent producer in the 1940s, film remained an assembly process of separately produced parts,[7] a mixture of cultural expressions,[8] at all levels, the blend being most dramatic in its music and song. As well as establishing itself as the dominant form of public culture, cinema reached into many other areas of popular culture, such as music, calendar art and even the print media, where it featured in magazines concerned solely with cinema (see Chapter 6) and in the national press. Meanwhile, Satyajit Ray, who made his first film, *Pather*

Panchali, in 1955 with help from the West Bengal government, established himself as one of the world's great film-makers. Although Ray's narratives are often taken from Bengali literature and have specifically Bengali locales and cultural milieux, his films belong to traditions of international art cinema and never established a national popularity except among the art house film-viewers.

In the 1950s, the new nation's media debated the creation of a national cinema and the government's role in its development.[9] Although Nehru was not fond of cinema, he realized the political advantages of Raj Kapoor's popularity in the Soviet Union and elsewhere, and kept good relations with the film world, although government enquiries into the rapidly expanding industry and its censorship yielded few benefits to the film-makers. In fact, the government's negative views led to a boycott by film music producers of All India Radio,[10] and resentment from the industry, which thought that it was viewed as a large taxpayer rather than a cultural resource. During this period the government established national academies of dance, literature and theatre but not of cinema. However, in 1960 it set up the Film Finance Corporation (which merged in 1980 with the Motion Picture Export Association to form the National Film Development Corporation, for financing and exporting films) and in 1961 established the Film Institute in Poona in the old Prabhat studios (soon augmented by the National Film Archive and later still extended to cover television). For the first time students could learn about film-making in an academic environment, and many of the art film personnel as well as a few of the Hindi film personnel were trained there. In 1973 the government established the Directorate of Film Festivals, whose brief was to organize an annual International Film Festival, which to this day remains one of the few places for the Indian public to see art and other international film.

This period marks the beginning of the separation of categories of film in India. Madhava Prasad argues that the Hindi film's omnibus genre of the social, with its underlying theme of the feudal family romance,[11] which long resisted generic differentiation, was segmented in the early 1970s. He sees this as part of a wider change in ideology, as the fragmentation of the national consensus brought about by political mobilization, as challenging the aesthetic conventions and mode of production of the film industry.[12] This resulted in the emergence of three major forms of the Hindi cinema: developmentalist state realism; identification-oriented realism of the middle-class arena; and the aesthetic of mobilization.[13] This model situates these changes in terms of wider issues of politics and ideology and shows how all these types of cinema to some extent draw on existing practices of narrative codes and signification.

These categories are somewhat similar to those suggested by Ashis Nandy, who argues that in the 1970s, Indian (not just Hindi) cinema split from the previous middlebrow, middle-class cinema into three categories: the art, the middle and the commercial.[14] The middle cinema is a continuation of the earlier popular cinema, while the other two forms, which derive from the latter, are significantly different. The art cinema criticizes tradition, seeming to support the 'survival sector' of Indian society, but in fact rejecting its values which the commercial cinema upholds and romanticizes. Nandy locates these changes in the social uprooting of this period, in particular large-scale migration to the cities which has resulted in the cultural displacement of people whose needs are catered for by the commercial cinema.

During the 1980s, the Hindi commercial cinema produced mostly films which belong to Prasad's aesthetic of mobilization, and this is regarded as the decade during which violence was the major attraction. While having roots in wider political and social trends of the 1970s, this phenomenon is also connected to changes in the composition of the cinema audience caused by the advent of colour television in 1982, followed by the increasing availability of the video cassette recorder. Thus the middle-class audience began watching the new television soaps and viewing films on video at home, while the cinema halls became run down and regarded as suitable only for lower-class men.

Prasad discusses two films of the 1990s, locating them within the cultural changes brought about by liberalization, noting certain significant changes such as the emergence of different techniques of production, styles and aesthetics.[15] This was due in part to the impact of south Indian cinema on the Hindi cinema, whose popularity seemed assured by the films of Mani Ratnam and other directors in the early to mid-1990s, but whose indirect influence has been greater than their own box office success. Despite the advent of cable and satellite television in India in 1991, the middle class has returned to the cinema halls to form a segment of the cinema audience, largely as the result of improved marketing and the vastly improved cinema facilities. This section of the audience will pay up to Rs100 to see a film in a fully equipped luxurious cinema, compared to the Rs10 in the cinemas of lower-class districts. The commercial cinema caters knowingly to different audiences, screening different genres in different theatres. These include the action film, the inheritor of the aesthetic of mobilization, which is screened in the cheaper movie halls, while another is the comedy, largely a one-man genre centred on Govinda, whose major popularity is among the lower classes, but whose talents have recently found a growing audience among the middle classes.[16]

However, the major hits of the 1990s, which have broken most previous box office records, are the big-budget, plushy, romantic films, which, I argue, mark the dominance of the values of the new middle classes as they find their audiences across social categories. These films revive a form of the feudal family romance in a new, stylish, yet unmistakably Hindu, patriarchal structure which, I argue, is connected to their contribution to the resurgence of the politics of Hindutva in the 1980s and 1990s.[17]

Prasad's and Nandy's models provide important ways of thinking about Indian cinema in the context of the new middle classes, locating it in shifting ideology and social and cultural displacement. I have chosen to use three slightly different categories, terms which are actually coined by the cinema-makers and their audiences, which are founded to some extent in different aesthetics, but are also useful as categories of taste: the art cinema, the Hindi commercial cinema and the popular regional cinemas. Unfortunately the terms 'art' and 'commercial' imply that one has noble aesthetic concerns, while the other is only concerned with financial rewards, but in the absence of good alternatives, they are convenient, widely used shorthands for grouping these varieties of cinema.

The Indian cinema that is seen at international film festivals, more rarely screened at cinema halls, is closest to western art cinema. Although its output is small, its range is vast, being made in a number of centres around India, in many different languages. The best-known of these film-makers is Satyajit Ray, nearly all of whose films were made in Bengali, drawing on modes of European and other art cinema.[18] Calcutta continues to produce a small number of Bengali art films which are usually critically acclaimed. From the 1970s, a number of Hindi films produced in Bombay have formed the 'new', 'middle' or 'parallel' cinema, which covers a wide range from Shyam Benegal's mostly realist, narrative cinema, to the avant-garde films of Kumar Shahani and Mani Kaul. South India has a flourishing art cinema, largely based in Kerala, with its most famous directors including Aravindan and Adoor Gopalakrishnan.

The art cinema is appreciated by a small elite which watches this and foreign art movies. Its aesthetic is the result of a dialogue between Indian and European culture which began almost two hundred years ago and manifests itself mainly in the Indian novel. Its preoccupations are local rather than global, it is politically oriented and it operates largely in a realist mode.[19] Art cinema is wrongly attacked for being 'not Indian' by many because Indian popular culture rejects western high culture, although it in turn embraces some aspects of lowbrow western culture. The audience for art cinema belongs to the elites or the old middle classes, and is linked to a wider audience of art cinema-goers overseas.

My second category of cinema is popular or commercial cinema, although these terms are felt to be derogatory, implying that it has no artistic merit, leading to its makers calling it simply 'Indian cinema' or by the language in which it is made, such as Tamil or Bengali. This category includes the films made in Bombay, often called 'Bollywood', which are popular all over the rest of India and have devoted audiences in Africa, the former Soviet Union and the Middle East, where they are often preferred to Hollywood or local cinema. These films are made in varieties of Hindi/ Urdu, a *lingua franca* widely understood north of an imaginary line between Bombay and Calcutta. Since this is regarded as the national cinema and Hindi is, disputably, the national language, it is called the Hindi cinema and this is the name which I shall use. However, its claim to be the national cinema is contested by a number of regional cinemas making films in local languages, notably that based in Madras (Chennai), which makes a larger number of films than does Bombay, mostly in Tamil and Telugu (the state languages of Tamil Nadu and Andhra Pradesh) but these films are seen only in the four southern states of India and where their diasporas have settled (Malaysia, Singapore, etc.). Other regional cinemas, such as those made in Panjabi, Gujarati and Bengali, are much smaller and have limited audiences. All these cinemas are different from the Hindi cinema, in that they mostly address local issues rather than national questions, and several of them deal with regional politics and nationalism.[20] In the Hindi-speaking areas, the regional cinemas are regarded as lowbrow, catering to the unsophisticated tastes of the small town and lower classes. Genres no longer so popular in the Hindi cinema are still produced in these smaller cinemas, such as the mythological, which often addresses a local deity, and the devotional, in which *bhakti* lyrics in the local language form a major attraction.[21]

The divisions between the popular and the art film are hotly contested, the makers of Hindi film rejecting them altogether, arguing there are only good and bad films and that art films are non-commercial precisely because no one wants to see them. By defining good and bad largely in terms of box office success, the commercial cinema falls into the trap of making commercial viability the predominant criterion, which is then levelled as a criticism of Hindi cinema, where box office receipts are valued more highly than creative or artistic contributions. Here again we see a return to the issue of class preference and to Bourdieu's concept of taste,[22] which manifests itself as a clash between the cultural legitimacy of the two cinemas. The era of the segmentation of the Indian cinema, namely the 1970s, is also when the new middle classes emerged and the divisions between the two cinemas were largely defined as the taste of different social groups. The art cinema shares the tastes of other cultural forms of the old middle classes, hence it is legitimated through state funding or government sponsorship and through its appreciation by members of this class – academics, intellectuals and other writers in India and overseas.

The commercial cinema is more diffuse, in that its audience is drawn from a wider social spectrum, while its films manifest a mixture of class tastes, some having the lower or working classes as its major social referent, while others share middle-class values in their depiction of the couple and of the bourgeois family. It is in the commercial cinema that the new middle classes are establishing their cultural hegemony, their depictions of lifestyle becoming those to which the lower classes aspire; hence its appeal to a broad social spectrum, and also its rejection by the old middle classes. Ashis Nandy argues that commercial cinema puts an emphasis on

> lower-middle-class sensibilities and on the informal, not-terribly-tacit theories of politics and society ... and the ... ability to shock the *haute bourgeoisie* with the directness, vigour and crudity of these theories.[23]

He suggests that this cinema is a reading of the haute bourgeoisie by the lower middle classes. This explains the medium's stylization, grandi-loquence, conventions and mannerisms and the fantasy of a peasant or rural past as a lost paradise, fearful of the city and its amorality. In my reading, this is a depiction of the culture espoused by the new middle classes, which may be close to that of the lower-middle classes, but differs from it in that its consumerist lifestyle opportunities are those of the rich. The old middle classes may well see this reading as a mimicry of their culture, hence their scorn of the medium which they see as a lowbrow interpretation of their values, anxieties, lifestyles and utopias. They find commercial cinema 'shamelessly rustic and blatantly cosmopolitan [its world] neither authentically traditional nor genuinely modern, a meeting of the mass and the popular'.[24] Nandy deftly sums up this attitude:

> An average, 'normal', Bombay film has to be, to the extent possible, everything to everyone. It has to cut across the myriad ethnicities and lifestyles of India and even of the world that impinges on India. The popular film *is* low-brow, modernizing India in all its complexity, sophistry, naiveté and vulgarity. Studying popular film *is* studying Indian modernity at its rawest, its crudities laid bare by the fate of traditions in contemporary life and arts. Above all, it is studying caricatures of ourselves ...

The popular cinema may be what the middle class, left to itself, might have done to itself and to India, but it is also the disowned self of modern India returning in a fantastic or monstrous form to haunt modern India.[25]

His argument is supported by Richard Dyer's contention that looking at the kind of escapism cinema is required to provide is likely to reveal a collective fantasy, a utopian solution to counteract anxieties.[26] The recurring motifs of Indian movies – such as the emphasis on family, the community and the individual's relation to them; poverty and wealth; and the opportunity for social mobility – can be seen as responses to the anxieties and fantasies of the cinema audience.[27]

It is partly on the grounds of these class divisions that Hindi cinema is denied the cultural legitimacy it seeks, notwithstanding the fact that it is one of India's major industries, taxpayers and employers. While the art cinema is simply ignored by the masses, Hindi cinema is routinely disparaged by Indian intellectuals, who define the legitimacy of culture. For example, Chidananda Das Gupta, a founding member of the Calcutta Film Society that was so central to the creation of an Indian art cinema ('the serious, realistic, "art" cinema is easy enough to understand'),[28] tries to understand the commercial Hindi film but keeps judging it on the terms of the art film, his resulting exasperation breaking into his writing repeatedly. In the case of film songs, he begins by writing of his irritation with their lack of intellectual rigour:

The inveterate didacticism of Indian cinema, both in its high art and pop forms, finds an outlet in the latter's songs. Invariably, they spout facile philosophy, giving vent to the Indian predilection, even among the illiterate, for moralizing and generalizing on every event.[29]

But he finds pleasure in their language and music,

Even if the sentiments expressed are sometimes trite, the songs are often written in felicitous language and perfect syntax, and their eclectic melodies come from folk traditions, the Urdu *ghazal*, even classical music or *Rabindra sangeet* and western pop music.[30]

while he loathes two of its most popular features, its action sequences and its dramatic dialogues:

It is only in the late eighties that one begins to come across a mindless streak ... that refuses to take off from the low average level of the action and dialogue sequences.[31]

Das Gupta continues in this vein, calling his final chapter 'The value of trash'. Satyajit Ray is regarded as a harsh critic of the commercial cinema, yet his view of it is distant yet sympathetic[32] as can be seen from his brief discussion of the Hindi film song, even writing about how it is mocked by 'a tiny highbrow minority who write about it in snickering terms in the pages of little magazines whose readership would barely fill a decent-sized cinema'.[33] He admits he has problems with the lack of realism in the use of music – in particular he does not like the way the song is integrated into the film, nor the mismatch of voices between actors and playback singers – but he finds the picturization 'a daring innovation, wholly cinematic and entirely valid', and is amazed at the inventiveness of the lyrics, and even concedes that the 'borrowing' of music is forgiveable:

> I feel less anger than admiration for the composer who can lift the main theme of the finest movement of Mozart's finest symphony, turn it into a *filmi geet* and make it sound convincing.[34]

The legitimacy of commercial Hindi cinema has been contested in other arenas, notably in film studies. Film studies has established itself as an academic discipline in the west since the 1960s. Initially based on structuralist semiotics, Lacanian psychoanalysis and feminism in the 1970s, it has broadened its terms of reference to include culturalism and identity politics in the 1980s, then added queer theory and subaltern studies in the 1990s. In India, although film studies has not yet become an established academic discourse, being taught at postgraduate level in only one university department,[35] an important group of film theorists has emerged.[36] Film studies has examined mostly the commercial cinema, and, to a much lesser extent, the avant-garde. The work of this group of critics has been important in integrating Indian cinema into the wider field of film studies, by creating new knowledge about this form of cinema and dispelling some widely held misconceptions. Yet as Colin MacCabe has pointed out, the study of popular culture often uses the highest theory,[37] its specialized language and references making it inaccessible to the non-academic, hence this important research has been largely ignored by non-specialists in India.[38] Thus one significant opportunity for granting the commercial cinema cultural legitimacy has been lost, for while this group has the highest educational capital, its limited reach shows the clear separation of academic and wider cultural discourse in India.

The academic work has not been taken up by the Indian film critics. The critics write in a more accessible language, but as journalists their intention is not to locate cinema within wider cultural or filmic issues, but to review individual films or to write features about film-makers, actors and certain current topics. Some journalists interact closely with the industry, while others have no personal connections, yet many of them have a deep ambivalence to commercial cinema, perhaps reflecting problems of their negotiating their own professional status in between the commercial cinema and the legitimate press. This ambivalence, along with the industry's association of journalism with gossip,[39] has led to a highly complex relationship between the critics and the industry. Several books have been written by the critics, but their quality ranges widely, from the informative to speculative gossip. Some of the more exciting critics have yet to publish their collected magazine and newspaper articles, which have appeared over several decades, but when they do so it will allow the Hindi cinema to be reassessed.[40]

The commercial cinema industry, while resentful of the criticism it has faced from all quarters, and its desire for legitimacy, has done little to further its own cause. It has not archived its own work, nor produced its own self-reflexive or analytical discourse, nor granted access to those who seek to research it. It is now beginning to compile websites which reveal how the industry sees itself.[41] Web sites are also compiled by fans, thus providing one of the few arenas for discussion of the cinema audience's views on cinema, although clearly only a tiny fraction of total viewers has access to the Net.[42]

It is perhaps ironic that the commercial Hindi cinema has been celebrated by the great cultural form of the old middle classes, the English novel, which has been India's major cultural export of the last two decades. Salman Rushdie's novels engage with a wide range of Indian public cultures, including the Hindi film, with many of his characters being actors, producers and movie fans. Others such as Shashi Tharoor, Shobha Dé[43] and several non-Indian authors (Clive James, Luke Jennings) have also written about cinema. For all these writers the commercial cinema appears as a grotesque form of Indian modernity, its personnel as amoral and sex-crazy. However, a new generation of writers, including Vikram Chandra,[44] has a great affection for Hindi cinema, which it regards as a cultural expression of emotion rather than an object of ridicule.[45] This reconsideration, along with the rising respectability of cultural studies, may mark the beginnings of a sea-change in the cultural legitimacy of the commercial cinema as its status is reassessed by a younger generation with a more complex understanding and acceptance of popular culture.

Textual grounds for refusing legitimacy

There are clearly criteria other than the aesthetic or commercial which distinguish the art and the popular cinemas – economic (concerning funding and production, distribution and exhibition), technical features, generic formation, the use of stars, the use of music and so on – which can be traced to their different histories. Some features of the commercial Hindi movie have prevented its gaining access to cultural legitimacy, including the lack of genre distinction; the absence of realism; the operation of a melodramatic mode; the centrality of song and dance or spectacle which has a complicated relationship with dialogue and plot; and the need to understand the star system.

The Hindi movie is often described as being formulaic, a *masala* ('spicy mix') of various elements which Hollywood would regard as belonging to separate genres. Genre is notoriously difficult to define even in the Hollywood context[46] but the audience, the producer and the distributor recognize a genre when they see one and use this category for a number of purposes. Hindi movies comprise only a few clearly delineated genres, such as the historical or the action or the nationalist movie (although these may still contain many features of other genres).

Since *Raja Harishcandra* (1913), Indian cinema has continued to develop its own unique styles, modes, genres and themes, drawing on a wide range of sources, both indigenous (including folk and urban theatre and mythology) and international (notably Hollywood). During the studio period (roughly the late 1920s to the late 1940s) a number of genres crystallized. It has often been argued that the random mixing of genres was brought about by the rise of the independent producer in the 1950s, eager to maximize profits at any cost. Nevertheless, a number of genres can be separated during the 1950s. Vasudevan distinguishes the following: - mythological, devotional, stunt, historical, social problem and social.[47] The last is a large omnibus category,[48] which approximates the category which Prasad argues dominated the 1950s and 1960s, namely the feudal family romance,[49] which he defines as a genre

> in which romance narratives reminiscent of early modern melo-drama, centering around aristocratic or otherwise exemplary figures, were presented in a loose, episodic structure with parallel sub-narratives and extra-diegetic interpolations. At the level of content, these narratives could register the contemporary in diverse ways (thus the central figures could be drawn from modern society: industrialists, well-behaved and pedigreed family, etc.) but the formal structure signalled a closure which evoked the pre-

capitalist not because it is in any way fully 'characteristic' of another era, but because it had become a full-blown convention before the arrival of cinema, in popular theatre.[50]

Prasad argues that this genre survives until the 1970s, when it comes under threat from the democratic genres of melodrama and realism.[51] These two modes have formed the central part of the critics' attack on the Hindi commercial cinema, which they have chastised for its absence of realism and its excess of melodrama, ignoring the 'rehabilitation' of these modes in film, literary and cultural studies.

While the commercial cinema has been criticized for its lack of realism, the latter is of course a mode of representation, based on assumptions about reality.[52] Meenakshi Mukherjee's work has looked at the specific problems of introducing realism into the Indian novel, since this aesthetic is often felt to be alien in India.[53] This can be seen in many narratives (folk tales, myths, etc.) and visual representations, notably pictures of gods and so-called calendar art. This question is further problematized by the movie, which incorporates narrative, visual and other regimes. A useful model of three main types of realism is provided in Ien Ang's work on the soap opera.[54] These include 'empiricist realism', in which art suggests our own experience, cinema being seen as a reflection of the outside world. Clearly this contravenes the narrative of Hindi films, which is unreal in the sense it is not portraying any kind of 'truth': there is not usually any psychological development of characters, dialogues are delivered rather than spoken 'naturally', song, dance and spectacle predominate, characters are usually fabulously wealthy, there is no reference to caste, and there is an emphasis on romance in a country where arranged marriage is the norm and so on. A second type of realism is called 'classic realism', a term Ang uses when the text presents itself as real, using fixed codes, the type of cinema we have become used to from classic Hollywood realism. These two forms of realism are upheld by art cinema, and used as a major source of criticism by the critics of the commercial cinema. However, it seems that Ang's third category may be usefully used for Hindi movies, that of 'emotional realism' where the emphasis is, as the name suggests, on being true to emotions rather than any other aspect of life. This type of realism often works through melodrama, as is the case with the Hindi film. This ties in with the industry's own views of its work, Yash Chopra categorizing his films' major themes as being 'about human emotions only'.

I am not attempting to find realism in Hindi cinema to fulfil criteria of taste. However, for whatever reasons, this value is upheld and discussed widely by the film-makers themselves[55] and by many of the audience.

Prasad defines two forms of realism in Hindi cinema:[56] 'nationalist realism', which is adopted by art cinema, and *mise-en-valeur* for popular cinema 'to designate the work of textual organization that produces the real as the rational',[57] in which the moral world is subordinate to the legal system, unlike the feudal family romance, and there is a drive towards an internal unity of narration, often focused on one character. Nationalist realism is clearly the mode legitimated by the old middle classes, while this new form of realism is associated with the new middle classes, who accept realism as a limited aesthetic value, being willing to subordinate it to what they regard as the more pressing concerns of the text. For example, the exotic locations of song sequences may be supported diegetically by a holiday or a dream sequence, but the use of song and the many costume changes undertaken by the heroine may suggest other concerns such as the need for spectacle and excess, and a need to step outside the narrative of the film.

The importance of the hitherto neglected or despised melodrama in western culture and cinema was highlighted in two studies which first appeared in the 1970s, Peter Brooks discussing its position within the realist aesthetic in nineteenth-century theatre and the novels of Balzac and James, while Thomas Elsaesser looked at the 1950s Hollywood directors such as Sirk, Minnelli and (Nicholas) Ray.[58] Both drew attention to the expressionism of melodrama, its connections with certain psychoanalytic formations, the use of music and nonverbal signs and its origins in the bourgeois revolution at the end of the eighteenth century.[59] Melodrama is used to describe cultural genres that stir up emotions, drawing on a 'tragic structure of feeling'.[60] It is often seen as cheap sentimental trash, which provokes ridicule for its failed, mundane tragedy, its straining for effect, its exaggeration of plot and characters, and its dominance of emotion over other considerations.[61] In melodrama the emphasis is not on the psychology and lifestyle of a unique individual but on the functioning of characters in situations that push their emotions to extremes. Melodrama needs to be read metaphorically rather than for its literary or other values. Melodrama is the underlying mode of Hindi cinema with its typical focus on the family, the suffering of the powerless good (especially through illness, family breakup, misunderstanding and doomed love), often at the hands of a villain who is known to the family. There are situations which can be resolved only through convenient deaths, chance meetings and implausible happy endings. Stephen Neale argues that the pleasure of melodrama or the pleasure of being made to cry is a fantasy of love rather than sex (in psychoanalytic terms, it is a narcissistic fantasy), hence the involvement of other family members and even the community and indeed the nation.[62] This explains the importance of mother figures who give protection and make self-sacrifices. In these pleasures the audience can overcome the meaninglessness of everyday existence and find reassurance for fractured lives.

Melodrama is such a broad category it can be hard to discern any specificities, but it is still an important and useful way of thinking about Hindi cinema, in particular those features which have led to the questioning of its cultural legitimacy.[63] While Vasudevan has shown how melodrama operates at many levels within the Hindi movies, I focus instead on language, a much-neglected area of the Hindi movies and a major arena of cultural contestation. As mentioned above, melodrama foregrounds language, as it makes all feelings exterior, through the characters' verbalizing, creating discourses on their emotions. In the Hindi film there is an opportunity to do this not just in dialogues or soliloquies but in the song lyric, where visuals and language are simultaneously foregrounded.

The first Indian talkie, Ardeshir Irani's *Alam Ara* (1931), had ten songs, and audiences were enticed with the promise of hearing the gods and goddesses talking in their own language. The language in question was Hindustani, a colloquial form drawing on a number of varieties of the language spoken over north India, including Hindi and Urdu.[64] The older films have a much stronger Urdu influence, while the modern films use a form of Bombay Hindi with a little English for dialogues, while the songs may still show strong traces of Urdu. The Bombay cinema's role as a national cinema has been created not just or even mainly through its subject matter, or its appeal to pan-Indian sensibilities, but through the development of a pan-Indian language. The decline of Urdu in India, since the association of Urdu with South Asian Islam, has meant that there is a scarcity of poets and indeed of an audience educated in the literary and lyric traditions of the language. Hindi has continued to develop a formal, Sanskritized register, which since it is taught in schools and used for many written forms of language is regarded as the language of the middle-class professionals. The movies use a colloquial language which is readily understood by speakers of Hindi and Urdu, but without any of the sophisticated connotations of the literary forms of either language, it is regarded by the elite as crude and lower class.

Nevertheless, Indian cinema has close connections with Indian literature. The 'art cinema' has frequently drawn on literature for its stories, notably Satyajit Ray's films of Tagore's and Banerjee's fiction, and recent years have seen Mahasweta Devi's fiction used by Kalpana Lajmi (*Rudaali*, 'The mourner', 1992) and Govind Nihalani's *Hazaar chaurasi ki ma* ('Mother of 1084', 1998). The popular Hindi movie has also drawn on several forms of literature, of which the most famous example is undoubtedly Saratchandra's Bengali novel *Devdas*, Bengali and Hindi versions of which were produced in 1935 by New Theatres, Calcutta; a further version was made by Bimal Roy in 1955. Since the 1950s literature has been used less for popular cinema's storylines, which are often inspired by Hollywood or western popular fiction, although the work of popular novelists such as Gurudatta and Gulshan Nanda has been used at least up until the 1970s.[65] I have been told that such scripts are subsequently published as novels but have yet to come across any.

The Hindi script is a colloborative effort involving storywriters and dialogue writers; while lyric writers supply songs for situations described by the producer/director.[66] The closest connection between literature and popular cinema in India has been in the number of literary figures who have made a living by writing for the screen. These include K. M. Munshi (1887-1971), politician, Gujarati novelist, playwright and critic, who wrote a number of film scripts in the 1930s. The closest of these connections was seen among a literary movement which began in the 1930s, the Progressive Writers Movement (PWM), many of whose members wrote scripts and dialogues for films. The PWM was largely a Hindi–Urdu group, and popular cinema is often seen as being the last great arena for the Urdu language in India. These writers included Krishan Chander, Rajinder Singh Bedi, Sadat Hasan Manto and Ismat Chughtai. Several of the actors have also had literary connections, notably Balraj Sahni, who wrote scripts and autobiography, and Rahi Masoom Reza, scriptwriter and novelist. Many lyricists were also published Urdu poets, including Sahir Ludhianvi and Kaifi Azmi; even today, Javed Akhtar, one of the most highly paid film lyricists, publishes Urdu poetry, albeit in two scripts. One of the top dialogue writers, Javed Siddiqui, writes in a whole range of cultures from art to commercial cinema, to middlebrow theatre. The cinema remains one of the few areas where Urdu writing has any commercial viability in India.[67]

It is often said that the modern Hindi movie does not use scripts, meaning that the script is not bound, or written before the film is begun, but is produced on an *ad hoc* basis, dialogue sheets being written on the sets. Some prestigious writers, like Salim-Javed, used to refuse to allow any changes to the bound scripts which they completed. Some of the younger scriptwriters write in English then translate into Hindi, yet still manage to produce dialogues which are highly acclaimed by critics and the audience alike.

One frequent criticism of the Hindi film is that one can watch one without understanding the language because the story is so predictable. This attitude reveals a total disregard for the dialogues which are an important source of pleasure to cinema-goers. They re-enact them with their friends, or they can buy film dialogues on disk, or look on the Net at pages of selected dialogues of certain actors. The language of certain films has attained a cult status, in particular Gabbar Singh's dialogues from *Sholay*, which almost any Hindi film fan can quote. Many films have a character speaking in a particular accent, which then becomes a craze in the region, whether exaggerated forms of Bambaiyya (Bombay Hindi), Bhojpuri (regions of Bihar), or as a source of amusement for other characters: the South Indian, the Goan, or the person who cannot speak English often being a figure of fun. Film catchphrases enter street language, while the rich language of abuse is a major source of pleasure to viewers. The theatrical style of delivery is enjoyed by the viewers, with particular actors being popular for their ability to deliver powerful monologues. Amitabh Bachchan's fame was due in part to his deep, dramatic voice and his impeccable timing in delivering comic dialogues and fiery speeches, and his dramatic way of remaining silent at key moments. Other actors are known to deliver dialogues whose meanings are read outside the film's context, such as political speeches (Nana Patekar has a wide following among the Shiv Sena, of which he is a known supporter).

In many films, the centrality of words is heightened in other ways. Often one of the protagonists is a writer, a poet or a journalist, someone who makes a living from words. Access to words is used as a narrative device: for example, narratives are often dependent on secrets and who has heard what is said; there are tensions generated when unspeakable events are visualized but never verbalized. Words from modern media intrude in the film: the telephone is used frequently to bring on speech without an actor and as a dramatic device for interrupting other people's speech; while television and occasionally radio act as conveyors of the state's ideology.

One area of life where language comes under great pressure is in creating a language for expressing love. Julia Kristeva, who has already established the heterogenous nature of poetic language,[68] recognizes the problematics of a language of love:

> The language of love is impossible, inadequate, immediately allusive when one would like it to be most straightforward; it is a flight of metaphors – it is literature.[69]

Roland Barthes, in his witty study of the fragments available to lovers,[70] argues that this most personal of all human experiences is structured and constrained by language:

> throughout any love life, figures occur to the lover without any order, for on each occasion they depend on an (internal or external?) accident ... the amorous subject draws on a reservoir (the thesaurus?) of figures ... the figures are non-syntagmatic, non-narrative.[71]

Sometimes love may be best suited to poetic language, where words are at more of a premium. Among the most important words of love are the declaration, 'I love you', which must be expressed in the Hindi movies. Indian languages have a wide range of ways to express love: nouns including *mohabbat, prem, ishq, pyaar, sneh* and *chaahat* in Hindi alone, and a variety of grammatical constructions to mean 'I love you'. Yet in cinema, where the expression or affirmation of love is demanded, it is often the three English words which are used rather than their Hindi–Urdu equivalents. This may be due to the language of love having been influenced by the English idiom, or could be simply a fashion in popular culture, showing the use of the global language. A likely cause is also that this is part of the prohibition of the display of the private which Prasad has analysed in the cinema's self-censorship of the kiss,[72] in that saying something in the formal register of English is less intimate than an expression in one's mother tongue.

The greatest arena for the creation of a language of love in Hindi cinema is undoubtedly the film song, found in nearly every Hindi movie.[73] There are several kinds (the comic, the diegetic, the spectacular) but the largest and most popular group is the love song. This has barely been studied at any level. I find Kristeva's analysis of courtly songs suggestive when examining the love songs of the Hindi film: They

> neither describe nor relate. They are essentially messages of themselves, the signs of love's intensity. They have no object – the lady is seldom defined and, slipping away between restrained presence and absence, she simply is an imaginary addressee, the pretext for the incantation. Like a dreamlike staging but without the narrative act, without even the ability to hold the vocabulary to a concrete meaning, let alone the vocabulary of love, the courtly song refers to its own performance. One should read it while hearing it and interpret it as a vast activity transposing univocal meaning outside of its limits, toward the two borders of nonmeaning and the mystical, metaphysical totality of Meaning.[74]

In other words, on the one hand there is the literal signification of the verse – the beloved, the heroine of the film; on the other there is the joy, the pleasure alone – the sign is not only the song, but the excess of meaning, brought about by indefinite syntax, paradox or metaphorical-ness in the very vocabulary. The first level is encouraged by the picturization of the song within the film, which is often filmed in exotic locations unconcerned with the film's main narrative, while the second is present not only in the film itself but also in the songs' life outside the films, on radio, cassettes and television. The first level lends itself to narrative and may be used as such within the film, whereas the second level allows for an ambiguity specific to play and joy found in the lyric. The erotic can become seduction and possession in the first level. Kristeva argues that narrative emerged from this first level of meaning in the west in the fourteenth century; similar patterns with their own variants may be seen with the emergence of the modern vernaculars in nineteenth-century India, yet the film song retains this spirit of lyricism to a degree not found in the western popular song, perhaps because of the continuing high valuation of poetry in India. However, the film song has its own connections with the modern vernacular literatures, especially that of Urdu, since most are written in Urdu by poets such as Sahir Ludhianvi, Javed Akhtar (formerly half of the Salim–Javed writing duo, who is one of the industry's most popular lyric writers), Majrooh Sultanpuri, Gulzar and so on. Its lyrics are written in the style of Urdu poetry, drawing on its language, images and conventions, albeit often in a simplified form.[75] Other discourses of love and desire can be drawn on, such as invocation of Hindu discourses on love through festive songs, in particular those referring to the loves of Krishna.[76]

The song forms one of the key pleasures of the film, in many ways beyond its lyrics. Song and dance is a feature of most Indian performative traditions, whether religious or secular. A Hindi movie has a song every twenty minutes or so, with a total of between six and eight in a film. Songs are sung usually by the hero and heroine, possibly the vamp, but never by the villain. Songs fulfil several important functions, including advancing the narrative, by setting the scene for future action or enacting crucial turning-points in the narrative. They also allow things to be said which cannot be said elsewhere, often to admit love to the beloved, to reveal inner feelings, to make the hero/heroine realize that he/she is in love. Many songs are presented as part of dance routines, which vary from modes based on classical Indian dance (mostly Bharatnatyam and Kathak forms), to folk dances, to the latest American styles. In the older films when the heroine's erotic display was more restricted, some actresses made a name as vamps or dance stars, such as Helen, but now all stars, male and female, are required to dance.

The song sequence is clearly marked as a separate event from the narrative, even though it may be integrated closely or even justified by the narrative (a common feature is to have a heroine who is a singer or dancer). The song usually stands somewhat outside the spectatorial regimes of Hindi cinema in that the narration invites *darshan* by its use of tableaux,[77] while some types of song, usually in conjunction with dance, present the body as a spectacle allowing for erotic display.[78] Such eroticism seems surprising when contrasted to the self-generated prohibition on kissing in Hindi cinema – which has only recently been broken. Prasad has argued cogently that this is based on the forbidding of the representation of the private in the public sphere rather than an issue of sexuality.[79]

The spectacular impact of the song is further heightened by the particular use of clothing. This may be a costume for a staged show or an MTV-type dance routine, or may involve numerous costume changes to display an excess of consumer choice. Such clothes are often richer, more elaborate and more erotic than those worn in the main narrative sequences of the movie. The song usually uses locations or sets which are also different from the main narrative locations. They may be justified by the plot, such as the use of stages for performances, or a holiday or a dream sequence which allow for images of beauty as the characters are transported to exotic overseas locales suggestive of conspicuous wealth. Gardens where fertility symbols of flowers and water abound are also popular. These locations not only fulfil the lyrics' requirements for an earthly paradise, but by their remoteness allow the characters to step outside the confines of their everyday lives, to savour movement and freedom but also to show the universal, spaceless nature of love.

The song and dance sequences are also outside the main narrative of the movie in other ways, being brought into the film almost as prepackaged items. The director gives the lyricist and music directors a song situation on which they work together, recording the music usually before the rest of the production begins. The songs are rarely sung by the actors but by 'playback singers'; that is, a professional singer records the song, which is played back on sets/locations while the actor or actress mimes the words. These singers have always been few in number, the most famous being Lata Mangeshkar, who has recorded tens of thousands of songs over fifty years. While her voice is instantly recognizable, the audience does not find her voice replacing the actress's voice in the film in any way disconcerting.

The music directors (composers and conductors) use an eclectic mix of styles from light Indian classical to folk to rap as well as western instruments such as the violin and the saxophone, western scales and ragas, harmony and rhythm. The classical music of India was never popular, as western classical music has been, but most of the music directors and singers are classically trained. Contemporary Hindi film music is despised by the old middle classes, although many still enjoy the film music of their youth.[80]

The film music is usually released several weeks before the film, and, while important itself in commercial terms, is also used as a marketing device. The old vinyl recordings were expensive and beyond the reach of many film-goers, who listened to film music on the radio and sang the songs themselves, often as part of games such as *antakshari* (literally 'final syllable'; a game in which the last syllable of a song is picked up and used as the first syllable of the next singer's song). However, the boom in the audio-cassette market from the 1970s[81] and the rapid increase in the number of film-music shows on cable and satellite television has increased the tendency for film songs to have their own life separate from the films. These song clips also play an important role in the circulation of images of the leading stars beyond the film itself, which forms part of the total viewing practices of Hindi movies.

The star in Indian cinema: ideals of beauty, desire and romance

Billboard posters advertising the latest films are a major feature of the Indian street. These images of the stars are several feet tall, painted in bright colours, their flesh pinker and plumper than it appears on screen.[82] The boards proclaim the names of the directors and producers but the stars are never identified. This is because they are instantly recognized, their images being in constant circulation in a variety of media including their earlier films, video clips of film songs shown on India's ever-expanding TV channels and in the film and lifestyle magazines which tell of their off-screen exploits. The film is their star vehicle and is classified as such by the audience who discuss films in terms of their stars rather than their directors. Even the songs of well-known playback singers may be sold on audio cassette under the name of the star who mimed to them.

The star is clearly at the forefront of the movie publicity business in India, yet we know little about the nature of Indian stardom and its implications for discourses of desire and ideals of beauty. In Chapter 5 I look at the deployment of Amitabh Bachchan's star image in Yash

Chopra's films, while Chapter 6 focuses on India's film magazines, which have reinforced the cult of the star and function as the place to narrate the star text, to undermine and to reinforce the image of the star; in Chapter 7 I look at the celebrity author and the star text in popular fiction.

There is no straightforward definition of the star nor of those elusive terms 'star quality' or charisma. John Ellis suggests the following: 'a performer in a particular medium whose figure enters into subsidiary forms of circulation, and then feeds back into future performances'.[83] The medium *par excellence* is of course film, for the star is part of the economic foundations of cinema, while star quality is encouraged by the very nature of film through the close-up and the viewing experience in the cinema hall. The glamorous star generates desire by an important elusive quality, that of being paradoxically ordinary yet extraordinary, largely through the 'photo effect', 'the paradoxical regime of presence yet absence'.[84] In India, this is enhanced by the mode of melodrama where the character roles are those of psychological, not psychologically rounded, individuals who function as transmitters of the action,[85] and the star text often leaks over into the performance.

Richard Dyer's work on stardom is the foundation of the study of this phenomenon.[86] He argues that an individual is said to be charismatic when he/she is the centre of attraction and seems to embody what is taken to be a central feature of human existence at a given time:[87]

> Stars matter because they act out aspects of life that matter to us; and performers get to be stars when what they act out matters to enough people.[88]

When social order is uncertain, this figure offers value and stability as the focus of the dominant cultural and historical concerns, thus creating interest in the life of the star and his/her whole off-screen existence.[89] Dyer draws together two main approaches to the star, those of semiotic and sociological study, bringing together insights from film studies and cultural studies in his notion of the star text, which is an amalgam of the real person, the characters played in films and the persona created by the media.[90] He argues one may look at the economic and institutional base of stardom, the cultural role of stardom, the audience reception of the star, social and/or personal reception; one may study stars as products of films' aesthetics, looking at issues of performance, text, genre and mode.

Although stars existed in pre-cinematic media practices, notably theatre and opera in the west, there is something in the very nature of film which generates stars, mentioned briefly above. While there were pre-cinematic stars in India, mostly from the theatre,[91] it seems that the popular press was more interested in other public figures than entertainers and it was not until the advent of the film that the star emerged. Mechanisms of involvement with the star are a central part of the pleasure of cinema. Murray Smith examines the spectators' emotional responses to cinema, arguing that 'identification' glosses over the relations between spectator and character. He sets up a model of character engagement (recognition, alignment and allegiance), while avoiding using psycho-analysis. He acknowledges the importance of the star system and his/her charisma,[92] but does not explore this in detail. In her classic study of scopophilia, the viewer's pleasure in sight in the cinema,[93] Laura Mulvey describes how in cinema-viewing the mechanisms of fetishism and voyeurism operate to make a denial of difference between the viewer and the star. The viewer identifies with the male star for illusory mastery, taking the female star as object of his gaze, turning her into a male fetish. Mulvey is arguing that the pleasure of popular cinema is rooted in a patriarchal unconscious and she draws attention to the problematic position of the female viewer who, it seems, must adopt a masochistic stance in her cinematic pleasure. In a later paper[94] she discusses this problem, arguing that the female viewer has to split her pleasure by taking both male and female identificatory positions. This leaves a problematic of an active male position and a passive female position as female desire has to be 'masculinized' to become active.[95] Questions about the homoerotic pleasures of cinema and the reason that many people prefer stars of the same sex are also left open.

For the study of Hindi cinema there are further problems in dealing with the premodern structure of spectation, *darshan*, whose hierarchies of the gaze reinforce the star quality.[96] Vasudevan argues that narration and the use of tableaux permit scopophilia and *darshan*, while the erotic display is confined to the song.[97] This gives few opportunities for a mechanism of identification but rather presents a spectacle which invites voyeurism and admiration.

The emotions the viewer feels for the star exist outside the cinematic experience. Jackie Stacey explores the question of the identification a female viewer may have with a same-sex star,[98] bringing feminist arguments to her study of the female audience of Hollywood cinema. She finds that the viewer adopts different attitudes to the star, ranging from an emotional tie to some perception of a common quality. These attitudes include devotion, adoration, worship, transcendence, aspiration and inspiration. Stacey draws attention to a number of extra-cinematic identificatory practices, namely pretending, resembling, imitating and copying the star. This line of approach has not been pursued in the context of popular Indian cinema, although Sara Dickey has taken an ethnographic approach to ways that members of fan-clubs in south India negotiate the stars' roles and their involvement in politics.[99]

The true star system in Hindi cinema emerged after the collapse of the studio system in the 1940s.[100] Films were made by independent producers whose rise is usually attributed to the need to launder money from the black market which expanded rapidly during the Second World War. It is a worldwide phenomenon that while many products of public culture can bring huge financial rewards, the majority incur losses. This is as true of the Hindi cinema as it is of the British record industry, where it is said that around 90 per cent of ventures lose money, around 5 per cent break even and only 5 per cent make any profit at all. The producers' primary aim was to seek the maximum return for their investment, hence they calculated that the best way to get good box-office returns was to hire the most popular stars, since this is what drew people to their films. Thus they hired stars who were able to demand fees according to their 'star quality'. The stars set their own prices at record highs, which further increased their stardom by enabling them to lead new glamorous lives, in the style of elites or nawabs. The need for money to maintain this lifestyle and to have high visibility not only through extra-filmic practices such as giving interviews and being seen at events, led to them appearing in as many films as possible. In India, a star will often act in six films at once, taking advantage of the industry's shift system that allows them to spend two or three hours a day on different films, leading producers to complain about the problem of booking dates with stars, who often refuse to give block bookings. A huge proportion of production costs are said to go in time wasted waiting for the star to arrive on the sets, which, along with their high fees, has led some to estimate that stars account for about 65 per cent of the budget of a film.[101]

The zenith of the power of the star was undoubtedly the multi-starrer, a film conceived with two or three heroes, heroines and baddies on the principle that if one star sold a film, six stars would sell proportionately more. The first of these was *Waqt* ('Time', 1965, dir. Yash Chopra). At least six stars acted in this film, presumably to justify the investment in colour film technology. While ten years later, *Sholay* had at least seven major stars,[102] the ultimate star count was in *Naseeb* ('Destiny', 1981, dir. Manmohan Desai), whose main narrative already had stars too numerous to count,[103] yet it also included a parade of stars[104] in the staging of a film party.

In the Indian context, the star is almost exclusively a film star, an actor or an actress, usually the hero or heroine of a film. The star text is created within the films themselves as vehicles for star performances which in turn build on images in other films and in other media to give them roles as national icons of beauty, desire and utopian beings. Television does not produce stars in the same way as film, given viewing practices and its status as a mundane, domestic activity. However it does create celebrities, mostly politicians,[105] the super-rich, sportspeople, the newly emergent pop stars, models, presenters,[106] and its own actors, many of whom are refugees from cinema. Rarely does a television star go on to film success, although Shah Rukh Khan is a notable exception. However, the star needs other media not only to maintain visibility beyond the brief moment of performance but also to allow the creation of a star persona. This is achieved largely through print journalism, notably the film magazines, discussed in Chapter 6 below. Despite dire warnings of the threat posed to cinema by the increasing availability of the video recorder in the 1980s, and of satellite/cable television in the 1990s, along with new technologies of the DVD, LD and CDV, these new media seem to have fed parasitically on the film industry, the only significant new forms generated being soap operas and game shows and the circulation of uncensored material. It is radio which seems to have suffered most from the impact of these more expensive media. India's music business continues to be largely dominated by the film industry despite the growth of non-filmic music in recent years.[107]

There is undoubtedly much overlap in Indian culture between the concept of the hero/heroine and that of the star, the major distinction being that the former is more concerned with narratives of the characters presented within a text (film, story, myth, etc.) whereas in the latter, the narratives centre on the actor/actress within *and* beyond the texts. A star may also be someone who is not a hero or a heroine, perhaps a villain,[108] or a dancer[109] or, more rarely, a comedian. There is also much overlap between categories when in the narration of the star text the star often becomes a hero/heroine within that text itself. The roles created for heroes and heroines by these traditions seem to have been inherited and developed by Hindi cinema, probably through its origins in several performance traditions sharing these models for the hero and heroine. These include the many forms of Indian theatre, including the folk and the Parsi theatre of the late nineteenth and early twentieth centuries,[110] from which the cinema took its traditions of spectacle, music and melodramatic modes. The aesthetics of classical drama (see Chapter 2 above) and non-mimetic modes of Indian aesthetics have been the subjects of scholarly enquiry, but serious questions have not been asked in terms of their intellectual transmission and influence. Characters have clear connections with Indian mythology and with folk tales and epics, in particular the *Ramayana* and the *Mahabharata* as has been manifest at least in their use of names.[111] Arguments in Mishra *et al.* (1989) about the creation of the actor as parallel text centre on their interpretation of mythological and epic elements in films. While this is of undeniable significance,[112] there has been an over-reading of some of these traditions to give an essential Indianness to this cinema,[113] ignoring the important influence and subsequent reinterpretations of Hollywood and other external sources.

Christine Gledhill argues that stars 'signify as condensors of moral, social and ideological values'.[114] There are two areas of particular interest here in the Indian context, namely the stars' roles as national icons and the opportunities they provide for debates around sexuality, in particular female sexuality. Hindi movie stars are chosen not only for their acting abilities but also on the strength of their looks. The importance of the gaze and the pleasures of scopophilia in cinema were discussed above. The Hindi film's ideal of beauty was the north Indian upper-caste Hindu, which is reinforced by character names, such Malhotra or Verma, or simply elided as 'Mr Raj'. The male characters' first names are often close to that of the actor, thus reinforcing the star text and off-screen knowledge of the star. For example, Raj Kapoor is usually called by the diminutive of his name, Raju, while Amitabh Bachchan is often called Vijay in his angry-young-man roles and Amit in his romantic leads. Heroines are more likely to have names which are merely fashionable (Neena, Chandni, Shobha), or names which have symbolic overtones (in *Shree 420* the heroine is called Vidya, 'knowledge', while the vamp is Maya, 'delusion'), or mythological resonances (such as Radha in *Mother India* or Ganga in *Pardes,* who both represent the essence of Indian womanhood).

The male stars were mostly Panjabis, whose height and fair skin approximated ideals of physical beauty. Discourses on Indian masculinities were set up by the British, some of which have become absorbed into everyday discourses in modern India. The British created a myth of Panjabis as a martial race, notable for a predominance of 'masculine' qualities, unlike the 'effeminate Bengali'.[115] The displacement of many Panjabis to Bombay in the 1940s, and their ability to speak Urdu, were also elements in their favour. However, their names were changed to remove regional and caste identity: Raaj Kumar (Kulbhushan Nath Pandit), Manoj Kumar (Hari Krishna Goswami), Rajendra Kumar (R. K. Tuli), a trend which has continued to the present with the 1990s star Akshay Kumar (Rajiv Bhatia). New names were given to stars from other regions, including Ashok Kumar (Ashok Kumar Ganguly), his brother Kishore Kumar, and Uttam Kumar (Arun Kumar Chatterjee).

There was also a playing-down of non-Hindu identities, as many Muslims began to use Hindu names. The most famous examples of this were Dilip Kumar (Yusuf Khan), Madhubala (Begum Mumtaz Jehan), and Meena Kumari (Mahajabeen). Nearly all these changes were made using the name 'Kumar' (Hindi 'youth, unmarried man, prince', also used as a title of respect for young men), there seeming to be only the one example of its female counterpart 'Kumari', that of Meena Kumari. These are interesting examples of the emblematic quality of names, changed to sound modern and 'ethnically neutral', a trend seen in Hollywood stars such as John Wayne (Marion Morrison) and Tony Curtis (Bernie Schwarz). In the 1990s, the decade of Hindu resurgence, there has been a reassertion of regional, caste and religious identity. The top three male stars of Bombay all use the Muslim surname Khan; two of them are married to Hindus, a topic which they discuss frequently in the press, talking of how love triumphed over religious and family prejudice.[116]

This renegotiation of caste and regional identities does not seem to have applied to women to such an extent, apart from the elision of some of the actresses' Muslim identities during the 1940s and 1950s,[117] although Nargis remains the notable exception. The first adult actresses were Anglo-Indians,[118] a minority community perceived as being 'fast', or sexually promiscuous, while the fairness of its women was seen as an additional attraction. One of the great stars of the 1930s, Fearless Nadia (1910–96), was a white Australian, with blond hair and blue eyes, yet this obvious racial difference from the film's other actors was not remarked on in the films themselves.

Female stars have often celebrated their regional origins, the most popular being the Bengali,[119] the Maharashtrian[120] and the south Indian stars,[121] most of whom have been upper-caste, usually Brahmins. There has never been a south Indian male star who has sustained success in Bombay, while from the 1960s there has been a steady stream of south Indian heroines in Hindi movies, many of whom have chosen to act exclusively in Hindi movies. This may be to do with their being seen as the object of the gaze of the high-caste, Hindu male, who is able to make any Indian woman the focus of his desire.

The cinema has had to deal with diverse issues regarding female sexuality. It was difficult in the beginning to get women to act in films, with men taking women's roles as they had in other performative traditions such as theatre. Phalke wanted a woman to take the role of Taramati, a highly respected mythological figure, in *Raja Harischandra* but could not find anyone who would act in films. It is said that not even prostitutes would agree to do this and thus the role was played by a man

(P. G. Sane). The first Indian actress was Phalke's daughter, Mandakini, who, with further gender reversals, took the role of the young Krishna in his *Shri Krishna Janma* (1917) and *Kaliya Mardan* (1919). It may have been because she was pre-pubescent that the issue of her appearing in cinema was less problematic or simply that her father flouted convention.

Since then cinema has been one of the arenas in India for women to emerge as professionals: producers, directors, actresses, choreographers, set-designers, make-up artists, singers, musicians, distributors and exhibitors. They have also been major consumers of cinemas, whether in the audience or as journalists, yet some hint of scandal has always remained around the female stars. Behroze Gandhy and Rosie Thomas discuss the gossip surrounding three leading female stars of Hindi movies.[122] Their information is drawn from widespread rumours and stories about the stars which still circulate and develop years after the events they describe. They note the on- and off-screen personae of the stars and draw attention to the fact that the star personae off-screen

> frequently encompass behaviours that are decidedly subversive of the strict social mores of Indian society and would be considered 'scandalous' in any other context, even by many of their most dedicated fans. Of course they do not simply transgress: stars are represented as finely balancing their transgressions with personifica-tions of ideal behaviour especially in the domains of kinship and sexuality. Both the films and the sub-text of gossip about stars are most usefully seen as debates around morality, in particular as negotiations about the role of 'tradition' in a modernising India.[123]

They find the stars are discussed in relation to issues of motherhood, sexuality and gender in the context of modernity and tradition, informed by deep-seated mythological attributes of women and the powers of goddesses.

The cinema of the 1950s gave the female stars a limited range of possibilities, for in this era the role of the heroine was contrasted with the glamorous possibilities of the vamp. The glamorous vamp was a 'bad girl' and was never quite the same grade of star as the heroine, even if she played leading roles. However, she was the sexy, glamorous, dangerous woman whose body was the focus of desire for the male spectator, made guilt-free by her ultimate defeat by the heroine's pure chasteness. The rise of Indian youth culture in the 1960s[124] exemplified by Shammi Kapoor, the 'Elvis of India', introduced a more overtly modern style, as spectacle triumphed over realism in terms of presentation of the stars, in rich, revealing clothes, outrageous fashions, location shots in Europe and in

Kashmir, sumptuous interiors and so on. The glamorous new heroine who combined the roles of heroine and vamp was typified by Sharmila Tagore, a discovery of Satyajit Ray: glamorous, liberated yet refined, elegant and traditional. Even though she was one of the first actresses to appear in a bikini[125] she seemed to be above any criticism. Sharmila formed star pairings on-screen with both Shammi Kapoor and Rajesh Khanna throughout the decade and off-screen with her husband 'Tiger' Pataudi, the Nawab and cricketer. Models and 'Miss Indias' began to enter the films as 'babes' who typified new ways and new lifestyles through their performances in cabaret and dance numbers, looking good in skimpy western clothes. This trend has continued. There have been fewer substantial roles for women in Hindi cinema over the last few decades, with the female stars taking more and more decorative and inconsequential roles.

To a large extent, films became star vehicles. The whole film is built around the roles, scenes and iconography of the star. This process was facilitated by the melodramatic mode of the Hindi cinema which eschews psychological realism but where the star functions as an icon of an emotion, a type or typical person. The highly individuated character of Hollywood cinema is not a feature of Hindi movies. This can be seen most clearly in the case of minor characters, who are often embodiments of essences: villains representing evil, fathers the law, younger brothers innocence, mothers pure love and so on. The presentation of the star is heightened in powerful dialogues, but most importantly in the film song, where his or her appearance is often most stylized in terms of cinematic technique and in the use of dance, costume and make-up which concentrate the essence of stardom:

> the actor text is propelled by a song syntagm that, effectively, ensures his entry into Indian consciousness as text. No actor without the support of the song has ever become a parallel text in Bombay cinema.[126]

The star has a total image created over a number of films which transcends the individual film.[127] This is a maximized ('best') image – the most beautiful, the most tragic, the sexiest and so on. The performance of this image in a character in a particular film has to enter into dialogue with this overall image.[128] The stars were always associated with certain roles and clothes, and they stuck to these roles because of perceived audience expectations. For example, Raj Kapoor[129] always played the common man, a pseudo-Chaplin, only appearing glamorous through his imitations of the wealthy, such as when he borrows clothes from the laundry where he works in *Shree 420*. Of course, in real life he was a figure of international stature, a major film producer, director and actor, who represented India on a cultural tour of the USSR, who met the great men of his day such as President Truman and Yuri Gagarin, as well as being the son of the famous actor, Prithviraj Kapoor.

Dilip Kumar took a wide variety of roles, thus putting his star status in jeopardy, ranging from the tragic hero of Devdas[130] – the modern manager in his roles as the other man in *Andaaz*, the factory manager in *Madhumati*[131] – to the dashing prince in *Aan*, to the anti-hero in *Ganga Jumna*.[132] He retained his stardom through the quality of his performances, which were of such high quality that he is often referred to simply as 'the thespian'. However, the instability of his persona and the over-identification with the roles he took led to a breakdown and subsequent psychiatric treatment, including advice that he took 'happier roles'.[133]

The later 1970s saw a new type of the hero in the greatest star of the Hindi cinema, Amitabh Bachchan. He first came to notice in the films of Hrishikesh Mukherjee, where he played mostly professional and upper-class roles, but he is best known for his roles as the man from the underclasses, the urban or industrial[134] hero, mostly in films scripted by Salim-Javed and shot by many of the great directors of the 1970s.[135] His long, lean, virile physique and his rich voice, coupled with his dramatic use of silence and his general stylish aesthetic, were suited to his role as the working-class hero, often expressing great anger, wronged through no fault of his own, made to accept responsibility for his family (often his mother and a younger brother), and who when failed by the state takes the law into his own hands. His anger, masochism and even a death-wish, lead to his becoming an outsider or outlaw. This involved taking on some of the aspects associated with the villain, but his heart remained pure and his motive was his family rather than himself. Nevertheless his lawlessness had to be punished and he often had to die at the end of the films. The combination of his physical presence and acting talent with the character roles he took and knowledge of his off-screen life (his elite background and his supposed and real relationships with actresses) produced a star persona,[136] which touched a nerve of the whole of India.[137] Madhava Prasad connects this to the political violence of the 1970s, which was represented by Bachchan's revolt against the system.[138] Bachchan retired temporarily from film in the early 1990s but failed to make a comeback in 1997, unable to reinvent his iconography as another type of character and unable to play himself.

The major media for the transmission of the narratives about the stars and the creation of the star persona and images of the star is the film magazine. There are no newspapers in India equivalent to the British tabloids which narrate the life of stars, although there is limited newspaper coverage in lifestyle columns even in the broadsheets. Outside largely undocumented gossip and rumour, the star text in India is narrated most widely in magazines. Among the many varieties of Indian magazines is found a group which are not film magazines, but star magazines, consisting largely of verbal and visual images of stars in narratives, interviews, photos, etc. These magazines are the place to find out about the private life necessary for defining the star. The magazine can show a variety of images of the star, focusing on morality, scandals, sexuality, the personal and the private. The photographs in the magazines are important in the construction of the image of the star. I return to a discussion of these magazines in Chapter 6 below.

Two special star roles: *Mother India* and the courtesan movie

Female star roles in cinema have often been restricted to that of the inferior partner of the male star. However, two of the most enduring images of women in Hindi cinema are exceptions to this rule in that they reinforce the female star, but also portray her as a symbol of the nation and national icon (Nargis as *Mother India*) and as a courtesan, the figure of desire (*Pakeezah* and other courtesan films).

The courtesan appears throughout Indian culture, her earliest representations being that of the cultured 'geisha' of Sanskrit erotic literature and drama, notably the heroine of Sudraka's fourth-century drama, the *Mricchakatika* ('Little clay cart'), the courtesan Vasantasena. This inspired the film *Utsav* ('Festival')[139] starring Rekha in one of her many courtesan roles.[140] While courtesans feature in many films, mostly in minor roles,[141] the two great films in which the main heroine is a courtesan are set in nineteenth-century Avadhi (Lucknow and Kanpur) (*Umrao Jaan*[142]) and in Delhi and Panipat in the early years of the twentieth century (*Pakeezah*[143]). These were two of the great centres of courtly Muslim culture of their time. It is the pleasures of these courtesan films to which I now turn.

Although the term courtesan is often used as a euphemism for sex-worker or prostitute, the true courtesan is to be distinguished from the prostitute. The miserable plight of India's prostitutes is well known, Bombay having one of the grimmest records with under-age girls being kidnapped or sold by their families, living in slums whose barred windows have led them to be known as 'cages'. They are also major carriers of

HIV/AIDS. The true courtesan, whose trade flourished in India until the early twentieth century, was more like a geisha or hetaira.

The most accomplished courtesans were said to be from Lucknow, the capital of Avadh. This city became north India's major cultural centre after the decline of Delhi, and was also renowned for the quality of its Urdu literature. It was annexed by the British in 1856 and was one of the major centres of struggle in the 1857 uprisings. Although landowners from Avadh maintained a courtly culture in Lucknow at least until Independence, it never achieved the sophistication of its earlier days, which is still remembered with great nostalgia by its elite. The world of the courtesan also declined during the British period, as other spheres of public culture emerged. The final blow was dealt after Independence as the loss of wealthy patrons came about with the abolition of *zamindars* ('landowners'), and salons were banned.

Veena Talwar Oldenburg[144] investigated the reality behind the life of the courtesans (*tawa'if*) in Lucknow, drawing on interviews with retired courtesans.[145] They tell how they lived in households (*kotha*) run by a chief courtesan (*choudhrayan*), who had acquired wealth and fame through her beauty, her music and her dancing talents, which she used to set up her own house where she would recruit and train younger courtesans. The courtesan had to learn music and Urdu poetry, and to dance the *mujra*, a dance where she pays her respects to the assembly rather than offer an erotic spectacle. The best houses kept skilled male musicians and were important patrons of music. The sons of the gentry were sent to the *kothas* to learn manners and Urdu poetry, and presumably the art of love-making. Other women lived in the establishment, including the regular prostitutes (*randi*) and a strange category of *khangis*, married women who were in *purdah* but were involved in clandestine relationships for financial gain. Although the profession of the courtesan has disappeared, she has remained an important figure in literature and later in film throughout the last century.

One of the first Urdu novels, Mirza Mohammad Hadi Ruswa's *Umrao Jaan Ada*, was published in 1899. Ruswa presents the story of Umrao Jaan, a courtesan of Lucknow and Kanpur, as supposedly true. It was set at the last moment of Lucknow's glory: the 1857 uprisings occur in the novel when Umrao Jaan is at the height of her power. The novel's popularity has continued to the present, although many know the story of Umrao Jaan in the eponymous film of 1981.[146]

The courtesan is found in later works, including those of the Progressive Writers' Association, which was founded in 1926 on a Marxist platform, stating that all literature should espouse a cause. In their writing the prostitute is a victim who is romanticized as a cultured, talented woman, famous for her accomplishments and beauty. In *Suitable Boy*, Vikram Seth describes the performance of a courtesan's *mujra* as an important aesthetic and social event in Bahrampur.[147]

The courtesan has also been a popular figure in film, where her attractions give rise to a variety of pleasures in the audience. She is portrayed as a victim of men's lust and as an object of the viewer's pity, but also delights the audience in being the object of the male gaze as she dances for his entertainment. The combination of a beautiful actress and the opportunity for music and dance to be incorporated into the narrative is important, but viewers also enjoy the spectacle of the body, the elaboration of scenery and in particular of clothing, tied to a certain nostalgia arising from the decline and disappearance of courtesan culture.

The courtesan in the film makes her living by her sexual charms, and so is presented as an object of desire to the men in the *mehfil* ('gathering') and to the cinema audience. This usually culminates in the *mujra*, where the film-maker emphasizes the details of lyrics, music, costume and *mise-en-scène*. The role of the courtesan in films has been given only to the most beautiful actresses, such as Meena Kumari as the eponymous *Pakeezah,* while the most glamorous actress of her generation, Rekha, has had numerous courtesan roles. Although the courtesan displays her sexual allure at all times in the film, she is usually presented as averse to her trade, calling her body a *zinda lash* ('living corpse'). An accomplished singer and dancer, she also writes *ghazals* in which she expresses her desire for love and marriage, which she knows will be denied her because of her profession. Yet one of her attractions is that she is the woman who is the opposite of the wife. Her sexuality is not associated with reproduction, nor is she expected to offer any nurture – she is the essence of female eroticism. (Oldenburg argues that most courtesans, like many prostitutes, practised lesbianism (*chapat bazi*), considering heterosexuality to be work, not pleasure.)

In Hindi cinema, the courtesan never appears in any way immodestly dressed. In fact one of the pleasures of the courtesan film lies in its elaborate use of clothing and make-up. While Stella Bruzzi has discussed the meaning of clothes in western cinema,[148] the semiotics of costume in Indian cinema has been little explored although it is an important source of symbols and signifiers of codes concerning status or class, westerniza-tion and the symbolic use of colour. Clothing in cinema is clearly a source of spectacle, sometimes taken to extremes in song sequences where the heroine, and sometimes the hero, has numerous costume changes to present a heady excess of consumption. As Bruzzi has argued, clothing is an important component of eroticism, seen in the courtesan film, where the heroine's clothes heighten sexuality by their opulence and rich colours and textures, and their elaboration presents an exaggerated exhibition of gender difference. The veil is used to effect in the film to hide and conceal, in a display of eroticism rather than modesty, seen in the first song in *Pakeezah*, where the courtesan sings how men have taken her veil or her modesty. The courtesan is the woman who is constantly available for the male gaze, yet she remains concealed within her *kotha*, outside the eye of wider society.

The courtesan film also displays fetishization of the woman's body, usually the feet. This is very clear in *Pakeezah*, where the lover leaves a note tucked into Pakeezah's toes on the train: *Aap ke paon bahut haseen hain. Inhen zameen par mat utariyega, maile ho jaayenge!* ('Your feet are very beautiful. Do not let them touch the ground, they will get dirty!'). Moreover, in her dance at her lover's wedding she lacerates her feet on broken glass to leave symbolically resonant bloody marks on the white sheet of her performance.[149]

The courtesan is a totally romantic figure: a beautiful but tragic woman, who pours out her grief for the love she is denied in tears, poetry and dance. Yet although denied marriage and respectability, she is also a source of power. The courtesans in the film live in splendid buildings, which are decorated exquisitely. As Veena Oldenburg has pointed out, the courtesan achieved her material and social liberation by reversing constraints on women's chastity and economic rights, succeeding through her combination of talent and education. The courtesans set up their own society within the *kothas*, where they inverted many of society's rituals such as celebrating the birth of a girl like the birth of a boy in mainstream Indian culture. Perhaps women enjoy the pleasures of the courtesan film as they find a figure of masochistic identification, a woman who cannot find the love she wants, yet knowing that a woman's sexual attractions can provide her with power. Men may also enjoy the voyeuristic pleasures of looking at a beautiful, sexually accomplished woman whose status as victim allows for male fantasies of 'saving' her – mostly from other men.

One of the greatest pleasures of the courtesan film is undoubtedly nostalgia, largely for a lost Islamic world, which is usually presented as a spectacle of excess and elaboration. The Urdu language is seen in its glory as the language of poetry and formal manners; the music and dance is a light classical style which is rarely seen today. This is seen best in *Umrao Jaan*, whose attention to detail and painstaking recreation of the glories of Avadh, in particular in terms of sets and costumes, has never been equalled.

The beauty of the actresses in the courtesan film was not their only reason for popularity. They were also women who had strong star personas, as the most beautiful, most tragic stars who themselves were never lucky in love. Their off-screen lives were read onto the image of the courtesan in the film, as can be seen most clearly in the taking up of these stars as camp and gay icons, notably in the case of Meena Kumari (1932–72). Her own life reads like that of one of her character roles. She was exploited by her parents and her lovers, despite her beauty and her talent as an actress and also as a poet. Gulzar collected and edited a collection of her poems, *Tanha Chand*, which she had written under the pen-name Naz.[150] One of the great lyricists of the Hindi cinema, Sahir Ludhianvi writes:

> She was an artist with a rare talent, a softspoken woman in white with the soul of a poet which she had to sacrifice to start work. Her youth was spent depicting various tragedies that befall Indian women, with no time to think of her personal tragedy. Her whole life was a sacrifice of her own emotions.[151]

Yet 'unofficial' views of her life also circulated, brought together in Mohan Deep's book, which, nearly thirty years after her death, still attracts readers by its vivid, and probably imaginative, account of her sexual relationships.[152]

These readings have led to Meena Kumari being taken up as a gay icon in a similar way to Judy Garland in the west.[153] The two women seem to be focuses of the same emotion by their fans, who do not identify with these women as failures (which was how they regarded themselves), but as beautiful, talented, successful, yet misunderstood people who had to cover up real feelings and be survivors, of their family, of society and of their own addictions. These figures were adored by the masses, but they did not have sustained happy relationships. We do not know if Meena Kumari had a gay sensibility, although she certainly had a love of the theatrical. She has been appropriated by the gay community largely through camp, an ironical, exaggerated and theatrical attitude, which focuses on the study of surfaces, and constructed nature of sex roles.[154] She has become the favourite role model for drag queens in India and in the diaspora, who find her a source of femininity and inspiration.

Mother India

Mother India (1957, dir. Mehboob Khan), has come to be regarded as the quintessential Indian film. It remains hugely popular and was the only

Indian film ever to receive an Oscar nomination as Best Foreign Film (1958) until *Bandit Queen*.[155] It has a powerful storyline, top stars and great music by one of India's best composers, Naushad Ali, with many of the life-cycle songs, such as the wedding, or the festive Holi song, still played on these auspicious occasions. Notable also are the sheer spectacular visuals of the film, especially the shots of Radha and sons with a plough, taken in the style of Soviet realism. These qualities were lost on western viewers: one critic is much quoted in India as having said it was a film about 'flood, mud and blood'. The Indian response to this is often that a foreigner could never understand the film because had Radha been a western woman she would have simply slept with the moneylender rather than put her family at risk. This reaction to western dismissal centres on the status of this film as a new national epic, in particular in its treatment of the essence of the Indian woman.

The time of the film's making was important for its initial and subsequent receptions. The 1950s are generally regarded as something of a Golden Age in India: it was the first decade of Independence, the country was one of the first to win freedom from colonialism and it was led by the renowned statesman Jawaharlal Nehru. It was also an era of optimism after the horrors of Partition and the subsequent mass migration. The Hindi cinema of the 1950s was still a middlebrow popular cinema, which often dealt, albeit in its own idiom, with wider social concerns, which the contemporary Indian cinema is felt to ignore. The 1950s were also, of course, the time when many of the present generation of writers were young, and it is a decade suffused with particular nostalgia both for the Indian state and for its cinema.

Mehboob Khan's life story is the archetype of the urban migrant's journey from rags to riches: the almost illiterate villager from Gujarat who came to Bombay in 1929 with three rupees to find work in films. He started off as an extra at Imperial Studios (run by Ardeshir Irani of 'Alam Ara' fame), then had roles as a villain and so learnt about film-making, ending up a director and producer of some of the classics of Indian cinema and the founder/owner of Mehboob studios, which are still in use today. He is still considered to be one of India's greatest film directors along with his contemporaries, Raj Kapoor, Guru Dutt and Bimal Roy.

Among his many hit films, Mehboob made a film called *Aurat*, 'Woman', of which *Mother India* was a remake, bringing the idea of woman as nation to the fore. 'Mother India' was the nation glorified by the Indian nationalist movement, in which European ideas about the nation as a woman dovetailed with Indian ideas about the earth (Prithvi) as a goddess, whether wedded to the king, or as the 'mother of the people'. The first literary mention of the nation as mother occurs in a nineteenth-century novel – Bankim Chandra Chatterjee's *Anandamath* ('Monastery of bliss'), where a group of rebels sings *Vande mataram* 'I hail the mother', which later became a song of the freedom struggle, along with the new image of Mother India. It was no coincidence that Mother India apppeared first in Bengal, where the mother goddess was a more prominent deity than elsewhere (see the discussion of female deities in Chapter 2).

Mother India has had other associations: it was the title of Katherine Mayo's 1927 book, which is an attack on rather than a critique of Indian society;[156] the term was also used to describe Mrs Gandhi, Prime Minister of India, in the 1970s as part of the creation of an image of her as mother of the nation. This film has only *Mother India* as an English title, which was transliterated, not translated, in the Hindi and Urdu credits. This was to avoid giving a Hindu bias, as the Hindi equivalent, the Sanskritic Bharat Mata, implies a Hindu goddess, whereas there is no Muslim equivalent for this figure, showing the implicit Hindu nature of much of independent India's 'secular' mythology. This silence on any Islamic component of the new nation remains throughout the film, where the village is entirely Hindu, despite the number of prominent Muslims involved in this production, including the director, Mehboob, the heroine, Nargis, and the music director, Naushad Ali. Nargis's plea to the villagers to stay in their village and the use of a map of pre-Partition India imply a rejection of the ideology of Muslim separatism.

Partha Chatterjee argues that the nationalist movement located women's issues in the sphere of culture while nationalism concerned itself with public and political power.[157] Indian nationalism divided the world into the public and the private, allowing nationalism to deal with public issues of politics and economics, while other key issues were incorporated into the private sphere, including women's issues. This film is a plea for women to enter the public sphere on the one hand and to choose to uphold the community (read nation) over her family on the other. The woman is also the judge of society, who beats or kills the wrongdoers, upholding the *izzat* ('honour') of herself, her family and her village; being admitted to a new sphere of values, she becomes the source of *izzat* for the modern state, honoured for upholding its values. However, her incorporation of public and private is incomplete, for she is beyond the reach of its legal sphere: rather than being punished for killing her son, she is asked to inaugurate a government project. Although the utopia of the modern state is shown in the film, it is eternally deferred for the woman who has gained a position of honour and respect, but has sacrificed her own happiness by killing her favourite son. This glorification of the woman–nation as a self-sacrificing, benevolent Mother India, shows a continuity with earlier valorization of women in non-sexual roles, since Mother India is a mother, not a wife, being one of the few goddesses who does not have a consort.

The film is not just about nationalism, a straightforward allegory of the suffering of India at the hands of colonialism. One of its most compelling attractions is that Mother India creates a new mythology for the new independent nation. The timing of the release of the film, ten years after Independence, was crucial as new models and mythologies were needed for the new state as society's patriarchal and feudal basis was shifting and millions of people had been displaced by Partition and urban migration. The film has a deep ambivalence, which is never resolved, between the traditional Indian village, where life is grim but lightened by moments of pleasure, and a utopian modern India which provides life's needs but at the cost of enormous human sacrifice and misery. One of the attractions of *Mother India* is that it eschews clear-cut answers, allowing the audience to experience the pleasures of its ambiguities. These contradictions are made clear in the opening sequences which show Mehboob's production banner: while the image of communism, the hammer and sickle, appears on the screen, the voice-over intones his fatalistic motto: 'No matter what evils your enemies wish for you, it is of no consequence. Only that can happen which is God's will.'

The film's treatment of women is one of its most popular features. It presents the nation as woman but it also presents the woman as nation. The shifting significance of these two images can be seen by contrasting the titles of Mehboob's two films, *Mother India* and the earlier version, *Aurat* 'woman'. Rosie Thomas draws attention to the film-makers' brochure on *Mother India*, a 22-page full-colour booklet in English with notes on traditional Indian beliefs about womanhood, nature and destiny. Mehboob gave his own view of Indian woman when discussing his earlier film:

> The story of *Aurat* ... was centred round the fact that the true Indian woman enters her husband's home when she marries and leaves it only when she dies, that she will never sell her chastity for any price on earth.
>
> Now ... times have changed and life is different ... But the main character has not changed: the Indian woman who is one with the land she works on.[158]

There is no mention here of the negative images of the other women in

Mother India: Sukhilal's lustful daughter and Shamu's foolish widowed mother who borrows money from Sukhilal thus precipitating the family's problems. In fact, the only entirely positive image of a woman is the teacher, the new, modern educated woman who has to sacrifice her own happiness, being unable to marry Birju.

This film concentrates on the lifespan of one woman, Radha, in the private and public spheres. As a Hindu woman, her life begins with her marriage, the start of her flashback which narrates the whole film through her eyes. She follows the role of the good wife (see Chapter 2 above), the *pativrata*, who comes to her husband's village as a bride and daughter-in-law. She is always the idealized good wife, beautiful, hard-working, loving to her family, and providing her husband with sexual pleasure and several children, mostly sons. At this level she can be identified with goddesses other than Mother India, namely the Sita-Savitri model of the ideal woman (Chapter 2), while her erotic love for her husband, portrayed so clearly here, links her to her namesake, Radha, Krishna's beloved. Her husband is called Shyam, one of the names of Krishna. Even Sukhilal identifies her with Lakshmi, the goddess of wealth, and it is she who protects her honour, presumably to avoid her own defilement. The preservation of Radha's chastity is more important than the provision of food for her starving children in a feudal society where her honour is central to the prestige of her family and the whole village.

Mehboob's own opinions, given above, and the booklet for the film ignore the other side of these images of Indian femininity and village life, although these are clearly presented in the film. Radha is an ambivalent figure and can be dangerous, destroying those in contact with her: she kills her son, while her husband loses his arms after she goads him to plough the rough land. She beats Sukhilal, and her older son, Ramu, is ineffectual in helping her or his brother. At this level, she appears more like Kali, the powerful goddess who punishes and destroys. Ultimately, at the beginning and the end of the film, she is Mother India or Mother Earth.

This view of Indian woman does not fit well with the idealized Indian woman described in other textual sources in Chapter 2 above. Radha is a good woman, but she is dangerous whether as consort or as mother. This depiction of a 'bad mother' is unusual in traditional mythology, although Sudhir Kakar suggests that this image emerges in the Indian male psyche when the mother–son relationship becomes too intense.[159] In my opinion, Radha becomes dangerous here because she is taking up the role of the father, the punisher. The image of the old woman with the gun is somewhat incongruous with our other images of Radha, but its very iconic power shows her as sacrificing her own honour to that of society as a whole and its laws (although its laws do not punish her for murdering her son).

Rosie Thomas has argued that *Mother India* takes up many of the themes of the Hindi film, notably its operation of an ideal moral universe,[160] in particular the central question of whether private duty should come before public duty. Radha's main choices are between these two spheres. Should she feed her children or protect her honour from the moneylender? Should she protect her son or Sukhilal's daughter on her wedding day? Birju is a good son in private, who protects his mother's honour, symbolized by the return of her wedding bangles, but he threatens the honour of other girls. His revolutionary tendencies are directed towards wider society, as he realizes the need for literacy, education and an end to feudal practices, but when he rebels against the family his behaviour is deplorable.

The story of *Mother India*, already reworked from Mehboob's *Aurat*, was later recast by Salim–Javed in their script for Yash Chopra's *Deewaar* (1975). This version undergoes two major changes in that it is given an urban twist, as the family migrates to the city after the loss of the father, but its major difference is that there is a clear shift to the anti-hero, Amitabh Bachchan, as the focus of the film.[161] The mother is crucial but Vijay is the central character, and the film concentrates on his lifespan and the wrongs he has suffered. In a further twist, his good brother, Ravi, is a policeman, a representative of the state, who has to hunt his brother down. Ravi knows that the law is unjust, but that his duty is to follow it to the letter. He is among the group of police who have to fire on his brother, resulting in Vijay's death in his mother's lap in a temple. The mother loves her bad son more but has to put her duty to Ravi and the state before her private feelings. The identification of these private values with the state becomes clear in that the mother's flashback is set not against the utopian future of the opening of a dam, but the award of a state medal to Ravi, which he asks her to accept on his behalf.

A further pleasure for the audience was the performance of the film's heroine, Nargis, one of the top stars of the 1950s Hindi cinema. She was famous both for her roles and her off-screen life which the audience could enjoy reading into the film and discussing in its subsequent readings of the films. *Mother India* was the last film she worked in, apart from a role she took in a film to help her brother out. *Mother India* in many senses was the culmination of her career as an actress, a film which helped to create her star persona but which also reflected her 'real' life.

Nargis was pushed into films as a child star by her mother, Jaddan Bai, a courtesan-singer. Her first adult film was with Mehboob, but it was her work with Raj Kapoor, with whom she is said to have had a long and publicly discussed affair, which made her into a top star by the 1940s. Despite the fact that he was married with children, she thought of herself as his second wife, and had hoped to marry him until Hindus were prevented from practising polygamy in the 1950s. When it became clear he would not leave his family for her, she ended their relationship and, in the small world of the Bombay elite, managed to avoid him for the rest of her life.

A striking feature of the film is the intense relationship between mother and son, with Birju the devoted son and Radha the doting mother. In psychoanalytical terms this could be read as the son's fantasy of the castration of his father by his loss of his arms, which leads to his disappearance, allowing Birju to replace his father. This is seen most clearly in the film when Birju puts Radha's wedding bangles on her hands. Birju can replace his father even in name, since they both have names of Krishna, Radha's beloved, unlike the older, good son who is called Ramu, that is Rama, the righteous king. The association of Birju with Krishna is further reinforced by his teasing the girls and breaking their waterpots, a frequent pastime of Krishna's. Unlike Krishna, who is recalled to his duties by Uddhava, Birju refuses to submit to the laws of society, or the law of the father, remaining in the world of his mother. This dangerous transgression leads to his being killed by his mother, who becomes a bad mother as she takes on the role of the father, upholding the law of society. While this reading has limitations in the application of a contested western theory of sexuality, it was reinforced by the text of the life of Nargis, in that the audience knew that it was during the filming of *Mother India* that she fell in love with Sunil Dutt, Birju, whom she later married. This reading of off-screen lives into cinematic relationships is seen clearly in the taboo in the Hindi cinema against playing roles other than real life (husband and wife, father and son). For example in the 1990s Anil Kapoor and Sri Devi, who were a hit pairing over many films, are no longer regarded as suitable partners since she married his brother.[162] It is possible that *Mother India* can be read as playing into this Oedipal fancy, since the audience can 'see' the desire of Nargis and Sunil Dutt in the characters they play in the film.

After this film, Nargis became known as an ideal wife and mother, her indulgence of her son, Sanjay, being regarded as the cause of his lifelong struggle with dependency on drugs and alcohol. Her eldest daughter married the son of Rajendra Kumar, who played Ramu in *Mother India*, another resonance of the film in her private life. Nargis took up the role of

Mother India in later life when she joined the upper house of parliament, the Rajya Sabha. When she lost her long battle with cancer, the nation mourned one of its greatest public figures.

Maintaining her star status, Nargis rejected the traditional patriarchy into which she was born, setting herself up as an icon of modernity, the secular Muslim, a working woman, who chooses her own lovers, then becomes a bourgeois housewife and doting mother on marriage, re-emerging as a political leader in later life. How did she manage to negotiate these roles as part of her star image? Behroze Gandhy and Rosie Thomas argue that the star personae off screen

> frequently encompass behaviours that are decidedly subversive of the strict social mores of Indian society and would be considered 'scandalous' in any other context, even by many of their most dedicated fans. Of course they do not simply transgress: stars are represented as finely balancing their transgressions with personifications of ideal behaviour especially in the domains of kinship and sexuality. Both the films and the sub-text of gossip about stars are most usefully seen as debates around morality, in particular as negotiations about the role of 'tradition' in a modernising India.[163]

They find the stars are discussed in the context of issues of motherhood, sexuality and gender in the context of modernity and tradition, informed by deep-seated mythological attributes of women and the powers of goddesses. Debates around Nadia and Smita have centred on roles for 'strong women' and feminist questions, whereas the persona of Nargis is the most complicated of all.[164] Although a number of events in her life[165] would be seen as shocking by many traditionalists (the alleged sale of her virginity, her supposed affair with Raj Kapoor), the gossip about her has never tainted her image and she has remained a figure of enormous respect, almost a consolidation of her Mother India image. It seems that allowances are made for stars as for gods, and so Nargis's good qualities – such as her fidelity to Raj despite his infidelity and her later devotion to Sunil, her family and her work – kept her image 'pure'.

Mother India has also been an important focus for debates about the cultural legitimacy of film among the middle classes. It came out only two years after Satyajit Ray's first film, *Pather Panchali*. Indian cinema is popularly divided into Ray vs commercial cinema.[166] Nargis attacked Ray in her first speech to the Rajya Sabha, saying that his films were giving images of India that the west wanted, namely that of abject poverty. In interview afterwards, she said *Pather Panchali*

Portrays a region of West Bengal that is so poor that it does not represent India's poverty in its true form ... And this is what [Ray] portrays in this film. It is not a correct image of India.[167]

When pushed by the journalist about how India should be shown on screen, she said she wanted images of modern India, suggesting these were represented by dams, as indeed in *Mother India*. In *The Moor's Last Sigh*, Salman Rushdie returns to these various themes of Nargis the star and as Mother India, the quarrel with Ray and the reading of the star text into the movie, in an episode in which the actress visits the narrator's mother in the novel:

Motherness – excuse me if I underline the point – is a big idea in India, maybe our biggest: the land as mother, the mother as land, as the firm ground beneath our feet. Ladies-O, gents-O: I'm talking *major* mother country. The year I was born, Mehboob Productions' all-conquering movie *Mother India* ... hit the nation's screens. Nobody who saw it ever forgot that glutinous saga of peasant heroinism, that super-slushy ode to the uncrushability of village India made by the most cynical urbanites in the world ...

'The first time I saw that picture', [his mother says to Nargis] 'I took one look at your Bad Son, Birju, and I thought, O boy, what a handsome guy – too much sizzle, too much chilli, bring water. He may be a thief and a bounder, but that is some A-class loverboy goods. And now look – you have gone and marry-o'ed him! What sexy lives you movie people leadofy: to marry your own son, I swear, wowie.'

'Dirty talk,' said the Living Mother Goddess. 'Filthy dirty, chhi. I heard tell that depraved artists and beatnik intellectuals came up here, but I gave you all the benefit of doubt. Now I observe that I am among the blaspheming scum of the earth. How you people wallo-pollow in negative images! In our picture we put stress on the positive side. Courage of the masses is there, and also dams.'

'*Bewaqoof!*' shouted Sunil Dutt, provoked beyond endurance. 'Bleddy dumbo! not oathery, but new technology is being referred to: to wit, the hydro-electric project, as inaugurated by my goodwife in the opening scene.'

'And when you say your wife,' ever-helpful Vasco clarified, 'you mean of course, your mother.'

'Sunil come,' said the legend, sweeping away. 'If this godless anti-national gang is the world of art, then I-tho am happy to be on commercial side.' [168]

The romantic revival

The 1980s are regarded as a low phase in Bombay commercial cinemas, a time when violence dominated the screen. Directors and producers report they were unsure of what would run at the box office and, given the popularity of action films, did not want to take risks with soft romances and family movies. It was only when the young Mansoor Khan released his *Qayamat se qayamat tak* (*QSQT*, 'From doomsday to doomsday') in 1988 that we see the return of the musical family-oriented romance. For the first time for years, film music became cool among the college crowd with everyone singing the catchy *Papa kehte hain* ('Daddy says'). The fresh-faced good looks of Aamir Khan, the male lead, appealed as a role model and a boyfriend. The story was a college romance but the plot still hinged around feudal structures: Thakors (rich peasants and landlords) engaged in a family dispute about a woman's, and hence the family's, honour, the young couple from opposing factions falling in love in a Romeo and Juliet situation.

Yash Chopra's 1989 hit *Chandni*, a bourgeois romance about a working woman, was saturated with romantic imagery (lovers showering their beloved with red roses from a helicopter) and romantic dilemmas as Chandni had to choose between two men. As in Chopra's earlier romances, eroticism and romanticism are carried as much by words (dialogues and lyrics) as by visuals. Hugely successful, it differs from the new kind of romance which emerged, with different forms of friendship, courtship, marriage and the family, in the other hit film of 1989, *Maine pyar kiya* (*MPK*, 'I have fallen in love').

MPK is a landmark film, partly as the debut of the director Sooraj Barjatya. Eroticism is almost absent in this film, apart from the monochrome opening sequences, where a modern dance is performed to a Hindi version of Stevie Wonder's 'I just called ...'. The female body is not presented for display – the heroine's appearance in a sexy dress is for the hero's eyes only as she seems to 'flash' him from behind a raincoat. Even her most romantic song, *Dil deewana* ('My crazy heart'), is replete with prayers for her beloved and a reminder of her procreative abilities made real by the presence of children. The images of fertility are reinforced throughout by foreground shots of fruit and vegetables, one song sequence showing the heroine waving bunches of vegetables above her head, while another bizarre sequence shows the lovers in a field full of apples but no apple trees. This is no girl with a career or a past, but a sweet, innocent traditional girl who certainly knows how to 'shell peas' (stated as a major requirement of a wife by the US-educated hero). She is maternal and nurturing, reserving her sexy performance exclusively for her beloved, not for the rest of the world. Even the vamp is unsexy, merely brazen, the focus of the viewer's desiring eye being the male body of the young Salman Khan, shown exercising and performing physical labour, shaved smoothly for a dance number in a red sequinned suit.

One of the most important emphases of this film is its certainty that the loving relationships offered by family ties and friendship are valued more highly than erotic love. In many romances, the problem facing the family is the incorporation of erotic love into the family's other relationships, but here the situation seems to be reversed as the couple's relationship was originally planned by the family (an 'arranged love marriage'), and is only temporarily blocked by a quarrel between the two families. A further striking feature of this film lies in the roots of the couple's relationship which arises from friendship rather than from passion, beginning with a glimpse of the beloved, in the *ghazal* tradition. Friendship in the Hindi movie had previously been concerned with male–male friendship (*dosti, dostana*).[169] This had been a major feature in many older films, where love for one's friends required one to renounce happiness, and if necessary one's life.[170] In this film, friendship is found as an important bond among men, but also between men and women, in particular in the *devar-bhabhi* (older brother's wife–husband's younger brother) relationship seen here in two generations, one of the few cross-gender friendships which is not taboo. In this film, the romantic couple is bound more by *dosti* than passion, which seems more suited to the wider requirements of family relationships.

However, the theme of friendship and teenage romance in this film has a clear genealogy. The story refers to the young romance seen earlier in Raj Kapoor's *Bobby* (1973), with many scenes in this film being a clear tribute to the former, although the questions of communal (religious) and class difference have been elided. Bobby's first words on meeting her future lover were the famous *Mujhse dosti karoge?* ('Will you be my friend?'), and her claim to be a 'twenty-first-century girl' is upheld by the influence she has had on subsequent teen romances. Barjatya updates his film by adding the 'Friends' baseball-cap, the incorporation of the servants into the family (the camp manservants and the bejewelled maid), the car-hopping pigeon and the need for the characters to say 'I love you', when '*Maine pyar kiya*' can no longer express their feelings. Not only were the clothes updated, but the look of the stars also changed. The unselfconscious but potent sexuality of Bobby, emphasized by her hotpants and miniskirts and her rolling on beds and heaps of flowers, is now the demure, pretty young girl who can barely touch the boy. However, the male is no longer the cute teenager, but a big-eyed, muscular hero, who displaces the woman's centrality as the focus of the woman's and the camera's gaze.

A whole spate of romantic, musical films was released after the phenomenal success of *MPK*. The hugely popular music, which was cheaply available on audiocassette, allowed music to reassert its position as a key contributor to a film's box office success, the film's *antakshari* sequence (showing a competitive game where verses of songs are connected by their first and last syllables) is a stunning piece of visual and aural nostalgia.

Passion remained a box-office attraction, but often in more disturbing forms. *Darr* ('Fear', dir. Yash Chopra, 1993), was one of several films in which Shahrukh Khan, another cute but muscular hero, played a negative role. Yet this film was unique and perhaps dangerous, in that it showed a lover obsessed and deluded to the point of madness, liable to arrest for his harassing the innocent girl, yet he displaces the girl's boyfriend to become the film's hero, leaving the viewer ambivalent about the morality of the film and the limits of desire.

The family film reached its apogee in 1994, with the release of Barjatya's *Hum aapke hain kaun ...!* ('What am I to you ...!),[171] a film entirely plotted around the family life events of engagement, marriage, childbirth and death.[172] The younger generation is prepared to sacrifice love for the welfare of their loving and supportive families, who are the entire focus of the film. Possibly the greatest box-office hit of all time, the film is also critical because its release brought about a crucial change in Hindi film-viewing when Sooraj Barjatya introduced the policy of 'video holdback'. When he released the film, he released only one initial print with seats selling at the then unheard-of price of Rs100. This publicity stunt aroused great curiosity, and as he released the film at a few more theatres, demand exceeded supply. When the film came out on general release and was still not available on video, the audience thronged to the cinemas. The unprecedented success of this film meant that big-budget, family-oriented films were once again commercially viable.

Yash Chopra's older son, Aditya, released his first film, *Dilwale dulhaniya le jayenge* ('The lover will take the bride'), in 1995.[173] A huge success, it showed clear marks of a Yash Chopra film in the romantic scenes, although closer to Barjatya in its more conservative deployment of the family in the couple's romance, yet having its own unique quality.

The Yash Chopra banner and the youth of the media-shy director misled many into believing they were seeing one of his father's romances. All the hallmarks were there – the gripping story, the visual beauty, the great locations, the unforgettable music. It would, however, be more accurate to see this as an affectionate tribute by an original film-maker, exploring his own cinematic vision while drawing on the visual vocabulary of romance his father has created for the Hindi cinema. The young couple do not challenge society's prohibitions and taboos when their passion unfolds, as Yash Chopra's lovers would, instead they persuade the harsh but well-meaning patriarchy to accept their love. Another difference is that Yash Chopra's cities are friendly homes for urban elites while here we have cold and anonymous London, an inappropriate location for romance. Like a Yash Chopra film, romance flourishes in Swiss idylls but reaches a state of passion only in rural Panjab, whose fields full of yellow mustard and village girls trailing their scarves become a place of the family and love, rather than a location for terrorism as Panjab represented to many in the 1980s and 1990s. Panjab is a place appropriate for religious occasions, such as weddings and the *karva chauth* (a fast performed by women to obtain a good husband). However, there is a significant change from earlier films where foreign locations were used only for spectacle. Here we see the beginning of the diaspora film,[174] which had begun to emerge with Yash Chopra's *Lamhe* ('Moments', 1991).[175] The new transnational Indian middle-class nuclear family is the norm in London, but it still seems pale in comparison to Panjab's extended family and traditional hospitality.

The film has as its central theme the hero's love for his heroine. It transforms him from brat to responsible adult, drives the story forward, gaining momentum as he wins over the whole of her family and friends through his relentless charm and good nature. Along the way it highlights the whole structuring of family friendships and emotions, bringing out tenderness and love in all the characters, reinforcing the belief that Indianness is not so much a question of citizenship as of sharing family values.[176] The success of the film is due more to its driving logic and its emotional richness rather than its overseas locations and the subsequent return to the *desh* ('homeland'). The great emotional highs – the scene when the hero refuses the heroine's invitation to her wedding or the scene when the heroine's mother urges her daughter to run away with her lover rather than sacrifice her happiness as she herself did – were among the high points of the movie. The exuberant and tender eroticism of the heroine which allows her to display her glorious sensuality as an innocent romp (*Mere khwabon mein*, 'In my dreams'), and the teasing of a wicked hero, who pretends to have taken advantage of her while she was drunk, display a new relaxed attitude to sexuality within the constraints of a traditional morality. A critical factor is the dynamic pairing of Shah Rukh and Kajol, one of the most popular screen couples in India for decades. The freshness and tenderness of the love they depict, their negotiation of modernity and tradition, their ability to charm and love all around them, touched the audience as much as the film's characters.

The success of these films and their new distribution practices encouraged the return of audiences to the cinema, but only for certain types of film: either the carefully crafted small-budget films which have mostly urban audiences or the high-quality, big-budget, star-studded movies. One of the biggest hits of recent years has been Yash Chopra's *Dil to pagal hai* ('The heart is crazy', 1997) whose hip style of romance is set in a theatre group, where the old American musical is updated by a bit of 'Friends' and lots of Bombay style. The Yash Chopra romantic touches are kept for Madhuri, who dances kathak, and wears chiffon Indian clothes, but even she barely gets a love song. The music, despite its lack of love songs, was an unprecedented success and carried this 'plotless' movie, which soon became a cult. That the other great success was *Kuch kuch hota hai* ('Something happens', 1998, dir. Karan Johar) shows how important Yash Chopra has become to the younger generation of film-makers. This film pays tribute to him and to Pamela Chopra in its credits, and the stamp of the Yash Chopra film is clear to see, along with references to the teen romance via *Bobby* and Sooraj Barjatya's movies.

Notes

1. Bourdieu, 1984.
2. Although there has been government finance for a specific kind of cinema since the late 1960s, the popular cinema was granted industry status only in 1998.
3. Mass media in India, 1992: 157, 198. Ref. from Nandy, 1998: 1.
4. See Rajadhyaksha, 1987; Pinney, 1997.
5. The most influential of the early studios were Prabhat Film Company (Kolhapur, 1929–33; Pune 1933–53), Bombay Talkies (Bombay City, 1934–54) and New Theatres (Calcutta, 1931–55).
6. Vasudevan, 1989. Vasudevan, 1993, shows how these codes are mixed in films, analysing sequences from *Andaz* ('Style', 1949, dir. Mehboob Khan) and *Awaara* ('The vagabond', 1951, dir. Raj Kapoor) in detail.
7. Prasad, 1998: Chapter 1.
8. Vasudevan, 1993: 56.
9. State governments also taxed the film industry, although some assisted film-makers, such as the government of West Bengal, which helped Satyajit Ray.
10. Barnouw and Krishnaswamy, 1980: 207–14.
11. See below.
12. Prasad, 1998.
13. Prasad, 1998: 118. He discusses these at length in Chapters 8, 7 and 6 respectively.
14. Nandy, 1995a.
15. Prasad, 1998: Chapter 9.
16. There are several professional comedians, whose presence in films, Prasad (1998: 73) suggests, offers a point of identification for the viewer.
17. In Bombay, the links between politics and cinema have drawn closer since the family of Bal Thackeray, the leader of the Shiv Sena, is becoming increasingly active in film production and has close associations at many levels of the film industry. Bal Thackeray has even acted as unofficial censor: Amitabh Bachchan visited him personally in his capacity as

producer of Mani Ratnam's *Bombay* (1995) to enquire how much of the portrayal of Thackeray in the film the Shiv Sena leader wanted cut.

18. Nandy, 1993.
19. Nandy, 1995a.
20. Baskaran, 1981; Pandian, 1992; Dickey, 1993a and b.
21. While there has been important work on the Tamil cinema, the other regional commercial cinemas have been neglected in favour of the Hindi cinema.
22. See also Chapter 3 above.
23. Nandy, 1998: 2.
24. Nandy, 1998: 12.
25. Nandy, 1998: 7.
26. Dyer, 1977.
27. Inden, 1999 and 2000.
28. Das Gupta, 1991: 90.
29. Das Gupta, 1991: 61.
30. Das Gupta, 1991: 62.
31. Das Gupta, 1991: 62
32. Nandy, 1990a, has pointed out that while non-Bengalis know Ray only from his art films, and hence regard him as a figure of high culture, Bengalis love him more for his detective fiction, which is of a middlebrow nature.
33. S. Ray, 1976: 73.
34. S. Ray, 1976: 75.
35. Jadavpur University, Calcutta.
36. Led by Ravi Vasudevan, Ashish Rajadhyaksha and Madhava Prasad. The study of film has been included in other aspects of social and cultural studies, notably by Ashis Nandy and Patricia Uberoi.
37. MacCabe, 1986, is entitled 'High theory/ low culture'.
38. Most reviews of Prasad, 1998, criticized the author for his 'jargon', a common attack on academic language, whereas his writing, while technical in places, is extremely lucid.
39. See Chapter 6 on the gossip magazines.
40. Important critics such as Maithili Rao, Khalid Mohamed and Iqbal Masud are largely unknown outside India.
41. Yash Chopra's (see Chapter 5) webpages have won awards for their design: http://yashrajfilms.com.
42. There have been few ethnographic studies of the cinema's audience. Dickey, 1993a, is the only significant work apart from Pfleiderer and Lutze, 1985. While it is widely assumed that the audience is largely urban, industrial, male and lower class, recent increases in ticket prices, to Rs100, indicate an audience with at least middle-class spending power, but this audience's views are available only in terms of box-office statistics.
43. See Chapter 7 below.
44. See Chapter 2 above.
45. Chandra's own background is firmly in the arena of the cinema of the new middle classes: his mother writes scripts, including Yash Chopra's *Chandni* (see below); one sister is a film critic for the new middle classes' favourite news magazine, *India Today* (see Chapter 6), while another is a film director.
46. See for example Bordwell and Thompson, 1990: 51–62.
47. Vasudevan, 1989: 29–50.
48. Vasudevan, 1989: 30: 'Though overlapping with the social reform film, this genre is not always so precise about the social ills it addresses. Set in modern times, the genre generates societal images that delineate ethical precepts raising questions of dignity, equality, honesty. The social referent is generally the plebeian or the *declassé*. It has become the characteristic genre of the post-independence cinema.'
49. Prasad, 1998: Chapter 3.
50. Prasad, 1996: 30.
51. On the 'democratic' nature of these modes see Prasad, 1998: 56–8. See also Brooks, 1995.
52. See Lukacs, 1972, on realism as a mode of literary representation.
53. Mukherjee, 1985.
54. Ang, 1985.
55. For example, Yash Chopra refers to his style as 'glamorous realism'. See Chapter 5 below.
56. Drawing on MacCabe, 1986.
57. Prasad, 1998: 63.
58. Brooks, 1995; also Elsaesser, 1985. Their work has been theorized further in a number of publications including Gledhill, 1987, Landy, 1991, etc.
59. See the 'Preface' to the 1995 edition of Brooks.
60. Ang, 1985: 61.
61. Ang, 1985: 61–8, is an excellent summary and analysis of the forms and functions of melodrama.
62. Neale, 1986.
63. Vasudevan, 1989, where he emphasizes cultural specificity of the Hindi cinema, drawing on Thomas, 1985. See also Vasudevan, 1993.
64. See Shackle and Snell, 1990.

65. For example, Yash Chopra's 1973 hit, *Daag*, 'The stain', drew on Nanda's *Maili Chandni*.
66. See below for a discussion of the song lyric.
67. Writers like Siddiqui write in Urdu, their work transliterated into Devanagari (Hindi) by their assistants.
68. Kristeva, 1984.
69. Kristeva, 1987: 1.
70. Barthes, 1990.
71. Barthes, 1990: 6–7.
72. Prasad, 1998: Chapter 4.
73. Yash Chopra has made one of the few successful Hindi films without songs, *Ittefaq* (1969). *Deewaar* is unusual in having only two songs.
74. Kristeva, 1987: 287.
75. Sahir Ludhianvi's poem, *Chakle* ('Brothels') was rewritten with simpler language for Guru Dutt's 1957 film, *Pyaasa* ('The desirous one'). The future of the Urdu film lyric in India does not look too bleak, for while fewer of the younger generation of film-makers are educated in Urdu poetry, their deep background knowledge of film lyrics and Urdu *ghazals* may encourage its survival, even though its development is unclear.
76. See Chapter 2 above.
77. Vasudevan, 1993; see also Prasad, 1998: 76–7, which draws on Babb, 1981, and Eck, 1985.
78. Kasbekar [2000].
79. Prasad, 1998: Chapter 4.
80. See Das Gupta, quoted above.
81. Manuel, 1993.
82. See Haggard, 1988, and Srivatsan, 1991, for discussion of these billboards.
83. Ellis, 1992: 19.
84. Ellis, 1992: 38f.
85. Ang, 1985: 64 (quotes Elsaesser); Gledhill, 1991b: 208.
86. Dyer, 1979.
87. Dyer, 1979, is the foundational work for the study of the star. He introduces the concept of the 'star text' in this path-breaking study of the star across a whole range of cultural practice through semiotic and sociological analysis. All later work on the star, such as the papers in Gledhill, 1991b, takes this as the point of departure.
88. Dyer, 1986: 19.
89. Dyer, 1979: 34–7.
90. See also Gledhill, 1991b: 214.
91. For example, in Gujarat an actor called Sundari, famed for his female roles, attracted a great following.
92. Smith, 1995: 193–4.
93. The pleasure of hearing is never discussed. This is foregrounded in the Indian cinema by music which is part of the spectacle in the film but has an important existence outside the cinematic experience. Recordings of dialogues are also found, the most famous being that of *Sholay* (now available on CD). A further example is that of the voice of Amitabh Bachchan acting, reciting poetry and even singing some of his own songs.
94. Mulvey, 1981.
95. For wider studies of female pleasure in consuming popular culture see in particular Radway, 1987, and Ang, 1985.
96. Prasad, 1998: 74–8.
97. See above n. 77.
98. Stacey, 1994: 130–8.
99. Dickey, 1993a and b; also 2000. See also Pandian, 1992.
100. On the history of the star in Hindi cinema see Kabir, 1985, which contains studies of some of the major stars of Indian cinema. Khalid Mohamed gives an overall historical survey in the introduction to this volume. A number of biographies of stars, musicians and directors have appeared in recent years, but these are all written for the general reading public, not for an academic audience interested in theoretical approaches to the star. They vary from the 'sex and scandal', via the popular, digressive style to important studies.
101. Karanjia, 1984: 151.
102. Dharmendra, Amitabh Bachchan, Sanjeev Kumar, Amjad Khan, Hema Malini, Jaya Bhaduri and Helen.
103. Three heroes – Amitabh Bachchan, Shatrughan Sinha, Rishi Kapoor; three heroines – Hema Malini, Reena Roy, Kim; and numerous villains including Pran, Amrish Puri, Kader Khan and Amjad Khan.
104. Raj Kapoor, Shammi Kapoor, Dharmendra, Rajesh Khanna, Mala Sinha, Waheeda Rehman and Sharmila Tagore.
105. Many major political figures in south India are former movie stars. See Pandian, 1992, and Dickey, 1993a and 1993b. On a national level, the cult of the personality and the celebrity family is seen clearly in the political dynasty of the Nehrus and Gandhis as well as in film dynasties like that of the Kapoors.

106. See Karanjia, 1984.
107. See Manuel, 1993.
108. Notably Amjad Khan after his role as Gabbar Singh in *Sholay*.
109. Helen's star status as a dancer has never been equalled.
110. See K. Hansen, 1992, for a discussion of the hero and heroine in *nautanki* theatre and [2000] on Parsi theatre.
111. The nature of epic heroes and heroines is discussed by Beck, 1989; Blackburn, 1989; Blackburn and Flueckiger, 1989; and Kothari, 1989.
112. See the discussion of *Mother India* below.
113. For example by V. Mishra, 1985, and Mishra *et al.*, 1989.
114. Gledhill, 1991b: 215.
115. See Fox, 1985, and Sinha, 1995.
116. Their Muslim identity may provide them with a hypermasculinity in that the Indian Muslim is perceived as a threat in Hindu nationalist discourses (Kapur, 1993), which use metaphors of impotency for those who do not oppose Muslims (Bharucha, 1995: 8), and which fear Muslim hyperfertility, imploring Hindus not to practise birth control (Bharucha, 1995: 7).
117. See above.
118. The great stars of the silent period included Miss Patience Cooper (?1905–), Seeta Devi (1912–) and Sulochana (Ruby Meyers, 1907–83), 'Glorious' Gohar (1910–85).
119. Sharmila Tagore, Raakhee, and recently Kajol and Rani Mukherjee.
120. From Durga Khote to Madhuri Dixit.
121. In particular Padmini, Vyjayanthimala, Hema Malini, Rekha and Sri Devi.
122. Fearless Nadia (1910–96), Nargis (1929–81) and Smita Patil (1955–86). Gandhy and Thomas, 1991.
123. Gandhy and Thomas, 1991: 108.
124. Mohamed, 1985: 36 per cent says that 60 per cent of spectators were aged 16 to 24 in the 1960s.
125. *An Evening in Paris*, dir. S. Samanta, 1967.
126. Mishra *et al.*, 1989: 58.
127. The politicians of the DMK and its branches have chosen their roles carefully. For example, MGR (M. G. Ramachandran), filmstar and Chief Minister of Tamil Nadu, always played the role of the dashing hero, the protector of the poor, both in his films and in his political life. See Dickey, 1993a, and 1993b; and Pandian, 1992.
128. See Dyer, 1979: 142–51, for an extended discussion of stars as characters in films.
129. Kapoor always attributed his success to his team in the 1950s which included the major figures K. A. Abbas, Shankar-Jaikishen, Shailendra, etc.
130. A role identified by Ashis Nandy in his study of P. C. Barua as the 'maudlin, effeminate hero'. Nandy [2000].
131. 1958, dir. Bimal Roy.
132. 1961, dir. Nitin Bose.
133. Interview with the author, May 1997.
134. Valicha, 1988.
135. See Chapter 5 for a discussion of his roles as romantic hero.
136. In an interview with the author Amitabh Bachchan said people were always disappointed that he was himself, not the character Vijay he played in many Salim-Javed films.
137. Ashwini Sharma analyses his role in *Agneepath* (1990, dir. Mukul Anand), a late and not hugely successful film, but has little to say about the nature of his stardom. See A. Sharma, 1993.
138. Prasad, 1998: Chapter 6.
139. Dir. Girish Karnad, 1984.
140. See also *Muqaddar ka Sikander* ('Man of destiny', dir. Prakash Mehra, 1978), *Umrao Jaan* ('Umrao Jaan', dir Muzaffar Ali, 1981) and *Kamasutra* ('Kamasutra', dir. Mira Nair, 1997).
141. Such as *Devdas* ('Devdas', dir. Bimal Roy, 1955) and *Sahib, bibi aur ghulam* ('King, queen and knave', dir. Abrar Alvi, 1961). See Chakravarty, 1993: 261–305, for a longer account of the history of the courtesan film.
142. 'Umrao Jaan', dir. Muzaffar Ali, 1981.
143. 'The pure one', dir. Kamal Amrohi, 1971.
144. Oldenburg, 1989.
145. Muslims formed the majority population of most north Indian cities before Independence, which is one of the reasons many of the courtesans were Muslims.
146. See below.
147. Seth, 1993.
148. Bruzzi, 1997.
149. See also Uberoi, 1997, on podoerotics.
150. Tharu and Lalita, 1995b: 364–5.
151. Tharu and Lalita, 1995b: 364–5.
152. Deep, 1998.
153. Dyer, 1986.
154. Sontag, 1983.
155. Dir. Shekhar Kapur, 1994.
156. See Mayo, 1998.
157. Chatterjee, 1986.

158. Chakravarti, 1993: 150–1.
159. Kakar, 1981a.
160. Thomas, 1989 and 1995.
161. Prasad, 1998: 144–53.
162. Married women usually retire from acting, although this taboo is now breaking down.
163. Gandhy and Thomas, 1991: 108.
164. See also Thomas, 1989 and 1995.
165. Gandhy and Thomas point out that these are, of course, entirely speculative.
166. Rajadhyaksha, 1996b.
167. Quoted in Robinson, 1989: 327.
168. Rushdie, 1995: 137–8.
169. See Chapter 2.
170. A good example is *Sangam*, 1964, dir. Raj Kapoor, where the couple sacrifice their love for the claims of their friend who fought in the armed services.
171. Uberoi [2000].
172. An English-language play based on the film was a great success in Britain in 1998. It ironically called itself 'Fourteen songs, two weddings and a funeral'.
173. Uberoi, 1998.
174. See Uberoi, 1998.
175. Dwyer [2000b].
176. Uberoi, 1998: 305.

5

The Flowering of Romance: Yash Chopra and the Hindi Romantic Film

In this chapter I discuss the depiction of romantic love by examining two well-known films of the renowned director, Yash Chopra. *Kabhi Kabhie* ('Sometimes', 1976) and *Silsila* ('The affair', 1981) epitomize his long-term attachment to love as a cinematic theme, and his preoccupation with the social and sexual mores of independent India's bourgeoisie. Both films contain well-loved examples of romantic songs which are integral to Hindi cinema, and I analyse their lyric content in order to shed light on both the visual depiction of romance and the literary roots of much Hindi film narrative. I also examine the off-screen personae of the stars, including Amitabh Bachchan and Rekha. This, I argue, affords another means of investigating the interstices of love, sex and romance among India's elite and their reception by the mass cinema-going audience.

Yash Chopra (1932–) is arguably India's most successful director of commercial films, where he has been at the top of his profession for almost forty years since his directorial debut, *Dhool ka phool* ('Blossom of dust; lovechild', 1959).[1] No other director of his generation has manifested such creative and box-office staying-power; indeed the careers of most directors of popular Hindi films rarely last more than a decade. Yash Chopra is one of the richest and most powerful producers in Bombay, now financing his films from his own pocket and arranging some of his own distribution. His position was enhanced recently by his production, directed by his elder son, Aditya Chopra (1971–), of one of the great commercial successes of Indian cinema, *Dilwale dulhania le jayenge* ('The brave heart will take the bride', 1995).[2] In 1997 the Chopra family consolidated its control of all aspects of its film-making by opening a London office, followed by a New York office in 1998, to handle overseas film distribution, and they plan to build their own studio in Bombay. This will be the first air-conditioned film studio in India;[3] it will also be sound-proofed, thus allowing for the introduction of simultaneous sound-recording in the industry, which still relies on dubbing dialogues. Although the old formula remains popular, Chopra's latest film, *Dil to pagal hai* ('The heart is mad', 1997), develops a new visual style in Hindi cinema.[4] It is the first film to feature jazz dancers,[5] has a new-look *mise-en-scène* created by young, high-flying designers,[6] and a music director new to Bollywood, on whom the Chopras gambled.[7] These are all indications that the Chopra film dynasty constantly takes risks in redefining itself and expands by adapting to the times, both creatively and financially.

Yash Chopra's cinematic output may be divided into three main categories. The first comprises a series of socially oriented films which were all produced by his elder brother's company, BR Films; the second is the action-film; and the third is the romance. He has had successes in all three styles, but the romance is his speciality and closest to his heart. Yash Chopra has also developed a unique visual aesthetic in his romantic movies which is manifested in his locations, sets and the way he presents his stars; instantly recognizable, this has frequently been imitated, notably his trademark shots of misty valleys, snow-capped mountains, lakes and rivers, women in chiffon, and fields of flowers. His films have always been regarded as being ahead of their time, in particular in their bold and controversial story-lines, which often feature love and sex outside of marriage. Many of these, unusually for modern commercial Hindi cinema, are heroine-oriented. His concentration on the depiction of the super-rich and images of beauty have led to his being dubbed 'the king of romance' and 'the guru of gloss'. I now turn to Yash Chopra's depiction of love in two of his best-known romantic movies, *Kabhi Kabhie*[8] and *Silsila*.

The romance is an ill-defined term in cinema studies; hence I begin by outlining some of the problems one faces in defining the term 'romantic'. I then look briefly at the question of the romantic genre in the Hindi movie, before discussing Yash Chopra's role in creating the genre, with reference to *Kabhi Kabhie* and *Silsila*. I selected these quintessentially romantic movies not only because they are among my personal favourites and for their enduring popularity,[9] but also because they subvert the trend of the 1970s in the roles played by Amitabh Bachchan, the greatest star of the Hindi film. At this point in his career Amitabh's star persona simultaneously embodied and represented its own sub-genre, namely that of the angry young man, or the industrial hero, as seen in a number of Yash Chopra's other movies, e.g. *Deewaar*, *Trishul* and *Kala Pathar*.

The discipline of cinema studies has concentrated on the erotic aspect of love. The erotic is largely focused on the look, hence its centrality to cinema needs no elaboration here. Laura Mulvey[10] has theorized the gaze in western cinema in her study of the pleasure of looking, the practice of scopophilia, which arises via the mechanisms of fetishism and voyeurism. The specificity of the gaze in Indian cinema has not yet been analysed,[11] although the visual anthropology of India and the problems of using a psychoanalytic framework in the context of Indian culture suggest the situation is complex. Nevertheless, a study of the erotic, which is always a culturally specific practice, is likely to be rewarding in the context of Indian cinema. An examination of the cinematic presentation of erotic images, songs and dances would be a vital component of such research, and note must be taken of the role of censorship in creating a suggestive visual vocabulary for the erotic; for example, flowers may suggest the wedding bed, or substitute for the lovers' lips in kissing scenes, etc.

Film studies have engaged with love or the romantic aspect of love mainly in the specific forms of the woman's movie and of melodrama. Yet romantic love is the central theme of film worldwide with nearly all movies, irrespective of their genre, containing a romantic theme. There are sub-genres of romance movies ranging from the teen love story to the great passion. Hindi movies are no exception and almost every Hindi movie has a love theme, love songs and themes of love extending beyond the romantic couple, yet it is not clear whether the romantic genre exists in Indian cinema as a specific and universally acknowledged category.

Viewers of Hindi cinema often refer to the star to categorize a film. For example, a film starring Rishi Kapoor will always have a strong romantic theme. While a 'Yash Chopra movie' is recognized by viewers, journalists and distributors of Hindi cinema in the 1990s as a category whose primary feature is romance, it remains unclear as to whether these films can be regarded as forming part of a romantic genre.[12]

It could be argued that *Kabhi Kabhie* and *Silsila* belong to the second segment in its extended form, which includes commercially successful middle-class cinema such as that of B. R. Chopra and the Barjatyas.[13] Nevertheless, in many other ways, these two films belong more to the mainstream commercial type than the other films, and part of Yash Chopra's success may lie in simultaneous appeal to the bourgeois and the plebeian. It has even been argued that Yash Chopra established the bourgeois aesthetic of Hindi cinema in *Waqt* (1965).[14] His protagonists are unmistakably bourgeois: in private they live in nuclear families, their lavish houses displaying their consumerist lifestyles, while in public their occupations depict them as citizens who control the media, law, medicine, architecture, etc. Some of them may be exemplary figures, but the key characters are people whose lives have been fraught by self-doubt and error, the mistakes they have made returning to trouble their lives. I shall discuss the division of the audience for these two films later in this chapter.

Yash Chopra's films feature a number of recognized melodramatic effects[15] (notably the emphasis on making all interiority exterior by speaking one's feelings, the role played by chance, the importance of secrets, the use of non-verbal signs, in particular of music and of the *mise-en-scène*), yet there are significant differences. The plots are largely concentrated around a single emotional question, and develop in a linear manner. There is no absolute good or absolute evil, the nodes of the plot arising from chance which leaves the characters to find their own ways of reconciling their desires with the happiness of their supportive nuclear families. The performance style adopted by his actors is somewhat restrained, largely different from their usual star personae (notably in the case of Amitabh Bachchan in the two films under discussion), and, apart from their wealth and beauty, his characters are fairly credible bourgeois figures. Yash Chopra's own term for his style is 'glamorous realism'[16] which I take to be a fairly accurate description of how his realism keeps melodrama in check.

I now turn to the three major components of his hallmark romantic style as manifested in these two movies: the narrative, the visual style, and the use of language, in particular that of the songs.

Although Yash Chopra states that his films are not just about romance but about the totality of human relationships, in India he is primarily associated with romance. One of the most distinctive features of his romantic films is their engagement with particular problems faced in relationships. Yash Chopra then offers a variety of ways of resolving these difficulties before suggesting and/or endorsing a solution. This denouement is somewhat similar to the way in which B. R. Chopra's films deal with social questions. Although Yash Chopra's films depict romantic love in many forms, they always uphold the sanctity of the family, albeit an idealized, 'modernized' nuclear family whose members are all friends who can discuss personal matters freely. The plots of his romances concentrate almost exclusively on emotions; there are no social themes other than those which affect love and the family. Evildoers feature only rarely; it is circumstances and emotions which dislocate people's lives. His characters rarely face any social problems other than those precipitated by relationships: his high-gloss films usually depict the super-rich. The family is a source of strength, not conflict, and society sets only loose controls on the characters' behaviour.

Kabhi Kabhie is not only one of Yash Chopra's personal favourites, but also one of his most popular and critically acclaimed films. It weaves together two different stories, contrasting romantic love in two generations in the context of love in the nuclear family unit. The first story, the Romantic poet who cannot free himself from the past, was inspired by the life of the film's lyricist, Sahir Ludhianvi, and by a visual image Yash Chopra has long cherished: a long shot with a man in the foreground whose beloved is marrying another man. The second story was developed from a feature his wife, Pamela Chopra, read in *Woman and Home* magazine about a woman meeting the daughter she had given for adoption. The presentation of the erotic is minimal; the film is almost exclusively concerned with romantic and familial love.

Amitabh Bachchan plays the role of Amit, who courts Pooja by reciting poetry in romantic landscapes.[17] Their love is depicted as being remarkably passionless, the only hint of eroticism occurring when she loosens her hair over him. Unwilling even to consider raising the matter of marriage with the girl's parents, Amit almost encourages her to leave him when they arrange her marriage. He abandons poetry, only reworking his great romantic poem, *Kabhi Kabhie*,[18] into a poem of misery and loss,[19] and one he composes for his young daughter.[20] He marries, becomes an ordinary businessman, seeming to resolve to live his life uncreatively, full of anger and misery, quite unbearable in his behaviour to others. His love is focused on his daughter, Sweetie, perhaps as a way of avoiding his wife, Anjali, who seems insecure even after twenty years of marriage. Even though Amit does not love Anjali, he cannot bear the revelation of her former love affair, the fact she has loved another, taking a harsh unforgiving attitude, calling it a sin. He refuses to see this as paralleling his own college romance and is unrepentant about his inability to forget it even after twenty years.

The other two couples of his generation are happy because they can live in the present, without dwelling on their pasts. Pooja weeps for her lost love on her wedding night, singing their love song at the request of her new husband, but as he discreetly and erotically undresses her, images of the two men merge in her song, and the sexual love between Vijay and Pooja is made clear by scenes of the couple in bed and her giggling in the shower on their honeymoon. Pooja asks Vijay to compose poetry for her. He says he cannot, but his whole persona is full of life and love, contrasting sharply with the brooding, silent Amit. When he learns of Pooja and Amit's college affair and the awful irony of his asking her to sing *Kabhi Kabhie* on their wedding night, he shrugs it off within a matter of hours, saying any sensible young man would have been in love with her.

The three members of the younger generation (Vicki, Pinky and

Sweetie) confide in their parents about their love affairs, the parents accept their choices and are willing to arrange their marriages. They encourage their children to fight for their loved ones. Vicki and his mother tease each other about courtship. She says: 'We were not like you: say "Hi," in the morning, drink tea in the afternoon, get engaged by the evening.' Vicki retorts: 'For six months you caught glimpses of each other through a window; after a year, "Hello, how are you? Good weather we're having!" and making a plan to look in each other's eyes. Then when you were ready to talk about love you found out that the girl's parents had fixed her marriage to someone else and the poor loverboy was left in the lurch!'

Vicki is like his father, Shekhar, happy and fulfilled in love, and he tells the world about it. Soon after his first appearance, he bursts into song: 'So what if I've fallen in love? Love is not a crime.' This music is in a different style from the slow love songs of the older generation, no longer a slow languorous lyric but a happy, upbeat song.[21] Nor are their love songs necessarily picturized with romantic and erotic imagery; the characters partake in modern urban life: they go swimming, ride motorbikes, go dancing and eat in restaurants.

The theme of family love is very strongly developed in this film and is used to establish a generational contrast. Amit does not struggle against the wishes of Pooja's parents but gives in without a fight, although Pooja makes it clear that she is still keen to marry him, arguing they do not have the right to destroy their dreams, while the love affairs of the younger generation are positively encouraged by the parents. The happy families are those who place emphasis on trust and love (the sooner we learn to trust our children). The norm is the nuclear family, with great love between husbands and wives, parents and children, whether natural or adopted, the joking relationships of in-laws and the love of friends for each other. The final scene allows Pinky's adopted parents, her natural mother and her new husband to take an equal part in the *kanyadaan* (gift of a virgin, the giving of a girl in marriage).

Silsila is the story of love, thwarted by society's demands, which reappears as adultery but cannot survive the demands of society. Although this film did not do very well at the box office on its release, it attracted large audiences overseas, is recognized as a classic and remains one of which Yash Chopra is very fond.[22]

After Shekhar dies leaving his fiancée Shobha pregnant, his brother Amit, although under no real pressure, marries her, thus abandoning his lover Chandni. Previously there had been no opposition to Amit and Chandni's marriage from either family: Chandni's parents were even

Raaj Kumar (Shyam) and Nargis (Radha) in *Mother India* (1957), directed by Mehboob Khan. © Mehboob Productions Private Ltd. Courtesy of Mehboob Productions Private Ltd.

Pakeezah (1971), directed by Kamal Amrohi. © Mahel Pictures Private Ltd. Courtesy of Mahel Pictures Private Ltd.

Rishi Kapoor (Vicki) and Neetu Singh (Pinky) in *Kabhi Kabhie* (1976), directed by Yash Chopra. © Yashraj Films. Courtesy of Yashraj Films.

Amitabh Bachchan (Amit) and Rekha (Chandni) in *Silsila* (1981), directed by Yash Chopra. © Yashraj Films. Courtesy of Yashraj Films.

Songbook cover for *Kabhi Kabhie* (1976), directed by Yash Chopra. © Yashraj Films. Courtesy of Yashraj Films.

Poster for *Silsila* (1981), directed by Yash Chopra.
© Yashraj Films. Courtesy of Yashraj Films.

Songbook cover for *Dilwale Dulhania Le Jayenge* (1995), directed by Aditya Chopra.
© Yashraj Films. Courtesy of Yashraj Films.

Karisma Kapoor, Shahrukh Khan and Yash Chopra (director) (left to right) on location for *Dil To Pagal Hai* (1997), in Shopper's Stop, Bombay. © Yashraj Films. Courtesy of Yashraj Films.

Scene from *Dil To Pagal Hai* (1997), directed by
Yash Chopra. © Yashraj Films. Courtesy of Yashraj Films.

Poster for *Dil To Pagal Hai* (1997), directed by Yash Chopra.
© Yashraj Films. Courtesy of Yashraj Films.

Shobha Dé at her workshop on creative writing at Chor Bizarre restaurant, London.
Photo courtesy of Rohit Khattar.

prepared to cancel arrangements with someone they had found for her. When Amit and Chandni meet again after Shobha's miscarriage, Amit woos Chandni again with words drawn from his play[23] and the affair recommences. While many Indian movies have dealt with extra-marital love,[24] this was the first film to show the consummation of adultery. While some justification for the adultery is given by the couple having been lovers before Amit sacrificed their love, the film raises the question: can adultery be romantic? The film portrays the quick decline of the relationship which collapses when they realize their loyalties lie with their partners: Chandni because Dr Anand's life is at risk; Amit because he finds his wife is pregnant. The innocent lovers become a sleazy couple, notably in the eyes of the state, embodied in the policeman who also turns out to be Amit's brother-in-law; in front of Amit's friends (Vidyarthi, Gurdip); and in front of older people who should be respected (Gurdip's parents). The sadness and silent suffering of the partners, who discuss the affair in riddles in the context of a medical examination, also make the lovers look shabby. Particularly reproachful and symbolic is Shobha's role as the archetypal Hindu wife, invoking absolute devotion to her husband through using Meera's discourse of her devotion to Krishna. Perhaps this creates grounds for the forgiveness of Amit's philandering by linking it to Krishna's dalliance with the Gopis. We later come to realize that she is pregnant in this scene[25] but that she saves this weapon until she fears he will risk his life and she will lose her second lover.

Yash Chopra's heroes and, more unusually, his heroines can fall in love more than once and even have sexual relations with more than one partner. However, one must make one's commitment to the bourgeois nuclear family, one must come to love one's spouse in whatever way one can and one needs to let go of the past, live in the present. Everyone needs understanding and forgiveness, and the bestowal of these virtues is always praised.

Kabhi Kabhie was hugely successful immediately on its release, whereas it initially appeared that *Silsila* was a flop, although it has become one of the most popular of all his films, especially with the elite. *Silsila* was and remains a highly controversial film for reasons within the film itself but mostly for off-screen aspects. A widespread rumour in Bombay was that Amitabh Bachchan and Rekha conducted a long-standing affair,[26] while he remained married to Jaya Bhaduri. This film was made at what was said to be the height of their affair and felt to depict their relationship. The controversy at the time was strong,[27] and was strengthened by the fact that this was the last film that Amitabh and Rekha made together and the last film Amitabh made with Yash Chopra.

Even the fact that the film was originally to be made with a different cast[28] and that it was Amitabh himself who suggested the eventual line-up was not enough to calm the rumours.

The film itself came under attack from many other directions. Some people of course argued against the film going too far by showing adultery. Others criticized it for not going far enough, for not taking real risks in depicting an extra-marital relationship. It gave the couple too many excuses: they were in love and about to marry but unable to do so because of social obligation. Some feel that the reconciliation was caused by the weight of tradition (the sanctity of marriage made clear at Gurdip's parents' Golden Wedding) and the necessity of motherhood (Gurdip's mother's conversation with Chandni on the virtue of motherhood, while it only becomes clear that Amit is returning to his wife when she announces her pregnancy). It seems Chandni has no motivation to go back to her husband other than that his life is threatened, but that this is a device to remove her from the story to avoid rejection by Amit. Many thought Shobha should have rejected the role of the forgiving wife and refused to take Amit back.[29] A more middle ground was that the film would have worked if Amit and Chandni had met again after their marriages, almost had an affair, but had drawn back. The problem lies in that the behaviour of Amit and Chandni is inexcusable. Although his private talk is about love, in public Amit behaves badly, whether getting into fights in a car park, or embarrassing his friends (Gurdip and Vidyarthi), and their partners (the Holi song). In a scene with his wife's brother, Kulbushan appears honourable while Amit is ignoble. Meanwhile their spouses take on the roles of hero and heroine. Although Chandni looks beautiful, her role in the film is just that of a girlfriend while Shobha has the better role as the widow, the wronged woman, the one who has faith that he will come back.

While *Silsila* was not an initial success it has gone on to be a landmark film, not just because of the 'reel life/real life' connection, nor because of the depiction of adultery, but because of its images of glamour and beauty seen particularly in its music and its songs.

I mentioned above that while many of Yash Chopra's films have appealed to a broad social class, several of his more controversial films which violate social taboos have appealed only to the more liberal or modernized elite. In his films, romantic and sexual relationships are the free choice of two bourgeois individuals whose social position allows them to disregard the rules of conservative society. This can be seen best in the case of Yash Chopra's own favourite film, *Lamhe* ('Moments', 1991), which divided the audience on a class basis: it was hugely popular with metropolitan elites and the overseas market, which allowed it to break even, but it had a poor box-office response largely among the lower class, especially the repeat audience,[30] because of its supposed incest theme.

Yash Chopra pays careful attention to all the visual aspects of his films, including framing, lighting, use of colour, etc., to create his style of 'glamorous realism', a total look of sensuousness. This can be seen clearly in the particular look which he gives his heroines. This is largely achieved through a particular style of clothes which he himself selects in consultation with the top clothes designers and make-up artists of Bollywood: his heroines wear much less make-up and jewellery than usual; chiffon saris, *malmal salwar-khamees* (muslin 'Punjabi suits'), *churidars* (churidar trousers), *mogras* (jasmine garlands), etc., to give a style which is tasteful, elegant and fashionable. For example in *Silsila*, Rekha's look was entirely remodelled in both costume and make-up. Previously she had been associated with an ethnic chic, handloom style.[31] Yash Chopra dressed her in a new blouse design, worn with chiffons or satin borderless saris,[32] pearl necklaces and her hair loose. This style was reminiscent of that of Gayatri Devi, suggesting a royal or super-elite look.[33]

Another Yash Chopra hallmark is his use of locations. In Hindi films, romance is traditionally set in paradisical settings such as gardens, parks, valleys and mountains, among flowering trees and plants, by lakes and fountains, with mist and rain, drawing on aesthetics developed in Urdu poetry and seen in calendar art, where space is remote and paradisical, usually a garden, and the season is often spring as an extended moment or the night in its beauty and tranquillity. Yash Chopra presents the most extreme glamorized version of this tradition. His preferred landscape for romance was Kashmir, which he used until the political situation made it impossible. His first overseas location was *Silsila*, for which he filmed a famous sequence among the tulip fields and the Keukenhof gardens of Holland, after seeing a holiday movie which Amitabh Bachchan had shot. Yash Chopra has now popularized Switzerland as a substitute and extension of Kashmir, to the extent that a lake has become known to the tourist office as 'the Chopra lake'. He has also filmed in Rajasthan and the UK, and now that other film-makers have followed his lead in shooting in Switzerland, he has experimented with shooting in Germany to keep ahead of his contemporaries.

While most of the songs and other key moments in the expression and development of the romance are filmed in these romantic locations, Yash Chopra's films most frequently site the protagonists' homes in New Delhi.

Delhi is seen as a happy, gregarious city, a place of delight, warmth and colour. The gracious lifestyle followed by his protagonists suggests the ambience of pre-Partition Lahore, where the nawabi culture of courtesy has been Hinduized, without any of the vulgarity associated with post-Partition Delhi. This contributes to the north-Indian feel of his films, augmented by snowy landscapes. He often gives a particularly Panjabi feel to his movies in the (upper-caste) names (Malhotra, Khanna, Anand) or diminutives (Pinky, Sweetie) in the script. Wedding ceremonies are explicitly Panjabi, and every film has at least a few verses sung in Panjabi, and some of the characters, usually Sikhs, speak Panjabi. Yash Chopra's characters move in the public space of the modern metropolitan bourgeoisie of Delhi: five-star hotels, restaurants, the Lodhi gardens, private hospitals, theatres, shops, airports, car parks, flower shows, and their workplaces. He also includes sites of the modern nation such as the police station and airforce bases. The characters' private space is again gracious and elegant and the camera enters the whole house, with scenes shot in the most intimate spaces of bedrooms and bathrooms. He portrays a wealthy bourgeois lifestyle, where characters travel in helicopters, holiday in Europe and go jogging, with no reference to the middle class, let alone the lower classes. Even servants do not intrude.

Yash Chopra deploys a feature of melodrama, that of iconic stasis.[34] Most of his films contain a scene when the characters form a tableau, standing back-to-back to deliver some of the most crucial dialogue of the film. In *Silsila*, this is typified in a scene when the wife and mistress confront each other in a misty garden, where they stand back-to-back as if they are to commence a duel. Their dialogue is stylized and symbolic of two types of love: the erotic love affair and the faith of married love:

Let him go.
I cannot do that. It is beyond me.
Amit is my husband, my religion.
He is my love and my love is in my destiny.
You will lose this game.
I am not playing a game.
Why are you breaking up my home?
I am breaking up my own home too.
If you think you can take him from me then you are wrong.
Is this your faith?
Yes this is my faith.
Live with your faith and let me live with my love.
If this is going to be a battle of love and faith, I accept the challenge.

The centrality of this debate is clear in the final title of the film: love is faith and faith is forever.

Yash Chopra deploys the star as spectacle in these films, reinforcing and confounding expectations. Many of the stars play roles close to their public star persona: Rekha the glamorous mistress; Jaya Bachchan the devoted wife; Rishi Kapoor and Neetu Singh the happy young couple; Raakhee the happy wife.[35] However, the use of Amitabh's star persona is more complicated.[36] When *Kabhi Kabhie* was made in 1975/6, Amitabh had just become a star with his depiction of the angry young man or industrial hero which was to become his trademark.[37] However, the role he played in this film was close to many aspects of his off-screen persona, and was strengthened by the use of his real name 'Amit', rather than Vijay of his action films, by the character's being from his elite social group, and by drawing on his literary background,[38] employing his voice and his skill in reciting poetry to full effect.[39]

In these two films, the centrality of words is heightened in many places. For example, the narratives are dependent on secrets and the tensions generated when these unspeakable events are visualized but never verbalized, the clearest instance being the Holi song where adultery can be *sung* in the context of carnival, can be *seen* but cannot be discussed, even by the spouses in the utmost privacy of the bathrooms and bedrooms of their own homes. The primacy of words can be seen in the occupation of the hero, played by Amitabh Bachchan: in *Kabhi Kabhie* he is a poet, while in *Silsila* he is a playwright. This means he has the opportunities not only of song but also of poetry and staged dialogues to verbalize his inner emotions. In *Silsila* this is taken to further extremes by his use of the audio cassette to send messages to his brother and to his lover;[40] and of the telephone for conducting his adulterous affair.

Yash Chopra's favourite poet and lyric-writer was his close friend, Sahir Ludhianvi (1921–80), aka Abdul Hayee. Sahir was also a journalist and editor, but was known primarily as a poet, although he published only two anthologies.[41] After his move from Delhi to Bombay in 1949 he began to write lyrics for film songs. His hugely popular oeuvre includes work with Guru Dutt[42] and with Navketan Productions, where he worked with the composer S. D. Burman. He also worked with B. R. Chopra on most of his films, and with Yash Chopra after he set up independently.[43] While most of the members of the Progressive Writers' Association were employed in the Bombay film industry,[44] Sahir, along with his colleague, Kaifi Azmi, was the most important of all these writers in bringing the new style of Urdu literature, in particular poetry, to the Hindi film.

Sahir was to have written the lyrics for *Silsila*, but when he died without composing them Yash Chopra's indecision was made clear in his hiring four lyricists, among them Javed Akhtar in his debut as a lyricist.[45] In subsequent films Yash Chopra has employed one of the most prolific of the modern lyricists, Anand Bakshi, who does not publish poetry other than his film lyrics, and sees himself as a professional lyricist rather than primarily an Urdu poet – a major difference between him and the earlier generation of lyric-writers, who saw film lyric-writing largely as a means of survival.

Kabhi Kabhie gives great emphasis to songs[46] and poems.[47] Practically all of the first reel of the film is taken up with song and poetry, using to the full Amitabh Bachchan's remarkably expressive recitation of poetry. The film opens with the poet's voice reciting a poem, then the poet sings a song in which he sees himself as a romantic hero, conscious of time and the transitory nature of this world. He is not important but his work may survive. There follows a brief poetic dialogue between the poet and a girl from the audience, who seems to be more in love with the poetry than with the poet. The next shot shows them as a couple lying under a tree, throwing snowballs, his voice-over reciting poetry again, very brief conversation about women and love, then song, so beautiful in Urdu, so banal in English:

> Sometimes the thought crosses my mind
> That you were made for me.
> Before this you lived among the stars
> You were called to earth for me.
> Sometimes the thought crosses my mind
> That your body, your eyes are in trust for me.
> The dense shade of your hair is for me alone,
> These lips, these arms are in my trust.
> Sometimes the thought crosses my mind,
> As if (wedding) music plays on the road.

This love song has a particular resonance in the film as its singer and addressee change. The first time we hear it, Amit is singing it to Pooja as the audience is expecting their love to develop. It then reappears as the title of a book which Amit brings to her as a present which then becomes her wedding gift from him. Vijay presents her with the book on their wedding night and asks her to sing him the song. As she sings it, he uses it as seduction, symbolically undressing her by removing her wedding jewellery. However, as the song advances, the film cuts to Amit, singing that he knows she now belongs to another, a rather abrupt intrusion into the wedding night. The visuals of the songs change from the romantic langour of Amit to the more physical love of Vijay. In a later moment in the film when Pooja interviews him on her chat show, asking him how he can live a life without poetry, he then recites his only poetic effort since their separation, a bitter, self-hating reworking of the poem that he first wrote for her.[48] Pooja is his poetry: he is unable to write without her. This song, in a simple Urdu, is totally concerned with the speaker not with the addressee. It focuses entirely on his emotions, and the other person is only an object created for his pleasure.

The film closes by showing the wedding of the young couple with the three sets of parents on stage, while the song with which the film opens is rephrased. It is no longer the song of the romantic hero, but a song about the love of one's children and joy in living every moment.[49] The closing title reads: love is life.

The lyrics of *Silsila* can be divided into two groups: those associated with rituals (a pregnancy: *sar se sarke* ('Slipping from my head'); a wedding: *pehli pehli baar* ('The first time'); Holi: *rang barse* ('Colour showered'); and a *bhajan*: *jo tum todo piya* ('What you destroyed, Beloved')), each of which has special meaning in the context of the characters' lives at the moment of singing, the latter invoking the ideal Hindu wife; and three private songs in which the hero and heroine sing of their love for each other (*dekha ek khwaab mein* ('I saw in a dream'), *neela aasmaan* ('The blue sky'), *main aur meri tanhaiyi* ('Me and my loneliness'))).

The film opens with a pregnancy song, with images of beauty, tradition, love and hope, as a chorus of girls waves scarves in the air in a paradisical setting. The song cuts from the chorus to Shobha and Shekhar, who sing of their love as the song binds them into its message: it is only later we find out that she herself is pregnant. This song is taken up again when Amit and Shobha are reconciled at the end of the film and Shobha is pregnant again.

Amit and Chandni meet at a wedding where they sing a song in which Amit swears his love, is ready to risk everything, but she warns him it will be dangerous for him. This song gives glamour to the couple and sets the scene for subsequent romance, although they never have their own wedding. They are united in a song in Amit's dream, which furthers the unreal nature of their relationship: he sings, 'I saw in a dream that this affair had begun, roses flower as far as the eye can see.' It is shot in the tulip fields of Holland and in the valleys and lakes of Kashmir. Yash Chopra's language of love is seen in the flowers, snow, boats and water which symbolize beauty and romance. The great love song of the film is poetry 'sung' by Amitabh himself, rather than by a 'playback singer', representing the idealized lover:

The blue sky has gone to sleep.
The dew falls, the night is tender, lips tremble.
My heartbeats want to say something but they cannot.
The song of the breeze is mellow.
Even the movement of time is slow.
You have come as shyly into my arms
As the moon moves slowly among the clouds.
This solitude and you and me
Even the earth has become silent.
The blue sky has gone to sleep.

The song is taken up later by Chandni, who has a different version in which she sings in her heartbreak as he marries Shobha.

One of the most important songs and one of the first film lyrics written by Javed Akhtar, is that sung to show their affair has begun, which returns to the tulip fields but includes shots of them in bed together. Amitabh recites the poetry himself while Chandni sings, in justification of their adultery:

He: My solitude and I often talk to each other.
How would it be if you were here?
You would say this or you would say that,
You would have been surprised at this, you would have laughed at
     that.
If you were here it would be like this,
If you were here, it would be like that.
My solitude and I often talk about these things.

She: Where have we come, walking together?
In your arms, my love, my body and soul dissolve.

He: Is this the night or your loosened hair?
Is this moonlight or has the light from your eyes bathed my nights?
Is this the moon or your bangle?
Is this the stars or your veil?
Is this the breeze or the fragrance of your body?
Is this the rustle of the leaves or something you whispered?
I think these things and become quiet,
For I know that you are not here, you are not here.
Yet my heart keeps saying that you are here, you are here.

She: You are the body, I am the shadow,
If you did not exist what would become of me?
My lover, I am wherever you are.

We had to meet whatever journeys we set out on.
My breath is softly fragrant like sandalwood.
Your love is the moonlight, my heart is like a courtyard,
(My heart is radiant with love like a moonlit courtyard).
My evening has become even more tender as it draws to a close.

He: A state of helplessness has overcome us both,
A night of loneliness has surrounded us both.
There is so much to say but to whom shall we tell it?
How long can we remain silent and suffer?
My heart tells me we should flout all society's rules,
Break down the wall that divides us.
Why should we suffer in our hearts?
We should say
Yes, we are in love, we are in love, in love.

His lines begin rather prosaically yet powerfully capturing the feelings of a lover in *viraha* ('absence'). In his second verse of poetry, his feelings of absence are voiced in the romantic trope of seeing his beloved all around him in nature, a flight into metaphor. His final verse is a verse of rebellion. Her song contrasts with his poetry as she sings a total submission to him and to love, using very physical and concrete imagery.

The Holi song (*rang barse*) emphasizes the north-Indian feel of the film, seen elsewhere in the images of snow, warm clothes and log fires. In this song Amit appears as a real Uttar Pradesh *bhaiyya*, singing the song again himself in a marked north-Indian accent. It is a traditional-type song by Amitabh's father, Harivanshrai Bachchan:

The (wedding) bed was strewn with flowers of jasmine,
The beauty's lover slept, while the husband looked on,
The colours of Holi showered.

As a traditional song in the carnival of Holi, this story of adultery is permissible, but the manner in which it is shown in the film makes the affair obvious to both their spouses, whose embarrassment is plain to see.

The end of the film reworks the opening song, as Amit has come to substitute his older brother. He and Jaya are reconciled and she is pregnant again in their paradisical world of the pregnancy song:

He: I decorate your hair with stars
I shall make flowers bloom on your lips
I shall forget the whole world for you.

She: Our whole garden will be fragrant

> My heart will rest in your arms
> The world will be full of joy for you and me
> A flower will blossom in our garden.

The title appears: love is faith and faith is forever.

The enormous changes in the depiction of love and romance in Hindi movies from the 1950s to the present can be traced within the oeuvre of Yash Chopra himself, but here I illustrate how cinematic romance has changed from the 1950s to the early 1980s by contrasting Yash Chopra with one of the Hindi cinema's great romantic directors, Guru Dutt (1925–64).

Only seven years older than Yash Chopra, Guru Dutt can be linked to him through the connection of Sahir Ludhianvi, who wrote lyrics and poetry for both the directors' films.[50] Guru Dutt's films are rooted in the romantic tradition. His *Pyaasa* ('Desirous', 1957) is one of his most emotional films, falling somewhere between melodrama and poetry. He adds a further element which Iqbal Masud[51] calls 'romantic anarchism', namely a brand of romanticism which leads him to despair and self-destruction. Pre-*Pyaasa*, Guru Dutt's films are light social commentaries, with the hero of the Dev Anand type, all surface and style. Sahir gives an elegiac feel to *Pyaasa* with the loss of the beloved and the fall of man from a paradise of social justice, seen most clearly in the song in the red-light area, *Jinhen naaz hai Hind par woh kahan hain* ('Where is a person who is proud of India?') and the *Yeh mehlon, ye takhton, ye tajon ki duniya*. Sahir contributed an important element to Guru Dutt's films, namely the search for the ideal, unattainable woman, whose loss is an unhealable wound. Sahir takes this further: even when he finds her, he will not want to possess her:

> *Tum meri ho ke bhi begana hi paogi mujhe*
> *Main tumhara ho ke bhi tum men sama sakta nahin*
>
> Even when you become mine you will find me a stranger
> Even when I become yours, your self will not hold me.[52]

In Guru Dutt the flight from feared disillusionment is concealed as 'noble' rejection, illustrated with genuine sorrow, as the poet contemplates beauty in the park by reciting stylized Urdu verse: *Yeh hanste hue phool, ye mehekta hua gulshan.* ('These palaces, these thrones, the monuments of the world'). This is the Romantic poet's plight: that all he can offer this scene of beauty is the tears and sights of a poetry of defeat (*Jaane woh kaise log the* ... – 'That is how people seemed').

Such defeated Romantic love, borrowed largely through the literary tradition of Urdu poetry, is far from Yash Chopra's depiction of romance apart from in *Kabhi Kabhie*. Here, one of the stories is the same pursuit of the unattainable or lost woman whose loss is such an open wound for the poet. Yet here, even his sorrow is rarely given a voice, only reworking his song of love. In *Silsila*, the unattainable woman is almost reached, then lost, then when she is finally reached his dissatisfaction leads to her rejection, although the ignobility of the rejection is hidden behind her husband's accident. The focus of Yash Chopra's movies is the happy lovers, the happy ending, a resolution of problems as the protagonists learn to separate the present from the past.[53] His films emphasize romantic love where beauty and happiness prevail, resulting in a seamless, bourgeois, loving relationship. In his bourgeois romances, the ultimate sanctity of marriage and the family is upheld. The family is the location not for eroticism, but for sex, reproduction and love. This allows the spectator to enjoy the forbidden erotic pleasures in the depiction of love affairs but the triumph of social conservatism and the restoration of family values makes these pleasures free from guilt. One of the major motifs in Yash Chopra's work is the tensions between conservatism and modernism. The young couple and the practical couple (Vijay–Shobha) are seen as having the answer to happiness in *Kabhi Kabhie*; in *Silsila* wifely faith is victorious as familial love is more important than erotic love. Perhaps we can argue that Yash Chopra has founded a new genre, the bourgeois romance, which is based on the nuclear family. In this moral universe, one must be modern, practical, self-seeking, and reject hierarchical relationships of man–woman and parent–child; but all this requires self-sacrifice, forgiveness, empathy for other people and a sense of duty.

This chapter has argued that Yash Chopra and his movies are deserving of reassessment as part of a long-overdue examination of the role of romance in the Hindi movie. But within Hindi cinema in general, is romance just a component of the 'formula film' or does it meet the criteria of a separate romantic genre? Opinion has differed widely on this question at all levels: from the viewing public to scholars and journalists. While almost all films contain some element of romance, the romantic film is often seen as a sub-genre of the social film, a broad omnibus category. This category, defined by the narrative, is adequate for many romantic Hindi movies (see Chapter 4), in which the couples fall in love early on in the movie, but before the interval romance is thwarted by their families, often because they are seduced by the lure of money or social status or because a villain has led them astray. The second part of the movie is often concerned with the young couple's negotiations with their parents and each other's families.

Yash Chopra's romantic movies, however, do not fit into this category of romance as a sub-genre of the social. His narratives are concerned with working out an emotional situation. His lovers' romances are threatened not by the family, but by fate or destiny or time, which places them in a moral dilemma. He eschews the easy plot opportunities offered by evil and villainy, preferring to explore inner emotional responses, notably where couples renegotiate their relationship in changed circumstances. The choices facing the lovers contain necessary compromises, with no polarity between wrong and right, but they must choose the best of the available options. They may make wrong decisions but are given the opportunity to change their minds. Perhaps the most distinctive feature of Yash Chopra's romances is that one of the choices which they may consider is that they can stop loving one another. Unlike the Hindi cinematic norm, in Yash Chopra's movies romantic love is not an eternal love which risks everything, but a pragmatic, urban, undisputably 'modern' love which has to adjust to the demands of others. Feelings of love do not wither at the moment of separation but may continue for some time until the demands of others in their lives claim their love. Contrary to popular expectations of mainstream Hindi movies, in Yash Chopra's films, depictions of the erotic are contained within a discourse of romantic bourgeois love.

Yash Chopra's cinematic romances preserve many features of romance from the social films of the 1950s, though they do not share the depiction of the Romantic, illustrated by the comparison with Guru Dutt above. Instead, Yash Chopra foregrounds emotional dilemmas, down-playing problems with family and society. Another of his innovations has been his drastic modernization of his films' visuals, *mise-en-scène* and music, all of which he supervises very closely. This modernization is seen clearly in Yash Chopra's most recent film, the top box-office hit of 1997, *Dil to pagal hai*. The story again emphasizes the centrality of destiny (its slogan is: Someone . . . somewhere . . . is made for you), thereby not only diluting the choices and emotional dilemmas facing the protagonists but also reducing the plot to a very simple level. The family backgrounds of the characters are barely shown, the lead male's family is never even mentioned, although he clearly has no economic concerns and can afford to live in an opulent flat. The dialogue and lyrics are mundane, the language being that of the wealthy Bombay elite. The key to this film's success is its enormously popular music, which consists of simple but very catchy tunes, and in its original and striking visuals, mostly showing a dramatically different type of lifestyle: urbanity is emphasized in Manhattan-style loft apartments, in theatrical performances in stadiums and warehouses, and by sophistication in the costumes (the lead heroine in floaty chiffons, the second heroine in skimpy designer outfits). The heroines appear in simpler maquillage and costume than is usual in the Hindi film, bringing a simple glamour and freshness to their ubiquitous images. The pandits predicted this film would bomb at the box office because of its simple story-line. Instead, it has re-emphasized the uniqueness of Yash Chopra's style which is widely acknowledged at a popular level, where people talk of a 'Yash Chopra woman', a 'Yash Chopra wedding', etc. This visual distinctiveness is his trademark and what has prevented other film-makers from copying his films. Yash Chopra's films are founded on a distinctive aesthetic, that of 'glamorous realism', a refusal to accept the dullness of everyday life, a glamorization of a middlebrow, bourgeois aesthetic.

Notes

1. This film was produced by Yash Chopra's older brother, B. R. Chopra. B. R. Chopra (1914–), a film journalist in pre-Partition Lahore, became one of India's great movie moghuls and spokesperson of the film industry. Known for his films on social topics, he made the record-breaking TV *Mahabharata* in 1988.
2. This film grossed a record Rs11.9 lakhs per week in just one cinema hall in Bombay. Rajadhyaksha, 1996c.
3. Famous, the only studio which is air-conditioned, is used only for still photography.
4. Mention must be made of the contribution of Chopra's cameraman since *Faasle* (1985), Manmohan Singh, who is widely acknowledged as one of the best in the industry.
5. Shiamak Davar's Bombay-based dancers.
6. Sets by Sharmishta Roy; costumes by Manish Malhotra. Malhotra was given a budget for Madhuri Dixit's outfits of Rs25,000 each.
7. Uttam Singh, who has previously worked in films only as an arranger although he has composed non-filmi music. The film soundtrack sold an unprecedented 3 million copies in the first week of its release.
8. The extra *e* is added to the second *Kabhi* to make it auspicious in numerological terms.
9. *Kabhi Kabhie* was a great hit and has

remained popular whereas *Silsila* was beset by controversy, largely for non-filmic reasons, but did excellent business in the overseas territories and has become a landmark in the history of Hindi cinema. See the discussion below. The songs from both films have remained popular, often re-mixed and re-released.
10. Mulvey, 1975 and 1981.
11. See Chapter 4, n. 77.
12. The publicity for Yash Chopra's *Dil to pagal hai*, 'The heart is crazy', 1997, described it as 'A Yash Chopra musical', thus employing a genre not usually recognized in the context of the Hindi cinema.
13. Prasad uses Yash Chopra's *Deewaar* to illustrate the third segment, that of mobilization.
14. Rajadhyaksha and Willemen, 1995: 360.
15. In the context of Steve Neale's suggestion (Neale, 1986) that melodrama is a fantasy of love rather than sex, in my forthcoming work I shall explore issues of melodrama in looking at the possible existence of a romantic genre in the Hindi movie or at least a sub-genre of the social movie.
16. This has coincidental echoes of the term 'emotional realism' used by Ien Ang to include the response of *Dallas*' audience to a value of 'realism' in the way emotions were depicted in the soap. Ang, 1985: 51–85.
17. See below for a discussion of the poetry.

18. See below.
19. 'You, grief for you, desire for you no longer exist. My life seems to be drifting along, without the need for companionship. No path, no goal, no light is necessary. In this dark void, my life stumbles along. And some day in this very darkness, I shall lose myself.'
20. *Mere ghar aayi ek nanhi pari* ('A little fairy came to my house').
21. As their other two songs: *tere chehre se* and *tere shish jaise ang*.
22. Its story was written by an airforce officer using the pen name of Mrs Preeti Bedi, perhaps explaining more clearly the use of the motif of the test pilot or airforce pilot, who dies leaving his beloved pregnant. This plot device is seen also in *Aradhana* (dir. S. Samanta, 1969) and *Kabhi Kabhi*.
23. In particular a long speech which forms an important part of Amitabh Bachchan's stage-shows in Europe and North America: 'Love is a relationship of hearts; a relationship cannot be divided like the earth by boundaries. You may be the moonlight of another's nights, but you are the pivot of my world.'
24. Early examples include *Andaz* (dir. Mehboob Khan, 1949); *Kaagaz ke phool* (dir. Guru Dutt, 1959). The depiction of pre-marital sex has become widespread by this time: an early example was Yash Chopra's directorial debut: *Dhool ka phool* (1959). Intercourse is symbolized by a thunderstorm: in 1975 in *Deewaar*, he shows the couple in bed having a post-coital cigarette.
25. This makes Amit look all the more sleazy, that he continues to have sex with his wife while he is having an affair.
26. Even in 1997, rumours of an Amitabh–Rekha reunion made front page of the film magazines.
27. *Stardust* magazine throughout 1981 and onwards referred to the film as *Sil(ly)sila*.
28. Padmini Kolhapure then Parveen Babi as Chandni and Smita Patil as Shobha.
29. This was the line followed by Mahesh Bhatt in *Arth* (1982).
30. The film gave good box-office returns in prestige locations such as Bangalore, Delhi and overseas. Within Bombay the division was even between certain cinemas; the expensive, elite cinemas had good returns while the lower-class cinemas did not.

31. In the late 1990s Rekha is said to have taken total control of her image, and remains the most glamorous of all the actresses.
32. This look was widely copied, the Rekha blouse and the oyster silk being a great craze. A similar phenomenon was seen after Yash Chopra's *Chandni* (1989), when white clothing became fashionable.
33. Jaya had a more conservative image, in bordered silk saris, although her long hair worn loose gave a strong suggestion of sensuousness.
34. See Brooks, 1995: 48, and Vasudevan, 1989.
35. Yash Chopra had to persuade her to return to films after her marriage to Gulzar to star in this movie.
36. See below for a discussion of the off-screen stories of *Silsila*.
37. *Zanjeer* (dir. Prakash Mehra, 1973); *Sholay* (dir. Ramesh Sippy, 1975) and Yash Chopra's *Deewaar* (1975). Yash Chopra was one of the key directors in the creation of this persona in *Deewaar* as well as *Trishul* (1978) and *Kala Pathar* (1979).
38. He is the son of one of Hindi's great literary figures, Dr Harivanshrai Bachchan.
39. The role he plays in this film is also reminiscent of the brooding, passionate bourgeois heroes he had played in earlier films, notably those directed by Hrishikesh Mukherjee (e.g. *Anand*, 1970 and *Namak Haram*, 1973), although his role as the father of a teenage girl and the husband of Waheeda Rehman, who, although only four years older than him, had been a great star in the 1950s and 1960s (when she was one of his idols) may have been thought of as something of a gamble. Its commercial success can be seen in the copying of this look as a 'poetic' pose in provincial photographic studios. See Pinney, 1997: 14.
40. 'Ask these flowers and they will tell you that I spent all day yesterday writing your name and mine together. Two names which apart are lonely but written together they can become a world, a universe, a search, a moment, a happiness. Try this and see for yourself. Amit, who is no longer his own.'
41. *Talkhian* (1945) and *Parchaiyan* (1955).
42. Notably *Baazi* (1951) and *Pyaasa* (1957).
43. Lyricist for *Dhool ka phool*, *Waqt*, *Daag*, *Deewaar*, *Trishul* and *Kabhi Kabhi*.

44. Including Krishan Chander, Rajinder Singh Bedi, Sadat Hasan Manto and Ismat Chughtai.

45. Akhtar is one of the few film lyricists who still places himself in the world of Urdu literature, where he is undoubtedly one of the most popular of all poets in India, not just in Urdu, whose survival in India is largely via the so-called Hindi film. He published his recent collection, *Tarkash*, simultaneously in Urdu and in Hindi scripts along with an audio version of his readings.

46. Another distinctive feature of Yash Chopra's films is his music, which has been enormously successful from his first film onwards. His music is usually slightly different from the mainstream and is regarded as being classy as well as popular. Although he used the most popular composers of the time, Lakshmikant-Pyarelal for *Daag*, he is willing to take risks: for example he used Khayyam, a composer B. R. Chopra had employed in the 1940s, at Sahir's recommendation. In his most recent film he introduced Uttam Singh, previously known only as a score-arranger. He earlier introduced the composer duo, Shiv-Hari, well known as classical musicians Shivkumar Sharma and Hariprasad Chaurasia, whom he has taken in seven of his films. Yash Chopra also uses a restricted number of singers: in all his films Lata Mangeshkar sings as the heroine, and now sings for him without a fee. Pamela Chopra usually sings one song in each film, often a Panjabi song.

47. Both the lyrics and music won the 1976 Filmfare awards (the 'Indian Oscars'): Mukesh for his performance of the title song, Sagar Sahardi for the best dialogue.

48. Sahir wrote this version of *Kabhi Kabhie* first. The more romantic version was written for the film.

49. The only time the parents sing, they sing songs about their love for their children. Cf. *mein har ek pal ka shair hoon* ('I am the poet of a moment') and *Mere ghar aayi ek nanhi pari* ('A fairy came to my house').

50. Yash Chopra's star-billing of Waheeda Rehman, Guru Dutt's most memorable heroine, as the older poet's wife in *Kabhi Kabhie* could provide a further link.

51. Masud, 1986. This section also draws on numerous conversations with Iqbal Masud.

52. Quoted from Masud, 1986.

53. One is tempted to connect this wish with a desire to heal the wounds of Partition, seen most vividly in Yash Chopra's *Waqt* (1965), where the family moves from the Panjab to Bombay but finally returns.

6

Shooting Stars: The Film Magazine
Stardust

Cinema reaches into almost every area of modern Indian urban culture, across every aspect of the media, from satellite and cable television, to the video industry, the popular music business, and magazine publishing. These domains are mutually dependent and form dense networks of narratives and images which contribute to the viewing experience in the cinema hall. Some of these media are so recent (satellite and cable TV appeared in India only in 1992) that it is not surprising if these key spin-offs of the cinema industry have been little researched.[1] One spin-off is the film magazines, which date back to the 1930s, and form a long-established central feature of this culture.[2]

Among the many types of Indian film magazines is found a group which may also be described as star magazines, since their major preoccupation is verbal and visual images of stars in narratives, interviews, photos, etc. They have among the highest circulation of any Indian magazines, and some even have international editions.[3] Perhaps they have been neglected because they seem too trivial, not about film at all, but consisting instead of stories of the exciting and scandalous lifestyles of the stars of the film world presented in a manner guaranteed to titillate bored, middle-class metropolitan housewives. I argue that it is these very assumptions which make these magazines so interesting. Although I question these assumptions (see below), this study forms part of my analysis of the great intellectual hostility to these new middle classes and to their culture.

Film magazines deserve serious study within the wider study of Indian cinema, not only for their coverage of the star, and their lively stories and visual images, but also because they have created and developed a new variety of English, the language of many of the magazines, notwithstanding their exclusive concern with Hindi movies; they provide a forum for the discussion of sexuality; they link the commercial interests of this class with the semiotics and economics of advertising and its generation of lifestyle and consumption issues. These magazines are central to the history of the printed media in India, a major economic and cultural phenomenon at this time.

One of the many important gaps in the study of Hindi cinema is the absence of any ethnographic study of the cinema audience. The only significant ethnographies are those of Sara Dickey[4] and Beatrix Pfleiderer and Lothar Lutze.[5] The latter describe how, after a screening in a rural area, the villagers rejected the film as entertainment, saying that it depicted a modern worldview which is of little interest to them. This research was carried out when the reach of television was far more restricted than it is today. There is likely to have been a great change in viewing patterns now that there are frequent film screenings on the various TV channels. However, on a recent field visit, the anthropologist Chris Pinney reported little interest in TV among the rural population of Madhya Pradesh. Nevertheless, one can make certain assumptions about the composition of the audience. It is widely known that cinema is a major leisure activity in India and since a pattern of wage labour and a division of work and leisure is required for there to be an audience, it is widely assumed that most cinema-goers are urban, male, lower-class industrial workers. This is supported by evidence internal to the film: Ravi Vasudevan points out that the social referent of the Hindi film is generally the plebeian or the declassé;[6] this view is supported by Dyer's model of the appeal of entertainment forms to the audience.[7] However, there is little information available as to the precise composition of the audience or variables such as gender, age, class and occupation.

It is clear from features such as the magazines' advertising and use of English language that the readership of the English magazines does not coincide with the cinema audience as described above. Rather, it is middle class or aspiring middle class, with possibly more women than men, and likely to be drawn from a wider age group.[8] It may be closer to the audience for domestic consumption of video cassettes of films. Since the boom in VCR ownership since the 1980s, many of the middle classes have preferred to watch videos at home rather than in the movie halls, which are seen as suitable only for lower-class men. The composition of this video-watching audience is even less clear than that of the cinema halls, but its economic status, in having enough money to afford the VCR and colour TV and in having domestic space and free time for leisure activities, suggests a middle-class or at least upwardly mobile status. The middle class has returned to the cinema halls in recent years to see high-budget films which are on cinema release only or 'video holdback', a practice which began with the 1994(5?) hit *Hum aapke hain koun …!*,[9] but these films represent only a handful of the annual releases. The change in audience can be seen in the massive hike in ticket prices: before this film the most expensive cinema ticket was Rs25; with this it rose to Rs100. While an analysis of the magazines in the *bhashas* or vernaculars would give a greater insight into the pleasures of the cinema-going audience,[10] the study of these English magazines sheds light on the role of the middle class, in particular women and adolescents, as viewers and consumers not only of the cinema and its stars but also of a new urban lifestyle.

In this chapter I concentrate on one of the most popular of these film magazines, *Stardust*, a gossip magazine about the stars of the Bombay commercial cinema, which has been published in English in Bombay since 1971. I discuss *Stardust*'s major concerns, looking at how it has constituted an 'imagined', interpretive community[11] of readers, and the activities of this social group in creating and consuming the pleasures of the magazine.

Approaches to magazines, popular culture

In the western context, the few studies of women's magazines[12] can be seen as part of a feminist reappraisal of women's genres of popular culture. These include Janice Radway's pioneering work on the romance,[13] Tania Modleski's analysis of women's fantasies through romance, Gothic novels and TV soaps[14] and Ien Ang's discussion of soap operas.[15]

While not adopting any of their lines of enquiry, I have found many suggestive ideas in them. I have been cautious in drawing on psycho-analytic approaches, which inform many of these works, trying to use them only for a general interpretation of pleasure. Ang's study of the consumption of the soap opera *Dallas* showed that most interviewees identified the motive for watching as pleasure, but no one could define what this pleasure is. One can only identify some of the mechanisms of pleasure which she found, namely the pleasures of melodrama and of 'emotional realism'. Radway expanded the study of pleasure to include the process of reading itself; the pleasure women took in setting time aside for reading; and pleasure in the narratives themselves. Hermes built on this in her study, arguing that readers of women's magazines enjoy the fact they can read them intermittently rather than having to set aside such long periods of time for themselves as they required for romance reading. Hermes identifies a further pleasure in the subversive 'camp' reading of magazines, often by men, which is part of the reader's repertoire of responses to the magazines.

I have used a less abstract version of semiological analysis of the magazine than that of Angela McRobbie,[16] following instead Christine Gledhill's model of negotiation,[17] where meaning is constructed through the meeting of institutional and individual producers, texts and audiences. In this model, the socio-historical constitution of audiences, as well as the production process, become integral elements in the dispersion of textual meaning. My research is focused very deliberately on the magazines themselves: I drew on archives, and talked to magazine production teams and to magazine readers on an informal basis. It became clear that the success of *Stardust*, whose origins are in the world of advertising (see below), lies in the close connection between the advertisers and their target audience of readers, a relationship consolidated by solid market research for commercial reasons.

The studies mentioned above are all concerned primarily with women's genres of popular culture and may not seem of direct concern to the study of these film, or rather star, magazines.[18] However, a number of generic overlaps[19] become clear. For example, in her study of the teenage girls' magazine *Jackie*, McRobbie identifies four major codes: romance; personal and domestic life; fashion and beauty; and pop music, the last of which discusses issues relating to stars and their fans. All these codes prove useful in analysing the film magazines where they centre on the Indian star. However, Hermes found that the reading of celebrity magazines was not very dissimilar from the reading of the more general 'women's magazines'. Nevertheless, since these magazines are one of the major media for the dissemination of narratives about Hindi film stars, I briefly consider theoretical work on the star. There are no tabloid newspapers in India equivalent to the British tabloids which narrate the lives of stars, although there is increasing coverage in the 'serious press' (*India Today* and most of the national papers) in their lifestyle columns. The gossip and rumour generated by the media in India is largely undocumented. Little has been written about the star in Indian cinema[20] but western film theory has proved useful in my analysis. I have drawn on Dyer's work[21] on the star, which considers stars' images in social and historical contexts, arguing that stars matter beyond their films when they come to act as the focus for dominant discourses of their time.

I begin by giving a brief history of the film magazines, their origins and their production. I then look at *Stardust*'s *raison d'être*, namely its advertisements and the female bourgeoisie it targets, before examining narrative, theme and language, to explore what they reveal to us about the readership and the nature of the magazines.

Indian film magazines

The earliest film criticism in India is found in newspaper columns, but film magazines in the vernacular languages[22] and in English first appeared in the 1930s.[23] The first magazine devoted entirely to cinema coverage was the Gujarati[24] *Mauj Majah*, published in 1924. One of the major magazines in English was the monthly *Filmindia*, which was published from 1935 to 1961. This expensive magazine containing advertising catering to an elite market, was nearly all written by one person, Baburao Patel. The paper published reviews, responses to readers' letters, etc. but editions from the final years contain lengthy polemics against western medicine and pages on homeopathic and other indigenous medicines.

The post-war period saw the decline of the studio system of production and the rise of the independent producer and the growth of the star system. This required new forms of information which were supplied by trade publications in English, the first being a roughly produced weekly review sheet called *Kay Tee Reports*. This was supplanted by the better-produced magazine *Tradeguide* (1954–),[25] which followed *Kay Tee Reports* by producing reviews of the week's films which journalists previewed on Thursday, in time for the Friday release. This and other trade magazines are aimed at distributors and exhibitors, so their most important role is to predict the success or failure of particular films (rarely proved wrong) and to publish the box-office statistics of recent movies. They contain no information about stars other than for commercial reasons.

Another type of magazine appeared in the 1950s, published by the major newspaper houses.[26] The *Indian Express* newspaper group launched its in-house publication, *Screen*, in 1951. Its major concerns were films under production and recent events in the film industry. *Screen* can be situated somewhere between the trade and fan magazines, containing enough hard news for the industry and interviews with people in the business; it is read by both audiences. It also discusses Hollywood films, mostly in the context of distribution in India. This weekly was in the form of a broadsheet newspaper with colour supplements, but it has recently remodelled itself in large-colour-magazine format and has substantial coverage of television.

The ground-breaking publication for the later wave of glossy English magazines was the launch of *Filmfare* in 1952 by Bombay's *Times of India* newspaper group. It was distributed throughout India[27] by the news-paper's good distribution networks. Its first issue contained a manifesto:

It is from [the] dual standpoint of the industry and its patrons, who comprise the vast audience of movie fans, that 'Filmfare' is primarily designed. This magazine represents the first serious effort in film journalism in India. It is a movie magazine – with a difference. The difference lies in our realisation that the film as a composite art medium calls for serious study and constructive criticism and appreciation from the industry as also from the public.[28]

Filmfare combined serious film journalism with coverage of glamour and had features about and interviews with the dominant figures in the industry. It was a sophisticated magazine, in keeping with the image of the *Times*, covering many cinema topics. It provided a forum for dialogue between the critics, the industry and the audience while fulfilling the further function of being an up-market family magazine with broad appeal to both the men's and women's markets rather on the pattern of the *Times*'s political and arts paper, the *Illustrated Weekly of India*. It assured its place at the forefront of the film world in 1953 when it instituted the *Filmfare* awards. These were modelled on the Hollywood Academy Awards with the major difference that the magazine's readers cast their votes. Regional versions in English are published with more information about local film industries. Even the Mumbai City edition caters to this regional interest; although its coverage of Marathi cinema is minimal, it carries voting pages for Filmfare Awards for Marathi films. *Filmfare* has evolved under various editors, who have included nationally known journalists like Pritish Nandy and Khalid Mohamed. It was bi-weekly until 1988, when it ran into financial difficulties, since when it has been monthly. Itself influenced in the late 1970s by the star magazines, although remaining much less scandalous and salacious, *Filmfare* has retained its distinctive blend of film coverage and star interviews and now some of the later publications have begun to follow its more successful features, notably its emphasis on interviews.

An important element of the magazine market is the vernacular magazines. These are quite different from the English monthly glossies (apart from the translated versions produced by *Magna* and *Chitralekha* publications[29]). They tend to be weeklies, have low production values, and are printed on cheap paper. Photos are scarcer, mostly in black and white with a limited number of colour pictures. Their downmarket advertising suggests they are aimed at a lower-class, male market. The majority of advertisements plug dubious-sounding tonics to restore male vigour, suggesting a great anxiety about sexual performance. This poorer, predominantly male, readership seems to coincide more with that of the cinema-going public and as such these magazines may reflect more closely the audience's concerns. Film-makers need to satisfy the demands of this readership, by covering their favourite stars from the angles in which they are interested.[30] Some of the more important titles seen in Bombay include *Film City* (circulation 100,000) and *Aar Paar* (45,000); others include *Kingstyle*, *Filmi Duniya* (1958– from Delhi, 118,000). *Filmfare* had a Hindi version (*Filmfare Madhuri Samahit*) from 1964 but it was not very successful and soon ceased publication. There are high-circulation film magazines in all the major languages including Urdu, Malayalam, Tamil, Telugu and Bengali.

The 1970s saw a whole new wave of magazines including the English-language glossies which are the focus of this chapter.[31] These introduced a new style of journalism in a new language, said to be invented by Shobha Rajadhyaksha (later Shobha Kilachand and subsequently Shobha Dé) (*Stardust*) and Devyani Chaubal (*Star'n'Style*), although some claim that *Blitz* was first. I shall concentrate on *Stardust*, one of the first of these magazines, which undoubtedly has been the market leader.

Stardust may well have the largest circulation[32] of any of the film magazines (in English 125,000; in Gujarati[33] 1987– , 75,000; in Hindi 1985– , 30,000. The international English edition 1975– ,[34] distributed in the UK, USA, Canada (specified on the cover) and South Africa and the Gulf, sells a further 40,000 copies;[35] no figures are available for the English-language editions, 1996– , which cover the four southern regional cinemas).[36] The only magazine with comparable sales is *Filmfare* (see above), which is said by its journalists to have recently reached 200,000 per month, although much lower figures are published for 1994.[37]

The recent *G* magazine (1989– , 15,000), edited by Bhavna Somayya, a former *Stardust* journalist, has fewer scandalous stories than *Stardust*[38] but has more chit-chat and less analysis than *Filmfare*. It is distributed by the *Chitralekha* group of Gujarati magazines, and has older versions also in Gujarati (*Jee*, 1958– , 97,000) and in Marathi (*Jee* 1988– , 48,000). The other English-language magazines seem to be very much on the lines of *Stardust* (*Cinéblitz* 1974– , 81,000; *Movie* 1982– , 75,000; and *Tinsel Town* ?1989– , which includes around ten pages of TV coverage). *Star'n'Style* (1965– , 15,000), which has suffered from industrial disputes, a warehouse fire and several changes of ownership, is now undergoing a revival under Nishi Prem, another former editor of *Stardust*. Her efforts to increase the gossip content have led to her being sued for libel by Aishwarya Rai, the former Miss World.[39] Most of the above magazines now have homepages on the Internet; some pages give all the magazine stories, whereas others just provide the covers and the headlines. There were some English-language magazines which seemed to be aimed more at a men-only market, including *Film Mirror*, published by Harbhajan Singh. Its lurid reports remain legendary and unsuitable for family readership or quotation here.

Video magazines, which were mostly borrowed on rental, including *Lehren* (1988–, now on the Internet only), cover events in the film industry such as birthday parties, *muhurats* ('auspicious moment; time of the first shot'), etc., although their popularity is on the wane since the explosion of film and film-star coverage on cable and satellite television in programmes ranging from reviews ('Chalo cinema') to star interviews, and mostly song sequences.

Stardust

Stardust is the flagship magazine of Magna Publications,[40] a Bombay-based publishing company owned by Nari Hira. Hira founded *Stardust* in 1971 as a marketing opportunity for his advertising business. The only major film magazine at the time was *Filmfare*, which ran film information and uncontroversial stories about the lives of the stars. His idea was to publish a magazine on the lines of the American *Photoplay* with celebrity gossip journalists like Hollywood's Hedder Hopper and Louella Parsons. Twenty-three-year-old Shobha Rajadhyaksha (later Dé), who had been working for Hira for eighteen months as a trainee copywriter, was hired as the first editor. She had no interest in the movie world and had never worked as a journalist, but was given the job on the strength of an imaginary interview with Shashi Kapoor, whom she had never met. She and a paste-up man produced the first issue in October 1971 from unglamorous offices in South Bombay.[41] Later they were joined by a production staff of three, and a team of freelance reporters collected stories which she wrote up. Dé stubbornly refused to move in the film world, only meeting the stars if they came into the office. The style of the magazine was established during her time as editor and has been maintained under the succession of editors who followed.

The first issue of *Stardust* appeared in October 1971. A statement of intent was given underlining the magazine's purpose in its 'Snippets' column:

> Very few movie magazines and gossip columns are either readable or reliable and hardly any are both. Most of them are inadequately researched and are the result of second and third hand reporting. One theory put forward has it that what often passes for news and fact is really much hearsay and gossip. Another claims that the people in the movie trade who are in a position to know are too busy to write or find it impolite to write down what they know.

175

So, this column – largely as its reason for being – will be a reporter's column and not a mouthpiece of publicists and ballyhoos of the film trade. And here we go . . .[42]

The magazine's manifesto is discussed throughout the whole issue, in particular in the Q&A page and letters page (presumably written by Dé since it was the first issue).

The production features were much less glossy than they are today. Colour was used only for the cover, an unflattering picture of the top box-office star, Rajesh Khanna, and a series of photographs of the leading female star, Sharmila Tagore. The front-page headlines were very suggestive – 'Is Rajesh Khanna married?' and 'Rehana Sultan: all about her nude scene' – but the stories were quite innocent. The main features were uncontroversial stories about Sharmila Tagore and her husband, the Nawab of Pataudi, the international cricketer. Along with the expected combination of photos, news and gossip, some of the staple features of *Stardust* appeared in the first issue, including 'Neeta's natter', written by 'The Cat', the letters page, and the Q&A columns. The trademark Bombay English is not much in evidence, and there is little innuendo and few of the double entendres that become a central feature in later issues (the only example in the first issue was the mention of eating 'red-hot pickles' on a date). Several of the features were later dropped, including Hollywood coverage, 'A day on the sets', 'What's shooting', cartoons, and film criticism, features which brought it closer to *Filmfare*. Within a year more of the staple features were established, including 'Court Martial' (October 1972), and the special use of language is soon seen throughout the magazine.

Many of the major themes which are discussed below emerged during the early numbers, including images of the body, and issues of sexuality centred around the affairs of stars and their scandalous behaviour off the sets. The magazines also have the usual self-reflexive coverage, writing about themselves, in particular about the special relationship of the magazine to the film industry, the definition of the star and discussion as to whether stars have the right to privacy.

The style of *Stardust* was firmly established in the first ten years and has remained largely the same to the present, even including the use of 1970s-style graphics. The style of production has also been constant. Nari Hira, the sole owner of Magna Publications, largely delegates the editorial work but negotiates with his editors over the final version. Ashwin Varde is the overall editor of Magna group publications, while *Stardust*'s current editors are Omar Qureshi and Nilufer Qureshi. These, like most of the reporters, are college graduates from middle-class Bombay families, without the glamorous social connections of Shobha Dé. Each of the eight reporters and two freelancers (all under 30 years old) has a set of stars to cover. Once the stories are collected they are cross-checked with the stars to make sure they are happy about the stories. If there is something controversial which is a good story they may run it anyway, but gossip about the star's family is taboo and they never write anything on this topic without the star's permission.

The stars usually collaborate with the magazines, but this does not always run smoothly. The first major quarrel was between *Star'n'Style*'s Devyani Chaubal and Dharmendra over her comment that his partner, Hema Malini, looked like a stale *idli* (south Indian dumpling). Amitabh Bachchan had a long-standing dispute with *Stardust* from the mid-1970s concerning gossip about him and Zeenat Aman. He refused to give interviews and the paper boycotted any mention of him, although they were ultimately reconciled without too much damage to either side. A serious dispute with the Cineartists Association in 1992 led to their boycott of six magazines (*Stardust*, *Cinéblitz*, *Filmcity*, *Movie*, *Showtime*, *Star'n'Style*). This has since been patched up by the stars, who felt they needed the publicity. Yet given the gossip, why do the stars collaborate with the magazines, and what is the extent of their involvement? Some stars do straightforward interviews only, while others seem to have a much more ambivalent relationship with the magazines. Many people in the industry argue that the journalists are not to blame – they are encouraged by the stars, who only later regret talking to the magazines – whereas others feel that the stars are persecuted by the journalists.

The stories cover fifty or more stars, concentrating on cover girls and glamorous figures who lead exciting lives or make controversial statements, rather than the top box-office stars. For example, Aamir Khan is a big box-office star and also a pin-up but since there are no interesting stories about him, and he gives few interviews, he features rarely in the magazine. Salman Khan, another pin-up but a more variable box-office star, is a more controversial figure and the magazine publishes many stories about his off-screen activities. *Stardust* also promotes stars by putting in glamorous photos, and making romantic link-ups with other stars. This promotion was evident with the model Sonali Bendre, who won a talent competition for a place on the 'Stardust Academy', an annual sponsored programme for would-be starlets. While few heroines have more than minor roles in the films (even an important heroine like Kajol may take such minor roles that they have to justify their choices in the magazines: 'I did *Karan-Arjun* because I wanted to know how it feels to be an ornament. I had nothing to do in the film except look good.'[43]), yet great importance is given to them in the magazines, especially on the covers, since the editors believe that a woman ('Cover girl') on the front generates sales. Some actresses have had magazine careers which outshone their screen roles, notably Rekha. Although she has acted in some great roles (in 1981 *Umrao Jaan* and *Silsila*), she has remained more famous for being desirable, beautiful and unattainable and for the scandal which has dogged her.[44]

This is part of the fairly fixed style of the magazine cover. In addition to the main picture, there is usually a woman or a star couple in an amorous pose, surrounded by up to four cut-outs of stars with sensational headlines, at least one of which mentions sex. The headlines are usually far more salacious than the stories inside the magazines.

The magazine's regular features include the opening quasi-editorial 'Neeta's natter', short paragraphs of gossip, written as if by a celebrity about her social life in the film world, covering openings, films' jubilees,[45] weddings, parties, etc. The stories praise those who are 'in' and mock those who are 'out'. This is where the exaggerated language of the magazines is strongest, full of innuendo and puns. There is some photographic coverage of industry events, but the majority of photos are the session photos found elsewhere in the magazine. The other insider-gossip sections are 'Star Track', which covers incidents in stars' lives, mostly stories from childhood, and events on the sets; and 'Snippets', which is more humorous, consisting mainly of jokes about stars' gaffes in English, in etiquette, and then short puns and jokes; 'Straight talk' covers other news items about the stars.

A number of regular formats for interviews include 'Spot poll', a Q&A session with stars; 'Court martial', where overtly hostile questions are asked to a controversial or fading star; 'Favourite things', where a star completes a cheesy questionnaire while the facing page features a signed glamour photo. Several interviews and articles about romances, quarrels and gossip are interspersed with glamour shots of the stars. The major feature is 'Scoop of the month', which is a big, gossipy story about an affair, a break-up of a relationship or a special interview.

Readers also have a chance to contribute to the magazine in two places: in 'Rumours and rejoinders' they address queries to stars over gossip about unprofessional behaviour or affairs and the star replies; letters to the journalists are published in 'International Mail Call', where readers seek information about their favourite stars; the stars' addresses are given for further correspondence.

Stardust has kept very much to the style established during its first decade, apart from the increase in the number of interviews by letter of the stars by the fans. Some of the graphics, such as those for 'Neeta's Natter', have remained unchanged and look very dated with their 'flower power' image, but these have provided the magazine with a recognizable identity. In fact, the black cat with a jewelled necklace smoking a cigarette in a long holder is printed on company stationery. The general consensus is that although the other glossies are of high quality and good reportage, in particular *Filmfare*, which many read in addition to *Stardust*, the latter still stands out from the other magazines because its gossip has more 'bite'.

Stardust: advertising and the consumer

'As easy as falling in love. (Even sweeps you off your feet.)'
[Advertisement for Bajaj Sunny scooter][46]

There are no detailed surveys of *Stardust*'s readership beyond the circulation figures given above. The best guide is to examine the magazine's other consumers, the advertising companies that provide the finance to produce the magazine. Market research gives the advertisers an idea of who forms a significant part of the readership and hence the important places to advertise, so some connection between the advertisements and the readers is to be expected. However, it is likely that there is an additional readership, namely readers with less purchasing power who aspire to the consumption of these products and the corresponding lifestyle. A large proportion of this 'Wannabe' readership is likely to come from among those who rent the magazines from their local 'circulating libraries'.

Stardust is heavily subsidized by its advertising: in 1996, a colour page cost Rs80,000. This allows the magazine to have a cover price of Rs20 although each copy costs Rs50 to produce. Advertisers rate it as one of the 'premium' magazines for advertising consumer goods and it has more advertisements than any magazine in India, the second being *India Today*. The latter's different market may be seen in the products advertised, which are mostly for male business executives including computers, shirting, luxury housing, etc.

Of the 66 pages of the first edition of *Stardust*, eighteen were used for advertising in black and white, for middle-class consumer goods: household utensils, saris, vests, creams, aftershave, furniture (mostly steel cabinets), fabrics and a camera. The only example of star endorsement was Shashi Kapoor's promotion of Burlingtons menswear.

Products advertised in recent Indian issues of *Stardust* range from household items (tea, mosquito mats, cooking oil, cleaning fluids, tableware, cooking pots, fridges) to small luxuries (greeting cards, beauty products such as cosmetics, shampoo, soaps, deodorants, aftershave), a wide spectrum of fashion (in particular foreign clothes and formal ware), to expensive hi-fi goods, holidays and scooters. There are also some unexpected government promotions for jute and state tourist boards, and more 'non-family' items such as condoms, whisky and cigarettes. Surprisingly, almost none of them features the stars who one might expect to endorse glamour and beauty products such as soaps and shampoos.

The advertisements do not show a strong gender bias towards products intended for consumption by women. While it is possible that men's products feature to a large extent because women may buy these items (such as shirts and aftershave) for their men,[47] the more likely explanation lies in the circulation of the magazine. *India Today*, a largely male executive magazine, is also circulated among the family, who may be less interested in the business and political pages but who want to read its coverage of the media or the arts, or features or gossip pages.[48] *Stardust* also seems to have a similar family readership, although the features do not show any particular gender divisions, even though this is possible according to the gender of star, type of story, etc.

The range of advertising allows a fairly clear idea of the magazine's purported readership. It is clearly aimed at an urban middle- or upper-middle-class readership, male and female, who have the purchasing power for these products. All the products belong to the category of luxury goods; even the cleaning fluids are a good deal more expensive than the usual varieties used at home. Although it is assumed the cinema audience largely consists of lower-class urban males,[49] there is clearly a significant middle-class group which has a deep enough interest in the Hindi film world to buy these magazines. The class emphasis here may explain the emergence of these new magazines in the 1970s as new class formations began to crystallize in urban India.

The only difference between the domestic and international editions is the range of products advertised. The majority of the advertisements in the latter are for the UK market with several for the USA and one or two for Dubai. This is one of the few places where these luxury South-Asian products can be advertised overseas. (The others are *India Today*, some of the language press (although such glossy advertisements are rare) and Asian TV and radio, with occasional advertising during national TV features made for the Asian community, such as the Hindi Night film series on the UK's Channel 4.) The international edition has advertisements on about a quarter of the pages, half in colour, half in black and white. Apart from Royal Navy recruitment, all are concerned with the South-Asian economy. Some are aimed at both men and women, such as marriage bureaux, astrologers, telephone companies, cable and satellite TV stations, music recordings, concerts, clubs and films, Asian hotels and restaurants, and varieties of *paan masala*. However, the majority are clearly aimed at women only, such as perfumes, jewellery, clothes, beauty products (from plastic surgery to hair products) and some advertisements for South-Asian food products. These give some impression of the NRI (Non-resident Indian) community reading the magazines for their 'Wannabe' lifestyles, and as a way of imagining India as 'home' and a world of glamour and style where the values they brought with them overseas can be fulfilled.

Issues of consumption reach beyond the advertising and are central to the magazines, since buying or renting the magazine is already an act of consumption. However, I wish to focus on consumption as part of the glamour of this public culture. Popular novels are often called 'sex and shopping' novels because of their emphasis on an excess of consumption of mostly luxury goods.[50] There are a whole set of overlapping perspectives on consumption presented in the magazines, in the photos and in the discussions. These include health and the body, which connects to discourses on sexuality, and consumption as a way of experiencing sexuality ('Buy this and you're this kind of a woman, you live this kind of a lifestyle, you too can belong to this kind of world'). The advertisements and their images are themselves sources of fantasies for pleasure.[51] Appeals are made to the aspirations to glamour of the target audience, with comments such as 'If it's good enough for Kim Basinger, Tina Turner and Diana Ross, it's good enough for you!' (although the model for this hair treatment seems to be Asian). Fashion is a key issue here since many women's interest in women stars is due to their display of conspicuous consumption (cosmetics, fashion, hairstyles, lifestyles);[52] in fact throughout the magazines, stars are presented as idols of consumption, not of production. This address to women as consumers blends discourses on femininity and consumption as do women's magazines in the west, but in India there is further emphasis on class and modernity. The necessity of money to participate in this lifestyle is unquestioned, it being required even to read these magazines. Perhaps this focus on consumption has been part of the reason for disparagement of the magazines by intellectuals. Shopping, a necessity for urban life, is often a pleasure enjoyed by women and as such is disparaged by many men.[53]

Stardust: language

The fact that the most popular magazines about the Hindi cinema are written in English is initially surprising. However, cinema features in these magazines as a source of glamour and way of locating stars rather than as the object of the discussion. The major connection of the magazine is with the world of advertising, the aim clearly being to cater only to a small section of the movie-going (or video-watching) public, the section which has the highest purchasing power. This group of people may use English as their first language or at least aspire to do so. The magazines use their own brand of language, a special variety of English. For example:

> Mayday darlings. The heat is on again. Time for beaches, martini-on-ice, bikinis and cold-showers. Not that our cooler-than-*kakdi* [cucumber] stars can lose their sizzle with mere *thandai* [cold drink]. The higher their temperatures, the better to use their libidoes with, my dears. I'm jetting to Eskimo-land already. Phew![54]

This variety is called 'Hinglish' or 'Bombay English', a mixture of non-standard varieties of English with the odd Hindi, Marathi or Gujarati word or phrase inserted. The English used here refers to other English texts to show an insider's knowledge ('The heat is on' is the title of a song) or to provide humour ('the higher ... the better ... my dears' has overtones of Red Riding Hood's wolf; 'Phew!' reminds one of comic strips, or tabloid headlines); it contains non-standard varieties (one can't *use* one's libido, and the standard plural is libidos; note also the psychoanalytic term) and non-politically correct English (Innuit is now preferred to Eskimo). The use of Hindi is not because of a lack of ability in English; the star whose English is not up to scratch is scorned as a 'vernac', a 'vern' (user of a vernacular) or a *ghati* (a Mumbaikar's derogatory term for someone from non-metropolitan Maharashtra, from the Ghats).[55] Although most Bombay English-speakers use a certain proportion of Hindi words in their everyday language, the use here is deliberately humorous ('cooler-than-*kakdi*' is a Hinglish calque which only makes sense if one knows the English – outdated – idiom 'cool as a cucumber'). Hindi is used elsewhere to add spice, to show exasperation or, more often, simply to sound 'cool'. A knowing use of *desi* (indigenous) terms when speaking English has become hip and is used by Mumbaikars and widely replicated in the media even by the hippest of all, the TV VJs. It is likely[56] to be traced to the exaggerated form (which is not used by anyone in Bombay) invented by these magazines, a code for insiders; knowing how to use it is part of the art of being cool.[57] One has to know it to gain admission to the circle of the film world, a group imagined to speak the language. It is also a way of distancing oneself from one's everyday language with its overtones of region and social group. Being able to read it also shows one has competence in English and in Hindi. It is a fun language for modern, fashionable people; one can write letters to the magazines in this language but any attempt to speak it out of context would result in loss of face. It also has the effect of providing a special language for the international editions. I imagine that many of the readers of these editions can understand sufficient Hindi to follow a film but are unlikely to have adequate reading skills in Hindi or other vernacular languages.

A more limited use of language is in the French phrases added for extra glamour such as 'Manisha analyses affaire d'Nana [sic]'.[58] I have heard the equivalent of 'pig-French' used by Indian college girls to sound cool, with knowing irony. For example, 'Pass le butter and le milk, s'il vous plaît.'

This delight in language and playing with it consciously for humour and effect is seen in the use of puns and word-play found throughout the magazines ('And if there's anything bigger than a Himalaya, it's actress Rambha's bulky posterior pets. Check out the circumference. I always said she had an hourglass figure. With all the sand settled at the "bottom" of course.'[59]) The magazines delight in the language that Dé developed in her initial years at *Stardust* and has used to critical outcry and her amusement in her novels:

> Surely there is no 'bakwas' about you. 'Abhinandan' for grinding to 'kheema' the casual remarks of stars. 'Arre bhai' what happened? I started to write in English and ended in using STARDUST'S 'apnihi pukka ghat' language.[60]

It could be argued that this language has been taken up by the Indian English novel. The Indian English used by Nissim Ezekiel in poems such as his 'From Very Indian poems in Indian English',[61] is a late survival of *babu* English whereas the magazines' Hinglish has been taken up by Shashi Tharoor[62] and has been reproduced best by Dé herself[63] and by Salman Rushdie.[64]

The style of the writing is exaggerated from the breathless style of 'Neeta's Natter', full of words of address ('pets, dahlings, darlings'), exclamations and an excess of punctuation (dashes, exclamation marks, inverted commas), to the purple prose of reports and descriptions of the stars. The stars' epithets (the 'sexy [Jackie] Schroff', the 'deadly [Sanjay] Dutt') and pet names (Dabboo, Chintu and Chimpoo, the sons of Raj Kapoor) are used regularly and this causes confusion to the new reader.

This is all part of the insider's knowledge, which has to be developed by continuous reading and accumulated knowledge.

The addressee is present in much of the writing. 'Neeta's Natter' is always addressed directly to readers (forms of address as above, sign-offs such as 'From one cat to another, meeow till next month!'[65]). This all adds to the feeling of a club, the close relationship of the fan to the magazine and the magazine to the stars. The readers have further opportunities to participate by sending in questions to the stars and writing letters for publication. The narratives provide the reader with a glimpse of a world of luxury and glamour, with events taking place in five-star hotels, de luxe restaurants and expensive clubs. For example, many events take place in one of India's most luxurious and famous hotels, Bombay's Taj Hotel. Readers learn of the 1900s (its nightclub whose annual subscription is Rs25,000), its Zodiac Grill (one of the most expensive restaurants in Bombay), and its Crystal Room (used for society weddings). The reader also learns about another favoured location, the Piano Bar nightclub, and its adjacent restaurant, the China Garden, run by India's top celebrity chef, Nelson Wang, who has featured in the magazine.

This marked style of intimacy is also seen in the narratives, which are usually written in the first person, giving a direct approach, a confessional mode, the feel of the eyewitness, often seeming to be in direct speech. The interviews with the stars themselves allow them to speak in the first person, furthering the effect of intimacy and revelation. The use of innuendo requires an audience and it seems as if direct appeals are made to the reader to judge the lifestyle of the stars.

Stardust: gossip

There are three major modes of narratives which may be presented in the form of interviews or told as narratives by the journalists. The three major forms of gossip outlined by Patricia Spacks[66] (gossip as intimacy, gossip as idle talk and gossip as malice) are found in the magazine.

The majority of the stories belong to the broad category of melodramas,[67] tales of heartbreak, struggle and survival. This is the gossip of intimacy. The tales of heartbreak may be due to the ending of a relationship, but the most powerful are the stories of family tragedy. For example the deaths of the mothers of Juhi Chawla and Govinda in August 1996 were written from a personal and emotional position, concentrating on the grief of the bereaved stars and listing all those who supported them. The tales of struggle are usually stories of male stars who rose from ordinary backgrounds and who, through luck, hard work and faith in their own abilities, have been able to triumph over life's difficulties. Their reliance on their moral qualities, their realization of the priority of home and family allow them to reach self-acceptance and maturity. For example, the career of Jackie Schroff features regularly in this mode.

The backgrounds of female stars are rarely discussed; for them the central issues are those of morality and acceptability. Male stars often repeat that they would not marry a girl from the industry or let their daughters go into films, and so women's backgrounds are given only when they are from star families or respectable middle-class homes. The stories are often about the star women who have reached a mid-life crisis, feeling they have sacrificed their education and are missing out on home and family. While the younger can say they are biding their time and intend to retire to family life, the senior stars have less room for manoeuvre. Women's struggle is to do with the lack of friendship and support in the industry; many interviews with women focus on rivalry between stars. These can be read as stories of outer happiness and inner sorrow, a typically melodramatic form. The moral of the women's stories is that success brings its own problems. The journalists put themselves in supporting roles here, while the reader is admitted to a world of emotion.

The second is the purely promotional treatment. This is usually reserved for newcomers, who are people like you and me but often have some 'star quality', or for the recently arrived crop of models. There is no gossip about these stars, just praise, flattery and a set of glamorous photographs. In fact, all photographic material is of this nature – scandals are not corroborated by pictures from the paparazzi, nor are emotional photographs shown (except of a life event). All the photographs concentrate on the glamorous aspects of the stars and there are usually plenty of studio photographs of the stars in the latest fashions or in theatrical costumes to accompany them.

The third category is concerned with malicious gossip and scandal. This is where the magazines derive their fame and notoriety. The gentler form is romantic gossip which exposes hidden love affairs, often between co-stars. A more malicious variety includes incidents of broken relationships, revenge, betrayal and jealousy. This is based on the understanding that public figures lead public lives and can have no privacy. It is a refusal to allow the stars to have too simple a life, because all their transgressions will be found out. In 'Neeta's natter' and other snippets, the magazine makes fun of the stars who are no longer fashionable and laughs at their appearance and delusions of grandeur. Professional rivalry is a major topic and stars are offered opportunities to attack each other and to respond to attacks on themselves by other people in the industry.

These three types of gossip have two main functions, namely as a way of understanding oneself and the world, and the creation of a sense of community, a feeling of belonging.[68] I discuss the former, largely sexual gossip, below. The second function is of vital importance to the pleasure of these magazines. The depiction of the inside world of films is the main focus, establishing the credentials of the journalists and the magazine. This has the effect of providing intimacy which stars shun in real life as they live often remote and sheltered lives, cocooned by security and air-conditioning. The magazine allows its readers to feel that they are participating in this world, a feeling which is reinforced by highly personal forms of address, creating solidarity and connections. The effect is one of intimacy and distance: the stars are personalities like you or me, but they are different in kind, in that they have an excess or surplus of everything. The creation of intimacy with the stars makes them figures who are near and yet remote and so can function as unthreatening figures for the projection of readers' fantasies and discussions. The melodramatic mode of the narratives is central to this, depicting the stars as emotionally charged, quasi-family figures.[69]

In summary, there is a dynamic of consumption. The magazine has an interest in creating a community of readers for its community of advertisers. The reader consumes these stories of the stars and the advertisements. This does not have to be in a passive way: she can read selectively, she can reinterpret the magazine in ways which are meaningful to her and has the ultimate power of refusal: not to buy or read the magazine.

Stardust: sexuality

The main concern of such gossip is to do with sexuality, the major feature of all gossip in any society. This is probably due to the fact it is now regarded as one of the most important and problematic areas of existence as well as one of the greatest sources of pleasure. A study of the issues raised in this context shows sources of anxiety and pleasure and, like all gossip, queries dominant values.

Sex without strings! The industry's orgy of immorality exposed![70]

The central concern of *Stardust* with sex and sexuality is emblazoned on every cover. The interest is not just with the sexual act itself, as is often assumed, but it discusses ideas, notions, feeling, images, attitudes and assumptions about a whole range of topics to do with sexuality such as romance, marriage, feminism, masculinity, femininity and gay and lesbian issues and the presentation of the body. This concern with sexuality is hardly surprising in the Bombay of the late 1990s where, along with lifestyle concerns, it is the dominant topic of conversation, especially among the young, upwardly mobile middle classes. These magazines are the sphere in which these major discourses on sexuality are sited outside of state locations such as educational institutes, medical discourse, population control and censorship.

India has a very limited and heavily censored pornography industry.[71] There are only two widely available men's magazines, the soft-porn magazine *Chastity*, which has many pictures of naked women, and is entirely concerned with the discussion of sexual matters whether in narratives or 'problem pages'; and *Debonair* (89,000), which belongs to the same proprietors as *Star'n'Style*. However, the latter is also known for its coverage of the arts, in particular poetry. Its present editor, Randhir Khare, is also a recognized poet; formerly it has had two of India's best-known poets, Adil Jussawalla and Imtiaz Dharker, working on its reviews and poetry pages. Its up-market playboy image can be seen as part of its attempts to widen the discussion of sexuality, but the soft-porn photos have caused some controversy. Women have no equivalent, which is to be expected in view of women's lack of interest in viewing the male body displayed in magazines. There is some discussion of sexuality in the health pages of women's magazines like *Femina* (available in English, 113,000, and in Gujarati) and *Women's Era*[72] (English, 101,000), but the majority of the writing is the usual female-oriented mixture of fashion, beauty, domestic tips and romantic stories in the numerous publications such as *Grhashobha* (Hindi, 315,000). In the last few years Indian editions of international magazines have begun, including *Cosmopolitan*. The contrast remains between women's magazines – lifestyle, fashion, beauty, romance – and men's magazines, which tend to be sports, news or business/financial. There has also been a rapid expansion of lifestyle magazines which can be aimed at both sexes, including *Savvy*, *Society* and more recently *Society Interiors*, *Verve* and *India Today Plus*.

The only magazine to give coverage to gay issues is *Bombay Dost*, mostly in English, with a few pages in Hindi and English. This is printed in black and white on low-grade paper and is mostly the work of one person, Ashok Row Kavi. Despite its struggle to acquire distributors and outlets, it has become an important publication for many gay activists in India. I know of no lesbian equivalent.

Apart from magazines, sexuality is discussed across a wide range of media. A discussion of the discourses on sexuality presented in films[73] lies beyond the scope of this chapter. However, while the commercial films may provide visual displays of a sexually explicit nature, they pay lip-service to a much more conservative view of sexuality than the magazines, leading to a complex and contradictory presentation of sexual desire.[74] Film songs and their picturization provide greater opportunities for sexual display than dialogue and narrative sections of the films, with their specific images of clothes, body and body language, while the song lyrics are largely to do with sexuality, ranging from romance to suggestive and overt lyrics. A number of the latter type have caused major controversies, famously the 1993[?] *Khalnayak* hit song '*Choli ke peeche*' ('What's underneath my blouse?'), and women's groups have demonstrated outside the home of Karishma Kapoor after her songs with Govinda, including '*sarkailo khatiya*' ('Drag your bed over here') and her 'Sexy, sexy, sexy'.[75] The films of the so-called parallel cinema, a term which covers films ranging from the middlebrow to the avant-garde, often deal with questions of sexuality in a more explicit way. The controversy faced by 1995's *Bandit Queen*, whose ban was subsequently lifted, was widely discussed in the press and showed the variety of problems such a film had to face from censors and women's groups, while the audience greeted scenes of rape and violence towards the heroine with the whistles and foot-stamping with which they applaud sexy dance sequences.

Television, which has been seen as a threat to the film industry, is actually largely parasitic on it. Much of the TV time of the new satellite and cable channels, which now number around fifty in Bombay, is given to film, whether screening of films, or programmes about stars, music shows or audience participation shows. TV's own unique genre, the soap opera, is hugely popular in India, presenting melodramatic family romances rather than sexual romances.[76]

Women's romantic fiction whether Indian or imported is more concerned with fantasies of love than of sex, although Shobha Dé has introduced a new form of popular, more sexually explicit writing in English, dealing with sado-masochism and lesbianism in a way not found elsewhere. In spite of a long tradition of erotic writing in India, I know of no academic study of its recent manifestations. Indian novels written in English, while not primarily erotic, contain frequent mentions of penises, masturbation and early sexual encounters. These tend to be highly narcissistic and are treated on the same level of fascination as lavatorial matters. Gay writing has become more widespread, whether overtly, as in the pioneering writing of Firdaus Kanga, or in more covert forms.

As one might expect, there is no single coherent discourse on sexuality. In the west, in particular in the USA, since the 1950s the major discourse has developed from psychoanalysis, but this has had a restricted circulation in India. However, one can identify two popular trends. One is that sexual permissiveness is one of the evils of westernization, and an Indian woman's major concern is her honour. The other is that there is a cover-up and deliberate obfuscation, a refusal to acknowledge the high number of prostitutes in Bombay, the AIDS problem, extra-marital affairs, etc. Nevertheless the abundance of discourses on virginity, the age of consent, the life of widows and Eve-teasing, etc. shows the centrality of sexual discourses.

'*I'm a virgin and I'm still at the top!*' *Mamta erupts!* [77]

This declaration by one of Hindi film's top sex symbols ('the *desi* sex symbol') that she is a virgin shows the high value put on controlled female sexuality. This contrasts with the images of Kulkarni in magazines and films, where she features as the most sexy of all stars. The ideal woman is presented in the magazines as in the films, as a virgin, but often turned on by her own body in a narcissistic manner, eager for her sexual encounter with her life partner. In other words, the woman must be sexually available but only for the one, right man, a position which can be occupied easily by the male spectator/reader. But how does the female spectator/reader find pleasure in this position? If she is heterosexual, is she obliged to take a passive, masochistic position as suggested by Mulvey?

It seems that women readers are at least equally concerned with female stars as sources of identification as with male stars as figures of sexual fantasy. These women can be seen as providing role models for the new urban woman. I argue that one of the reasons women enjoy reading about female stars is because of the opportunities these features give for questioning standard views of sexuality, by setting up opposites and negotiating new possibilities. The off-screen star is as vulnerable in her own life as the reader is in hers, leading the reader to adopt attitudes of empathy and protectiveness. The star must face questions such as: Is it all right to sleep with someone without being married to him? Is it acceptable to live with someone without being married? What about having a child without being married? How should one deal with one's husband's infidelities? Are women always vulnerable?

The magazines have also supported the female stars. For instance, it is often said that some of the major actresses began their careers as porn stars. *Stardust*, in February 1985, responded to these charges on behalf of the stars by claiming that they were tricked into acting in pornographic films, where sequences with body doubles were added later.

From its beginnings the cinema has been seen as unsuitable for respectable women. Famously, Phalke could not persuade even prostitutes to act in his films and the first female stars were from the Anglo-Indian community. This concern with respectability remains one of the major concerns for the female star. Early issues of *Filmfare* depicted female stars in traditional saris, in their homes, engaged in domestic light chores such as flower-arranging, or looking after their sister's children, or in refined activities, such as painting or embroidery. Stars had to be presented as unmarried daughters or housewives. There were articles on how they liked to relax and spend their time at home. It seemed that any reference to labour was avoided, apart from the efforts the stars make to cope with their busy professional and private lives. There is no direct reference in these magazines to women's domestic work or even the 'servant problem'. In fact one of the major features that distinguishes these magazines from women's magazines is the silence about domestic life (except in advertising).

Nargis, who trod the line of respectability very carefully,[78] argued forcefully for women stars to be more highly regarded. The lack of success of this viewpoint can be seen throughout the industry, whether in the much lower pay for women, or their diminished roles. It is seen clearly in contemporary magazines where male stars claim they would never marry an industry girl or let their own daughters go into the business. Female stars will rarely admit affairs, while male stars seem to boast of their conquests whether married or single.

It may be surprising then that most of the female stars are not seen to take an interest in any form of feminism. They mostly reject feminism with trite remarks such as, 'Who wants to be equal to men? We're better!' A few women (Pooja Bedi, Pooja Bhatt, Anu Agrawal) step beyond the limits of female behaviour, but this is reactive rather than suggesting meaningful alternatives to those on offer.

The stories show a lack of female bonding and emphasize rivalry, unless one group of women are ganging up on another woman. This is particularly disappointing in view of the fact that there has been numerical dominance of women among the magazine's reporters and editors.[79]

The photographs of the female stars can be interpreted by the female viewer as images of the inner person, following the widely held belief that the female body expresses the idea of female sexuality, where the inner life and sexuality are the same. Women can also enjoy the fashion, the clothes, the make-up and the hairstyles of the stars which they may copy; they can also enjoy the pleasure of identifying with their beauty.

The photographs are always of the most glamorous women, who are not necessarily leading heroines. For example, many magazines carry photos of the actress Raveena Tandon, who has not had a big box-office hit for a long time. The actresses are beautiful and elegant. The larger ideal has been marginalized, although not replaced by taller, thinner women with smaller breasts and hips like western models.[80] The actress is heavily made-up, wearing a particular type of western costume which is more high street than high fashion. These often look cheap and vulgar and are not infrequently fetishistic outfits in black PVC. The actresses rarely wear Indian clothes for these shots, which is a sharp contrast from the early *Filmfare*, where the women wore saris. The outfits tend to reveal rather than to conceal; camera angles are often invasive, with many cleavage shots, as well as some (depilated) groin shots. However, nudity is not even considered, *Stardust*'s cover of Mamta topless, even though covering her breasts, is still discussed, and much has been made over the scene in *Bandit Queen*, where Seema Biswas (Phoolan Devi) is stripped naked. Close-ups usually emphasize eyelashes, lip-liner and heavy jewellery. There are frequently staged shots of a couple in passionate clinches, pre-orgasmic, orgasmic and postcoital.

Hot! Are industry men sex-starved? [81]

While the images of the male stars are more complicated than those of female stars, the story-lines are simpler. The male star can be the subject of scandal, which he can reject or enjoy, he can utter threats to would-be rivals, he can reveal himself as a sensitive soul or a survivor. These seem to approximate quite closely to the roles that the man takes on screen, unlike the woman's which is so different.[82] Cinema provides mostly positive roles for male stars, the obvious exception being the villain. The villain, however, is a lower category of star, even when hugely popular, for the male star is almost identical with the hero, or anti-hero.

One of the most interesting star texts is that of Akshay Kumar, a box-office and magazine idol. He is discussed as a relentless womanizer and superstud; endless stories circulate about him and Raveena Tandon – that they may be secretly married, may be a couple or may have ended their relationship – but he is also important as a gay icon.

Bombay Dost ran an interview with 'the new Eros of eroticism',[83] accompanied by a review of Akshay's film '*Main khiladi tu anadi*' ('I am a player, you are innocent'), finding numerous homoerotic overtones and gay codes in this two-hero film. The picture accompanying a story in *Stardust* which referred directly to the *Bombay Dost* interview, has Akshay dressed in uniform with his arm around action hero Sunil Shetty. Akshay Kumar's statement in *Stardust* ('I feel nice about being a gay fantasy!'[84]) was reported with delight in *Bombay Dost*,[85] showing an intertextual link between the two magazines. Akshay's status in the gay community may explain the numerous photographs of him in uniform, leather and bondage gear.[86] Akshay himself is careful in all his interviews to offend neither his homosexual fans nor homophobes; his portrayal in film magazines is usually hypermasculine, as a body-builder and a compulsive seducer of women, which is open to gay readings.

While many other photographs of male stars suggest gay readings, this is often inherent in the subject matter, photographs of the male body, rather than necessarily saying anything about the stars' sexuality. Codes of looking (men look, women are looked at) make it difficult to eroticize the male body for the female look or to allow for the voyeuristic female.[87] Dyer argues that images of the eroticized male body appear as gay images because the active gaze is thought to be male.[88] This requires men in photographs to avert their eyes to deny the gaze, to appear as action types or to be hysterically male. Whether these rules apply in an Indian context is unclear. However, the direct look of the male star, the recent craze for body-building – which on small men heightens the gay effect, as does the tight clothing required to display their muscles – and the use of soft textures and gentle lighting in the photographs certainly do not inhibit a gay interpretation of the images.

However, the magazines rarely speak directly about gay issues. There are infrequent suggestions that stars are gay, and, more rarely, coded references to their orientation,[89] suggestions of a gay readership,[90] and the occasional photograph such as *Stardust*'s picture of two female stars, Farah and Khusboo, engaged in a passionate kiss.[91] The style of the magazines certainly lends itself to camp readings, and camp interpretations are unpredictable. For example, the camp following of top female stars such as Sharmila Tagore and Meena Kumari, the preferred role models for drag artists, is likely to be because of the excess of femininity of the former and the tragic on- and off-screen images of the latter.[92] There seems to be little similar to the western prepubescent desire of girls for androgynous, non-threatening males as typified by boy-groups such as Boyzone. However, the above views show a western interpretation which may not stand up to scrutiny in the serious analysis of Indian sexuality which is so far lacking.[93] The major stories are about heterosexual love and sex; the photographs of couples are almost all male and female.

The appearance of the hero indicates popular perceptions of beauty. He must be tall and fair, usually north Indian and clean-shaven. His clothes are nearly always western; a number of shots are designed to emphasize the physique; his clothes may be torn, or he may be topless, covered in sweat with his slicked-back hair, or dressed as western actors (Shah Rukh Khan has been photographed dressed as Rudolph Valentino). In other words, the presentation of the male star is as hypermasculine or active.

In addition to the male practice of body-building mentioned above, two other major forms of body-shaping have emerged in India in recent years. One is dieting, the other is plastic surgery. Stars are regularly criticized for putting on weight and praised for weight-loss. Although this is seen in early issues of *Stardust*, it was clearly absent from early issues of *Filmfare*, where many of the stars were large by today's western ideals. Anorexia and bulimia are not known as such in India, and a tracing of these images of the body remains to be seen.

Far more drastic is the use of plastic surgery. Several stars have talked about it in public; several have clearly gone under the knife. However, a major feature on plastic surgery in *Stardust* was the most public and controversial discussion so far.[94] It began by saying how common plastic surgery is in Hollywood and reported Dolly Parton's revelations about her own plastic surgery. There then followed an interview with two cosmetic surgeons, Dr Narendra Pandya and Dr Vijay Sharma. The magazine then gave its own list of male and female stars who seem to have had work done on them. The most frequent operations are breast implants for younger female stars, who often demand excessively large breasts with prominent nipples. Across the board the most popular operation is the nose job and more rarely liposuction, and breast upliftment, while many older stars have undergone face-lifts. The often impossible demands of the stars reflect the beauty priorities, namely to be taller and to have lighter skin. Perhaps the most surprising part of the whole piece was Sharma's advice on which stars need what sort of plastic surgery, which seemed very close to British tabloid newspaper discussion.

Despite these forms of body-improvement, health trends such as reasonable exercise, healthy eating, sensible drinking and quitting smoking are discussed less frequently, and stars are even featured smoking.

The majority of the stories in the magazine are concerned with sex, love and romance. These give different values to romance than the images portrayed on-screen. On-screen the focus is on the struggle with the ultimate happy ending, usually a wedding or at least the promise of one. In the magazines the emphasis is on the problems of romance, its scarcity, its lack, the failure of marriages, the infidelities rather than on the successes. This can be interpreted as a specialized form of reading romance:

Romance reading, in this view, is escapist, cathartic and addictive, and serves the same gender-specific functions for women as does pornography for men.[95]

Although the terms 'escapist, cathartic and addictive' raise more problems than they answer (escape from what to where and why? etc.), this remark raises an important issue avoided by Radway in her study of the romance, namely the question of whether readers find the narratives of romance sexually arousing. It seems more likely that the pleasure in *Stardust* is found in the melodramatic mode, in that the stars have everything – looks, money, fame – yet they still have to worry about romance and they still are not happy. The stories of stars are heightened versions of romance along the lines of betrayal by one's partner with another desirable person, and the public knowledge of the situation. This also allows readers, among whom dating is restricted, premarital sex is taboo and arranged marriages – however loosely we use the term – are still the norm, to fantasize about such relationships and to learn about how they would behave in certain situations. They allow readers to discuss issues of romance, love and sexuality.

Despite the prominence given to romance and sexual liaisons, there is clear emphasis on the family and on controlled sexuality, especially in the case of women. There is an underlying theme about reconciling individuality with wider duties. The stories endlessly go over problems of romance and love in heterosexual monogamy.

Marriage is a key issue in the magazine, and there is no questioning the respect given to marriage. Occasional discussions on 'living in' always see it as a poor or unacceptable substitute for marriage. Marriage and a career in cinema are seen as irreconcilable for women. Women are expected to retire from the industry after marriage, partly because fans will not accept a married woman in romantic roles and also because her place is in the home. The only possibility is of a return to play mothers and character roles.

A regularly occurring feature is of the secret marriage between star couples. In 1995/6 a major story was published concerning the possible marriage of Akshay Kumar and Raveena Tandon. There were rumours of wedding photographs, although these were never seen. The issue of *souten* (co-wife) is usually silently acknowledged: an article about Dharmendra's (star) children Bobby and Sunny Deol will not mention Hema Malini while an article about Dharmendra and Hema will not mention Bobby and Sunny. Divorce is seen as rather scandalous, with even the divorce of star parents reported. The issue of whether to divorce or to take a second wife is frequently raised; for example Sri Devi (who was reported to be

Mithun Chakraborty's second wife in 1990) is now pregnant and recently married the already-married Boney Kapoor.

All melodrama highlights the importance of the family. Even if characters in a melodrama are not relatives, they take on functions and roles of relatives to assume any importance.[96] Another melodramatic feature is that the families of stars take on the star's aura. The names of star partners are well known; stories are run about how wives of unfaithful husbands are forgiving, how the star has suffered due to the ill health of a partner, etc. Star children are a regular feature and are rarely mentioned without some reference to their parents, such as Sanjay Dutt (Nargis and Sunil Dutt), Karishma Kapoor (Babita and Randhir Kapoor, son of Raj Kapoor), Twinkle Khanna (Dimple and Rajesh Khanna). On the occasion of a marriage or the birth of children to stars, all enmities are dropped and congratulations, purple prose and smoochy photos are in order.

I conclude this chapter by looking at the pleasure of reading these magazines. Following Ang,[97] I argue that although readers would accept that they read the magazines for pleasure, no one can define what these pleasures actually are. Instead, I look at some of the mechanisms of pleasure.

The most obvious of these is often overlooked, which is the act of reading itself. Radway's study of the reading of romance fiction found that one of the central pleasures was in designating time for oneself, refusing the demands of one's family.[98] Hermes builds on this and finds that reading women's magazines is a secondary activity for passing time, the readers saying they read magazines instead of novels because they fill gaps in the day and yet are easy to put down.[99] This can clearly apply to the consumption of magazines in India, but there has been no study of domestic reading practices. Personal experience suggests those times while waiting for food to cook, during the afternoon rest or, in Bombay, on the long journey to the office, as a way of shutting out the rest of the commuters, is when such reading occurs. In India, the magazine circulates among the household, some of whom may just pick it up briefly, and enjoy only the visual pleasure such as the photographs of beautiful people, clothes and consumer items.

However, although Radway focused on reading in her research, she was unable to draw firm conclusions about the pleasures of reading. Most importantly, readers did not give enough information about whether they found the stories erotic or sexually exciting. The problems of eliciting such responses remains.

A second central pleasure is also extra-textual, namely the pleasure of an 'imagined' community of readers,[100] providing an imaginary and temporary sense of identity and of seeing the community as an extension of the family for the siting of melodramatic events. Gossip is circulated by the magazines through melodramatic stories, narratives in which the readers 'get to know' the star, are addressed directly by the narratives and share the consumption fantasies of the advertisements. This is encouraged by the style of *Stardust*, which invites the reader to become part of the inner world, where the stars also read the magazine. The discussions of the stars and their lives, romances, marriages and reconciliations become like interventions by other family members. The focus on sexuality is because the stars negotiate the concerns the readers face in their own lives.[101] Although the concept of finding oneself through sexuality has prevailed in the west since the seventeenth century,[102] the strength of this growing belief in India remains unclear.

An examination of the stories raises the question: Why do the stories contradict all 'normal expectations' of behaviour and the roles associated with the star personae on-screen? Clearly the audience are not passive receivers of these messages but they can interpet them in a wide variety of ways. The active role of audience in folk and other performances in India has been noted in that the audience uses texts as ways of dealing with inner dramas, not as models of behaviour.[103] This has been noted also among viewers of soap operas in the west, where the emphasis is not on 'escape' but on ways of dealing with one's everyday life.[104] Dyer argues that the lives of stars are places to discuss sexual morality, the role of the individual and of the family, the understanding of the body and the nature of consumer society.[105] Gandhy and Thomas follow his approach in their study of three female stars of Hindi cinema[106] and draw attention to the fact that the star personae off-screen

> frequently encompass behaviours that are decidedly subversive of the strict social mores of Indian society and would be considered 'scandalous' in any other context, even by many of their most dedicated fans. Of course they do not simply transgress: stars are represented as finely balancing their transgressions with personifica-tions of ideal behaviour especially in the domains of kinship and sexuality. Both the films and the sub-text of gossip about stars are most usefully seen as debates around morality, in particular as negotiations about the role of 'tradition' in a modernising India.[107]

An undoubted source of pleasure lies in the creation and fulfilment of the desires of the readers in a new urban, consumer society. The links between cinema and desire, consumerism and capitalism and desire are highly complex.[108] While mass media and popular culture embody and communicate society's dominant ideology they also give grounds for resisting them. The magazines must seek and create their market, but the readers also choose what they prefer. The magazines can create desires and fulfil them, but the readers can subvert them so that their own desires and needs are met. The content of the magazines must be relevant to the fantasies and anxieties which dominate the readers' concerns. Hermes identifies two dominant fantasies which can be fulfilled by such magazines, namely control through understanding other people's emotions; and the control of imagining difficult scenarios and how one would cope if faced with them in real life.[109]

We should be wary of thinking that the reader absorbs these magazines passively at face value. Readers may have their own ways of reading. They can choose which stories to read and which photos to look at; they can read with a sense of irony and humour, whether a camp style as identified by Hermes, or just as part of being a cool, urban person. The magazine sends itself up, notably in 'Neeta's Natter', and the stars themselves point out they should not take it all too seriously:

> 'Stardust' proudly flaunts that it is a gossip and fun-seeking magazine, and that teaches us to have a sense of humour.[110]

The impact of the language of *Stardust* on South-Asian writers in English was mentioned above, but the magazine's star stories are also appearing in the novels of Dé and Tharoor.[111] India's daily papers are now taking on star stories as features; new cable and satellite TV links are allowing more and more of this gossip to circulate to the new aspirants to this world of glamour and modernity. For example, Zee TV now offers a whole spectrum of film spin-offs in addition to the films themselves, including song shows, chart rundowns, quizzes, etc. The magazines have not stood still: *Stardust* along with other magazines now makes its own weekly TV show using the language of 'Neeta's Natter' and is already available on the Internet.

Taking these magazines seriously allows us to have a closer look at the concerns and aspirations of an emerging social group. A study of the consumption of these magazines by the diaspora would provide further rewards. Almost universally condemned as trash, an analysis of the magazines reveals the creation of an 'imagined' community of readers and consumers of a new public culture. Unlike readers of women's magazines who fantasize about perfect selves, the study of film magazines shows multiple points of identification and enunciation of fantasies.

In looking at the magazines it is clear that the central underlying themes are the issues facing these new classes, at a time when values are shifting rapidly, and massive social changes are taking place in Bombay. This can be seen in anxieties about class and respectability. For example, a recent issue of *Stardust* dealt with the issues of class, money and 'modern' views in one article.[112] Some film stars were hired by a diamond merchant to perform at his brother's wedding for large sums of money. In conservative terms, being hired to dance at a wedding has overtones of the *mujra* and hence associations with courtesans and prostitution. The magazine solicited the opinion of a number of stars. One admitted she had performed and taken money but claimed to feel degraded. Some stars denied any knowledge of the event, some said they had been tricked, while others said that it was shocking and degrading to the industry that any of its members should have behaved in this manner. A few of the younger female stars said that they thought that a big fuss was being made over nothing and there was no problem in performing at such events. This presentation of a whole range of views allows the reader to consider this story of the breaking of a taboo from a number of perspectives. Since the magazine does not give an editorial line, the reader is allowed to draw her own conclusion on the issues raised.

Stardust does not stand apart from other cultural products, but it is a major source of pleasure among a whole range of forms. Its economy of pleasure centred around leisure, consumption, fantasy and humour, its new language and modes of expression have reached the upwardly mobile middle classes in a national and international (diasporic) readership, tying together this class across the nation.

Notes

1. The exceptions include studies of billboards: Haggard, 1988, and Srivatsan, 1991; Manuel, 1993, touches on concerns important to cinema in his wider discussion of the music cassette industry; and there has been some work on soap operas including Mitra, 1993, and Lutgendorf, 1995.
2. This reflects the wider academic neglect of the long history of Indian newspapers, magazines and literary periodicals which began in India in the early nineteenth century, and has expanded to include film magazines, women's magazines and lifestyle magazines. These now number 28,491 according to the *Lintas Media Guide India*, 1995.
3. See below.
4. Dickey, 1993a and b.
5. Pfleiderer and Lutze, 1985.
6. Vasudevan, 1989: 30.
7. Dyer, 1977.
8. See below for a discussion of the readership of the magazines.
9. See Uberoi [2000].
10. See below.
11. Hermes, 1995: 121, uses Anderson's term 'imagined community' to describe the readership of women's magazines, while Radway, 1991, extends Fish's term 'interpretive community' to cover non-academic reading communities.
12. Winship, 1987; McRobbie, 1991; McCracken, 1993; Hermes, 1995.
13. Radway, 1987.
14. Modleski, 1982.
15. Ang, 1985.

16. McRobbie herself revised her 1980 study in 1987. Reprinted as Chapters 5 and 6 in McRobbie, 1991.

17. Gledhill, 1988.

18. The stars who receive the most coverage in the magazines are not necessarily the biggest box-office stars. It could be said that there is a separate category of 'magazine stars'. Rajadhyaksha and Willemen, 1995: 186, suggest this is true of Rekha.

19. Genres of magazines are not altogether clear-cut. There may be overlap between the various genres in formal terms and consumers may categorize the magazines differently. For example, Hermes, 1995, finds that what she took to be a 'feminist magazine' is seen as a 'women's magazine' by most of the readers in her survey.

20. Karanjia, 1984; Kabir, 1985; Mishra *et al.*, 1989; Gandhy and Thomas, 1991; Sharma, 1993.

21. The papers in Gledhill, 1991a, show how central Dyer, 1979 and 1986, is to the study of the star. Ellis, 1992, is also an important contribution. He shows how the star is created within the films themselves as vehicles for star performances which in turn build on images in other films and in other media. He argues for a study of these performances which touches on the star's cultural meanings, acting, performance, personality and national status and the implications of these for identity, desire and ideology. He asks: How do stars relate to social meaning and values? How do they reconcile, mask or expose ideological contradictions? What are their roles as utopian fantasies? Who generates and directs the images of the stars? How does the star as a cultural figure generate tension around glamour but also hard work and dedication? What is the star's role as a national icon? While such a study lies beyond the scope of this book, I plan to focus on such questions in a forthcoming paper.

22. Film magazines began at this time in other regional Indian cinemas, but unless otherwise specified the discussion here focuses on those which are published from Bombay.

23. Rajadhyaksha and Willemen, 1995: 17–30, give details of mostly non-star magazines in their chronology of Indian cinema.

24. This was the silent period of cinema, so language issues were important only for title cards. Many of the key figures of the Bombay film industry were Gujarati speakers; at this time Gujarati was the main commercial language of Bombay so its use in the cinema industry alongside Hindi/Urdu was not surprising. However, by the 1950s it seems that English had come to replace Gujarati and was the second language of the Bombay film industry.

25. Other trade publications include *Film Information* (1973–), *Super Box Office* (1985–) and *Complete Cinema* (1986–).

26. A further type of publication are the journals dedicated to Indian art cinema such as the *Indian Film Quarterly* (1957–), *Deep Focus* (1987–), etc.

27. The magazine was distributed in Pakistan and the cover gave a separated PRs price, although this was the year since which Indian films have been banned in Pakistan.

28. *Filmfare*, 7 March 1952: 3.

29. See below.

30. A point made by Ashwin Varde, former editor of *Stardust*, interview, Bombay, December 1994.

31. The social and economic reasons underlying the rapid expansion of Bombay's advertising industry at this time are harder to discern, though international comparisons suggest that advertising only really took off in the late 1960s. The political situation is also unclear: I have found no evidence of censorship during the national Emergency (1975–7) when journalists were strictly curtailed.

32. Note that these figures are only numbers sold; most magazines are lent through 'circulating libraries' where they can be rented for around Rs5 per night; the purchase price is Rs20. Most copies are read by several people before they are sold and recycled at an even lower price.

33. The Gujarati version contains a page or two of information on the Gujarati film industry, but the main features are translated from the English version. The advertisements are considerably down-market.

34. The only other magazines with international editions are *Movie* (1989[?]–) and *Cinéblitz* (1989–). They both give cover prices for the UK, USA, Canada and Holland.

35. The major difference between the Indian and overseas versions is that the advertising caters to different markets (see below). The same stories may run in different months' editions of the magazine.
36. The circulation figure for the whole Magna stable is said to be approaching half a million.
37. The *Lintas Media Guide India*, 1995: 42, suggests 113,000.
38. Amitabh Bachchan cited it as the only film magazine he enjoyed, interview, Bombay 1996.
39. Devyani Chaubal, queen of gossip columnists, was the star journalist in the magazine's heyday. She wrote about herself as a star and carried stories about how the stars were in love with her. The magazine folded in 1990 after a journalists' strike and was sold by the Somani group to a Delhi buyer along with the 'men's magazine' *Debonair*. Early copies are said to be unavailable after a fire at the offices.
40. Other Magna publications include *Showtime* (1984–) (a star magazine), *Savvy, Health and Nutrition, Parade, Society, Society Interiors, Society Fashion, Island* (a Bombay magazine), *Family* (a Bangalore magazine) and *Citadel* (a Pune magazine). Magna also publishes romantic fiction and has recently published Mohan Deep's biographies of the stars, including Deep, 1998.
41. The Magna group now has its own seven-storey building in the inner suburb of Prabhadevi.
42. *Stardust*, October 1971: 39.
43. *Stardust*, March 1995: 112.
44. 'One of the few contemporary Indian film stars with a legendary status far outstripping her screen roles.' Rajadhyaksha and Willemen, 1995: 186.
45. Celebrations of the number of weeks a film has run. Hence, a silver jubilee means the film has had a twenty-five week run.
46. *Stardust*, January 1995.
47. All women's magazines have a high male consumption in the west. Hermes, 1995, draws attention to the overlap in men's reading of the magazines between serious consumption and ironic or camp consumption.
48. The advertisements in these pages are not distinguishable from others in the magazine.
49. See above.
50. This is seen in the novels of Shobha Dé. See Chapter 7 below.
51. Winship, 1987.
52. Stacey, 1993.
53. Shopping has been seen as a gay male activity in the west, as mocked in a chant of the early 1990s: 'We're here, we're queer and we're not going shopping.'
54. 'Neeta's Natter', *Stardust*, May 1996: 7.
55. Used for Mamta Kulkarni, March 1995: 79.
56. The use of *desi* images (street barbers, old women dancing), found on music videos and films by fashionable directors like Mani Ratnam, may suggest a wider phenomenon.
57. This use of language is seen in Dé's novels. See Chapter 7 for an analysis of the criticism and Dé's defence.
58. *Stardust*, August 1996: Cover.
59. *Stardust*, April 1996: 17.
60. 'Surely there is no *rubbish* about you. *Congratulations* for *mincing* the casual remarks of stars. O *brother*, what happened? ... STARDUST'S *our own proper* language.' *Stardust*, December 1972: 51.
61. For example, Ezekiel, 1989: 268. Many attempts were made in literature to produce an Indian English, notably in Raja Rao, 1989. Desani's unique brand of English (Desani, 1972) seems to have been the role model for that of Rushdie (see bibliography) although no direct genealogy can be traced.
62. Tharoor, 1994.
63. See Chapter 7.
64. See Rushdie, 1995, especially the passage on Nargis and Sunil Dutt (Rushdie, 1995: 137–8), reproduced in Chapter 4 above.
65. *Stardust*, August 1996.
66. Spacks, 1985: 4–7.
67. Gledhill, 1987 and 1991b.
68. Cf. Hermes, 1995: 121.
69. Brooks, 1995: 4, argues that characters take on essential, psychic features of family relations, including father, mother, child.
70. *Stardust*, February 1995: Cover.
71. I know of no study of this industry in India. Imported pornographic films are said to be widely available for hire and screened in cafés, and I have heard of a series of pornographic films in Malayalam. Posters in urban streets advertise the showing of 'hot' films but

these include medical films and western films appropriated as pornography. In Bombay in 1991 a much-advertised 'hot' film was Peter Greenaway's *The Cook, the Thief, the Wife and Her Lover*.

72. See Naipaul, 1990, for a discussion of this magazine.

73. Very little has been written about this. Uberoi, 1997, gives a lively account of female desire in Guru Dutt's 1962 *Sahib, bibi aur ghulam*.

74. See Kasbekar [2000].

75. *Raja Babu* and *Khudda*.

76. Neale, 1986, argues that melodrama is a fantasy of love rather than sex.

77. *Stardust*, January 1994: Cover.

78. Gandhy and Thomas, 1991.

79. See a feature on women reporters in *Filmfare*, 23 April 1996: 3.

80. See below for a discussion of the body.

81. *Stardust*, November 1994: cover.

82. See below the discussion of morality.

83. *Bombay Dost*, 4(1)(1995): 8–9.

84. Akshay Kumar, *Stardust*, June 1995: 82.

85. *Bombay Dost*, 4(2)(1995): 5.

86. A cover of *Filmfare* showed him dressed as the 'patron saint' of gays, Saint Sebastian.

87. Theories of the gaze are mostly Eurocentric. See Chapter 5, n. 11.

88. Dyer, 1982.

89. For example, a leading male star (referred to by name) is called *mamu*, which is gay slang for a gay man. *Stardust*, May 1996: 12.

90. 'It wouldn't be surprising if the mercilessly handsome Bobby Deol is someday voted "Most Likely to Guest Star in Masturbation Fantasies" by both men and women alike.' *Stardust Annual*, 1996: 221.

91. No date, see *Best of Stardust*, vol. 3: *1981–90*: 16.

92. Dyer, 1986, analyses the camp following of Judy Garland.

93. Kakar, 1989a, being the only study.

94. *Stardust*, May 1996: 44–52

95. Singh and Uberoi, 1994: 94.

96. See Brooks, 1995: 4, and Neale, 1986.

97. Ang, 1985.

98. Radway, 1987.

99. Hermes, 1995.

100. Hermes, 1995.

101. Dyer, 1986.

102. Foucault, 1981: 6–7.

103. E.g. by Beck, 1989, and Kothari, 1989.

104. Ang, 1985: 83.

105. Dyer, 1986.

106. Gandhy and Thomas, 1991. They discuss Fearless Nadia (1910–96), Nargis (1929–81) and Smita Patil (1955–86).

107. Gandhy and Thomas, 1991: 108.

108. Laplace, 1987.

109. Hermes, 1995: 48.

110. Rekha, *Stardust*, August 1996: 46.

111. 'The novel parodies other genres precisely in their role as genres; it exposes the conventionality of their form and their language ...' Bakhtin, 1981: 5.

112. *Stardust*, May 1996: 60–6.

7

Pulp Fiction? The Books of Shobha Dé

Shobha Dé's novels[1] have been something of a *cause célèbre* in India. These were the first Indian novels in English which approximated western popular or pulp fiction, in that they were by a celebrity author, their story-lines and style were typical of this genre, and they rapidly became bestsellers. Dé's introduction to India of this form of writing in English marks the beginning of a new cultural product of the new middle classes, leading to much of the controversy and inappropriate criticism which has surrounded these books.

Shobha Dé has been a celebrity in India for more than twenty years, famous as a model, society hostess and journalist. Founder of three English-language magazines covering fashion, films and gossip,[2] and writer of many columns in the Indian press, she has also written a long-running soap opera for Indian television,[3] has since 1988 published several highly successful novels, and has recently published her autobiography. Born Shobha Rajadhyaksha in 1948, the daughter of a district judge, she grew up in Maharashtra and Delhi, reading for her BA in Bombay. She became one of India's first models, appearing in *Vogue*, before she married into one of the city's wealthiest families. They divorced and she married the shipping magnate, Dilip Dé, one of Bombay's *bons viveurs*; they now have six children between them. Shobha Dé is a prominent figure in Bombay society; details about her life are known to many outside this circle, and talk centres on her great beauty, her wealth, her art collecting and her sharp tongue. Her gossipy and acerbic columns in the newspapers are read avidly, and well-known Delhi intellectuals confess (off the record) that they are their favourite items in the press.[4]

Looking at Dé's novels and other writings in chronological order, one can see how she has kept her finger on the pulse, creating and following social trends and other fashions. Her major concern remains the same, namely women's search for meaning in relationships and, unusually for most forms of popular fiction, in their work. Bombay is not a mere backdrop for her novels but features as the city that enables her characters to pursue their dreams and explore the widest range of opportunities. Her presentation of the several layers of Bombay society from the lower-middle-class suburban to the downtown elite and their use of the city's spaces provides one of the most vivid portraits of this city in fiction.

In Dé's first two novels the major focus is on Bombay's brittle glamour. Men are exploiters and betrayers of women, who are struggling to get a foothold in this society. The first novel, *Socialite Evenings*, like many first novels, has several autobiographical links. It depicts the dream of a girl from the provinces who enters the Bombay social scene, but concentrates on the nightmare it becomes, as she becomes enmeshed in the struggle for survival among the key figures in this world (including many recognizable composites of real people), who are shallow, callous and ruthless. Although a lot of sex takes place in the novel, most of it happens, as it were, off the page, with relationships rather than sexuality being presented as more central to a woman's self-fulfilment. The woman's determination to survive disasters and betrayals, to move on in terms of relationships and to find her own place in the city is the central theme of this first novel.

Her second novel, *Starry Nights*, is set in the film world, widely regarded as India's epitome of glamour and scandal. This is Dé's closest to a 'sex and shopping' novel, although its focus is on the negative aspects of this world and its ultimate trashiness. Again, the lead characters, the starlet who sleeps her way to stardom and the number one hero of Bombay cinema, are clearly based on composites of well-known actors of the Hindi cinema. The exploitation of the female star by her family and by the industry is also drawn from many stories about the film star presented in the film magazines. The emphasis again is on the heroine as survivor, able to endure appalling treatment by almost everyone she meets, and ultimately finding her own place from which to negotiate her future.

The third novel, *Sisters*, set in the Gujarati business world of Bombay, contrasts the lives of two sisters, one legitimate, the other illegitimate, in their struggle to gain control of their dead father's business. This is a story of many melodramas, but the difference here is that the relationship between the sisters and their position in the family is not presented in black and white terms, nor is it the only concern of the novel. Again, Dé returns to the theme of work, as this novel is set in another of Bombay's major concerns, namely its business world, looking at the opportunities for women in this field, and the routes that women from different parts of society must take in order to get a foothold in this traditional male domain. Again, another part of glamorous upper Bombay society has its underbelly exposed.

In her fourth novel, *Strange Obsession*, Dé examines one of the most important contemporary images of women in the modern Indian media, the latest role model, the supermodel. The supermodel has become a key figure for adolescent girls in the west, who long for the glamour, beauty and wealth of these women, whose tall, emaciated bodies are so different from their own changing bodies. In India, these women's role is celebrated, although contested, by a wider section of society, enhanced by the survival of media coverage of the beauty pageant, a long-forgotten media event in the west, interest in which was boosted by the titles won by Indian models (Sushmita Sen as Miss Universe in 1993, Aishwarya Rai as Miss World 1994 and Diana Hayden as Miss World 1997) and the controversy created by the hosting of the Miss World contest in India in 1996. The acceptance of these western ideals of beauty can be seen in the dieting rage, although eating disorders have not received the widespread media coverage, nor has there been the level of blame ascribed to the modelling industry for generating women's dissatisfaction with their body image, that there has been in the west. Fascinating as one of the few Indian novels to discuss lesbianism, its sado-masochistic elements make it a disturbing work.

Sultry Days has a lighter theme, being set in another work culture, one of the important domains of employment for the upwardly mobile, younger generation, namely an advertising agency. Several characters can easily be recognized as prominent figures in the Bombay advertising world, while the presentation of one of the city's leading poets as DOM (Dirty Old Man) seems to provoke deliberately the literary world of Bombay. Once again, the focus is on sex, relationships and work among young metropolitan professionals.

Dé's next two books are not centred around a single heroine but about several women and their relationships with one another and with their families. *Snapshots* is about six women college friends, whose meeting after many years is the narrative device against which they reflect on their youth and the different trajectories of their careers, marriages and families and the ageing process; *Small Betrayals* is a collection of short stories on similar themes.

Her most recent novel, *Second Thoughts*, is about a woman from Calcutta who moves to Bombay on marriage. Rather than finding the glamour she had dreamt of, she is trapped in the boredom of a suburban marriage, and feels neglected by her husband, whose primary relationship is with his mother. The loneliness caused by the lack of intimacy, romance and sexual relations between the couple creates the conditions that lead her towards an affair with a young neighbour, disregarding all the obvious dangers. The young lover's major attraction is that he provides the young housewife with her only opportunity to get to know the city of Bombay. The deglamorized, 'realistic' tone of this book is in contrast to Dé's earlier works, which were set against a backdrop of high society. This book is about the stifling boredom many readers of romances wish to escape, their pleasure perhaps being in the woman's rebellion even though it does not bring her happiness.

In Dé's tongue-in-cheek (innuendo intended) *Surviving Men*, she presents the modern urban Indian male as an ill-mannered, overgrown child, spoilt rather than socialized by his mother, who can be easily exploited by his more intelligent wife in her ruthless pursuit of her major aim (money). A woman must train and control or ignore her man through a strategy of suffering silently his lack of physical and social charms, indulging his whims and providing him with his major needs, *khana–peena–dena* ('food, drink and sex'). In a deliberately provocative manner Dé raises issues which other women would only discuss among themselves in private. Her caricature of the macho Indian male slob is highly insulting, but she pulls her punches with a number of acutely accurate and amusing observations. However, she never quite comes to the point about why women still want to live with these unredeemably ghastly creatures, nor does she discuss the existence of more sophisticated and attractive Indian men. The book is written in the style of a self-help manual for women, but is also about refinements that the modern Indian woman wants from a man in terms of relationships and behaviour, while this particular kind of man clearly needs to be hunted to extinction.

The final chapters have a sting in their tail. 'Things our mamas didn't have to do for men' can be read as praise for the traditional, non-modernized Indian woman who had to deal with a more attractive version of masculinity. She laments the pressures of modern urban society, which sets impossible standards for women in terms of physical appearance, sexual athleticism, personal relationships and career achievement. The previous generation had to cook, keep home and in bed 'shut their eyes and think of Dilip Kumar'.

Selective Memory, Dé's autobiography is important for revealing a carefully selected view of her private life. Its twin themes, like those of her novel, are between her career and her family life. Dé describes her orthodox, Brahminical upbringing, and her move into the fashionable world of 1960s Bombay's new youth culture, culminating in her success as one of India's top models. The development of her career as a writer is presented episodically and her ambition and driving force remain somewhat concealed. Her love of glamour and style, and her desire to be in the hub of happening events, is clear. Bombay's resident and visiting celebrities appear in a number of vivid thumbnail sketches, but her own attitude to herself is often hidden. Dé's relationships with her family are standard, affectionate and occasionally fraught, but her love for them is sincere. The one episode presumably too personal and too painful to tell concerns her divorce. We are not even told her first husband's name, let alone how their relationship developed and how it fell apart. She details her depression and her material hardships when she moved out, but how did her friends and family really react to what must have been a great scandal at this time? Did it damage her relationship with her older children? Her romance with Dilip Dé is presented in the style of a romantic novel, with no discussion of how they felt about each other's previous marriages. This discretion is very much part of the Shobha Dé celebrity status, whose dynamic arises from the tension between the private person, the religious Hindu, the mother of six, the good wife and her public figure as a *femme fatale* and writer on sexual relations. It is this status which gives her the authority to discuss the unmentionable, ranging from women's desires and sexual pleasure to issues of promiscuity and alternative sexualities. In her status as celebrity and in her writing, Shobha Dé promotes a new kind of modern, bourgeois family, a modern Hindu family for the next millennium.

Dé's work has many commonalities with the other texts of the new middle classes discussed in previous chapters. Like these, her work shows a new dynamic between social and familial conservatism tied in to ideas of self-determination and a quest for fulfilment through relationships. Her texts are also women-oriented, seeing women as the bridge between the public and the private, and the source of change. Though she is by no means a feminist in western terms, Dé's women are dealing with central concerns of all women: namely how to reconcile their desires and duties, how to build loving relationships within and beyond the family, to explore the limits of sexual fulfilment within the boundaries and conventions of everyday life.

I argue that it is this association of Dé's writing with the new middle classes which has caused much of the controversy surrounding her writing. Again, the issue of taste (see Chapter 3) becomes a major criterion in the reception of these works.

While there has been no research into Dé's readership,[5] these novels have made Dé the best-selling writer in India since Independence.[6] Moreover, the books have been given some sort of a seal of respectability by being published by the prestigious Penguin India. However, their critical reception is mainly negative, typically summed up as 'filthy, semiliterate, semi-autobiographical airport-slush novelettes'.[7] This chapter explores the gap between the popular and the critical responses to these novels.[8]

It is known that her novels are marketed exclusively for an Indian audience, not for an international readership, and so far her books are distributed mainly in India.[9] Dé receives fan-mail about her novels from all over India, from men and from women. Nothing is known about the age or background of these fans. Nevertheless, a few groups of readers may be identified. Many of Bombay's social set were targeted by the publicity campaign for her first book. This was called 'Are you in it?' and is said to have led to many reading it in the hope or dread that they would find themselves featured and for the fun of recognizing characters. Another group of readers is likely to be that which knows about Shobha Dé through her other work, in particular her newspaper columns, the nearest one finds to society gossip. A further group undoubtedly reads the books to be shocked and titillated by the lifestyle of Bombay's rich and famous, whose central concerns they perceive as being the large amounts of 'sex and shopping' described in the books.

In the absence of any research, the reasons underlying the popular reception of Dé's work remain open to discussion. However, the reviews may be analysed more easily. Many condemned the novels as trash. For example,

> To her, the novel is an extension of the Media Column ... conspicuous absence of plot, character and prose panache is self-evident: one doesn't read De to discuss the inner depths of human nature (one reads her to be amused ...).[10]

While many criticized them for being pornographic:[11]

> a smorgasbord of sex, sleaze and glitz ... dollops of souped-up sex, bitchy one-liners and high society kinks.[12]

Some reviews are more ambivalent in their assessment of Dé:

> I couldn't put down Shobha Dé's new book, 'Strange Obsession,' and I didn't even like it.[13]

and

> One can't say much about the literary merit of the book, except that one emerges more knowledgeable about the names of leading international labels in wines, perfumes, undergarments and leather goods. [But nevertheless Dé] writes with remarkable ease and felicity.[14]

However, it is interesting that a major theme of the criticism of Dé is that of supposed or possible influences in her work. The most important are seen as being western pulp fiction,[15] the Hindi movie[16] and the film magazine.[17] Many of the criticisms of Dé's writing are made of these genres. For example:

> De's [newspaper] columns are far more readable and better instances of fiction [than her novels] ... The story is vapid [its] cardboard characters ... do not even possess the merits of stereotypes ...[18]

> her characters ... have been churned out of gossip columns of a film magazine ... blatant plagiarisms from the cine magazines that provide such melodramatic overtures week after week for gullible and naive readers ...[19]

I argue here that methods used for studying these genres may be used towards an understanding of Dé: popular fiction for questions of readership, the Hindi movie for the underlying aesthetic and the film magazines as a foundation for style and the narrative construction of Dé herself. These genres are all despised by the old middle class and seem to have their major markets in the new middle classes, showing once again a return to the theme of 'taste', discussed in Chapter 3 above.

There is a large market for popular English fiction in India, whether Mills & Boon-type romances or airport novels. It is not written in India but is either imported or reprinted in cheaper Indian editions. Although a large number of romances are published in the vernacular languages, Dé is the first to write 'sex and shopping' novels in India. There are clearly western parallels for this type of novel; Jackie Collins and Judith Krantz are the most frequently cited in connection with Dé. While there are undoubtedly links between Dé's novels and this genre of English writing, the complexities need to be explored, the issue being clearly more complex than the relocation of western popular novels to an Indian situation.

This genre receives little critical attention in the west from the critics of literary magazines and the broadsheet newspapers, where it is largely ignored. (It is itself noteworthy that Dé's novels have been reviewed alongside art novels written in English, rather than being categorized as belonging to a different genre.[20]) However, the popular novel has not been ignored by western academics, and the use of similar approaches to Dé's work may be more rewarding.

This would involve surveys of readership, a study of the economics of publishing,[21] a study of consumption (such as the surplus of detail throughout the novels about possessions, people's backgrounds, what people read, etc.). For example, ethnographies of reading may give insights which are supplementary to textual interpretation. These may suggest answers to the questions as to the popularity of Dé's books, the importance of variables such as age, class, education and gender among the readers, the pleasure that is obtained by the reader, the other books that her readers read. This may involve a project like Janice Radway's classic study[22] of the romance, using methods of ethnographic research (questionnaires, discussion, interviews, informal observation), drawing on a feminist revision of psychoanalytic approaches to reading, to look at questions of why, how and what in a group of women who read romances. The insights she gives as to the fulfilment of the pleasures of reading met by these narratives would provide insights into the pleasures found in Dé's texts.

Dé's novels make their links with the world of the Bombay cinema clear. Not only does this form the setting for many of her novels, but the original cover of *Starry Nights* has a painting by M. F. Husain, now one of the most famous artists in India and formerly a painter of movie hoardings in Bombay. The cover photograph of the author is a glamour-shot by India's top glamour photographer, Gautam Rajadhyaksha (Dé's cousin), whose work is mainly seen in film magazines, while Kaifi Azmi's verse opposite the title page is a lyric of a song in a classic Hindi film of the 1950s.[23] The original cover of *Socialite Evenings* has a photograph of the actress Neena Gupta, the first woman in India to identify herself as a 'single mother'.

Dé's characters mock the art cinema (see above, Chapter 4):

> It was Nitesh's frequent boast that he made films for money – first and last. He was not an aesthete he sneered. He made movies for moolah – mega-moolah. '*Arrey, chhodo yeh sab* art-fart *ki baatey*' ['Quit talking about all this arty-farty stuff'] he'd say to journalists who accused him of crassness. 'My movies sell. They're seen by millions. I give audiences three hours of *masala* [spice]. That is all. See it. Flush it. Forget it. But see it. At least, I'm better than all those pseudo art-film-wallahs whose films win awards in Timbuctoo. Nobody watches them – even when they are shown free on Doordarshan! *Bilkul faltu; ghatiya cheez* [useless nonsense].'[24]

The same criticisms of the popular Bombay cinema are made of Dé's novels: the ways in which a story is developed, the excess of emotion, mostly as melodrama, and the integration of spectacle – in film, the songs, dance, fights; in Dé's novels the emphasis on the glamour of consumption and sex – which interrupts any idea of realism. It is significant that Dé's critics see her use of *masala* and overloading as detracting from the merits of her work:

A tawdry tale thus far, but realistic enough as it is based on real life stories, but Shobha De moves on to a second part where her art goes to pieces, melodrama takes over.[25]

Further essential features of the Hindi film mentioned below are also highlighted by her critics as negative points in Dé's works. The analysis of these features and an exploration of their significance to the audience in recent studies of the Hindi film[26] may prove fruitful for a study of Dé's work.

The major theme of the Hindi film is the conflict between good and bad.[27] The film occurs in the operation of an ideal moral universe, the narrative often being constructed around tensions within this universe, usually those based on kinship or morality. In the ideal world fate and religion are accepted and there is respect for kinship, controlled sexuality and, most important of all, emotional bonds. Bad is the polar opposite of good. Good is most often traditional and personified by a mother figure, evil is often explicitly westernized and personified by a male villain and/or a female vamp. The hero and/or heroine mediate and restore the balance of good, often reconciling modernity and traditionalism.

Many of these features are shared with Dé's novels. A closer look at the second novel, *Starry Nights*, itself set in the world of the Hindi movie, shows this clearly.

A south Indian actress, Aasha Rani, pushed into Bombay films by her mother, becomes the reigning sex symbol and sleeps with a number of actors and producers. She then makes her 'fatal career-move – she falls in love' (cover blurb) with the reigning superstar. He soon tires of her and after trying various ways of getting rid of her finally succeeds by provoking a public confrontation with her and exposing her past in porn films, at which he humiliates her. She runs off to Dubai, then Madras, experiments with lesbian affairs and attempts suicide before going to New Zealand with the son of a business magnate. When his father lures his son back with money, she is left stranded until she meets and marries a New Zealand fan of hers. Five years of suburban domesticity follow before she returns to Madras to find that her sister has usurped her throne. She separates from her husband and goes to live in his flat in London, where she unwittingly enters the underworld of arms-dealers. Forced to flee to Bombay, she attempts a come-back which goes disastrously wrong. Her sister falls foul of the underworld and is attacked by an acid-hurling Mafia don, while Aasha Rani is beaten up by a gang of toughs. All this suffering leads to a family reunion. They go back to reopen the family studio in Madras in the hope that Aasha's daughter will one day become a star.

There are also a number of important differences with the film story, the most notable being in the role of the hero. In the Hindi film, the hero is always the central character, the person who is the focus of the whole story. In Dé's writing the hero is largely absent, inadequate or marginal and the men are important only in their relation to the heroine. The heroine, in turn, is key to Dé's books, whose central narratives chart her development from innocence/ignorance to self-awareness, although, like the film, her sexuality is always brought under control.

Bombay is the desired place to be in Dé's novels. The west is not seen as being of great importance to anyone; it is sketchy and unreal, more of a giant supermarket than a place of interest. As in Hindi films, those who go there do not interact with it in any meaningful way, but deal only with other South Asians. This provides a strong contrast with the English 'art' novel in India, where the encounter with the west is nearly always a major feature. Bombay may be a city of 'ecological imperialism' in its physical appearance but it now wishes to be an independent, cosmopolitan city on the lines of Singapore.

The critics have seen clearly the connection between Dé's novels and the film magazines. These lie in two major features: the construction of the star and the use of language. Dé was editor of one of the most popular of these magazines,[28] and it is said that it was she who was responsible for bringing in the most scandalous stories. She is also said to have introduced the use of Bombay English with a smattering of Bombay Hindi, full of innuendo, *double entendre* and puns.

> Don't worry. Akshay will come back to you. Leave it all to me. I'm expert, *yaar*. The number of *filmi* marriages I have saved. *Toba!* I've even lost count by now. Your husband must have been seduced by that whore in his weak moments – all men have them. ALL! Or she may have used *jaadutona*. Black magic. Who knows? And these South Indians! They just can't leave our men alone. Their own must be impo *yaar*. They look pretty limp.[29]

The star magazines (see Chapter 6) feature in her writing:

> Aasha Rani had seen *Showbiz*. Everybody read it – cover to cover. Even in Madras. She had known that if she got a write-up in it she'd immediately get the attention she'd been craving for. But after that? She had wanted to wait. She'd wanted to sign a film before being picked up by the press.[30]

This view of the star is significant in constructing a star persona and makes the star herself (or himself) into a text, running parallel to the roles played on-screen, and indeed even intertwined with it.[31]

The negotiation of the role of the heroine in Dé's novels has many similarities with the life of the heroines described in the film magazines. Rumour and gossip surround the heroines in the magazines, but they tread a delicate balance between scandal and the traditional values of kinship and sexuality. Dé's style also shows features of the film magazine, in the lifestyles of the stars, the demolition of characters, the very nature of the gossip and the use of the same form of language for the dialogues – a form unique to Bombay.

Some of Dé's narratives draw on specific narratives from these magazines. For example Aasha Rani's story weaves together strands of narratives from the lives of a number of top stars, such as Rekha (a father in a high position in the Madras industry, who disowns her mother), Zeenat Aman (the hotel brawl), Parveen Babi (the disappearance), while Akshay shares a number of features with Amitabh Bachchan, the greatest superstar of all time. However, she includes details about the underbelly of the film world which are never included in these magazines – the underworld financiers, the casting couch, lesbian film journalists, gay heroes, etc.

In the same way, Dé herself has become a star, her life being as famous as her work. Dé is undoubtedly one of Bombay's most prominent celebrities and is certainly its first celebrity author. Western TV programmes about the glamour of Bombay all contain the obligatory interview with Dé to reveal this side of the city.[32] The critics are uncertain how to deal with the celebrity author, and some of the reviews of the novels are more about Dé than her work, whether banal comments of the type,

> Shobha is very good-looking and refined and polite in real life.[33]

or comments about her talent as her ability to write filth and to gain publicity.[34] One reviewer suggests that Dé is trapped by her public image ('as the acid queen who spares nobody') and that people criticize her novels without having read them.[35] Another suggests that

> the cause for the carnivalesque reviews is not the novel. It is the fact of a woman (married with six children etc.) 'daring' to write such stuff.[36]

These magazines are published in English and I have already mentioned that one of the important features of Dé's work is her use of English for the popular novel. English is used in other genres of popular culture in India, including media (cable and satellite, newspapers to some extent), women's magazines, etc. Although Bombay films are made in Hindi, the most popular star magazines are written in English, and within the movie world jokes are made about stars whose English is not very good.

Although 'Bombay Hindi' is spoken by nearly everyone in Bombay, a number of groups use English as a first or at least as a second language.[37] These groups are the younger Bombayites, educated in English-medium schools, who live or socialize in mixed ethnic groups. They often have restricted competence in speaking languages other than English, and certainly have very limited competence in reading and writing. However, the language used by Dé is not British English, nor even Indian English, but a form of Bombay or filmi English. Just as Bombay Hindi has a large admixture of English, so Bombay English is mixed with Hindi. Dé's characters speak a very marked form of this Bombay English, with Gujarati or Tamil pronunciations added where appropriate:

> Aasha Rani ... genuinely believed she had finally found the friend she was looking for. A trendy, up-market, Bombay friend. 'I'm a survivor, *yaar*,' Linda loved to say. 'In this *badmaash* [of bad guys] city and this *badmaash* business, you have to be one. You are a real *bachchi* [kid] – a mama's girl. You should be on your own. Live life for yourself.'[38]

Dé developed this language when she wrote for the popular English magazines. It has been taken up by the 'art' novel, notably in the writing of Salman Rushdie. This language is difficult for someone who doesn't know Hindi and doesn't have some acquaintance with specifically Bombay slang.

There is no doubt that Dé delights in the rich language of abuse, and she is criticized for this by her reviewers:

> The language of the work ... smacks of the gutter in its putrid contents. ... It serves no real purpose.[39]

> peppered with four-letter words, ... words like *randi* [whore] and *haramzaadi* [bastard] spice up the pot-pourri.[40]

However, the reviewers themselves cannot resist imitating her style by alliteration and constant punning on Dé's name, calling her 'the rani of raunch',[41] 'the sultana of sleaze',[42] and finding titles for articles about her such as 'Porn again De'[43] and 'A De in the life of popular culture'.[44]

It is clear from this preliminary analysis that what Dé has done is not derivative but innovative in that she has harnessed a number of features from dominant forms of Indian popular culture, the Hindi cinema and its magazines, into the Indian novel.[45] While various kinds of popular novels are found in the vernacular languages, Dé's novels represent a radical departure from the whole tradition of the Indian novel in the ways outlined above.

The novel in English continues to maintain its hegemonic grip in literary circles and over literary studies in India. Even fifty years after Independence the Indian university syllabuses are dominated by the teaching of non-Indian, usually British, English literatures.[46] Some of the writings in English by Indians are included on certain papers in the syllabus; agitation by some academics, notably Meenakshi Mukherjee, has led to the more progressive academic institutions giving these authors a more prominent role and even to including the study of other Indian literatures translated into English. (The study of literatures in indigenous languages at university is seen as a pursuit to be followed only by those who cannot gain admission to the more prestigious courses.) Apart from the films of Satyajit Ray, the Indian English novel is the only product invested with cultural capital in India which has achieved worldwide recognition. Dé's new form of writing is seen as being in defiance of values of this novel and her role as the first popular, best-selling novelist in English has precipitated the debate in the English press in India about the high/elite and the low/popular forms of fiction.[47]

It seems that it is here that the furore over Dé's work lies in this tension between the culture of the old and new middle classes. In the west, bestsellers in English are seen as a separate genre and are not reviewed in the 'serious' press. Works of celebrity authors are barely mentioned in the literary pages although they may be the subject of the feature pages. Reviews of Dé's novels have appeared in the Indian press alongside works of 'high' literature and they are taught in prestigious universities around the world. Dé launched her autobiography in the UK at the cultural wing of the Indian High Commission and she runs courses in creative writing. This has led to her work being, to some degree, legitimized. Dé is amused by this critical reception of her work:

> 'I didn't set out to write a textbook,' smiles the Prescribed One, 'And if many more layers of meaning emerge from the books than I'd intended, that'll be a hoot. It'll amuse me no end.'[48]

Dé's work has been dismissed largely as part of the rejection of the new middle classes, who form much of her readership and whose lifestyles are depicted in her fiction. Dé's own social ambiguity – as wife of a rich business man, yet a successful career woman; a journalist for the broadsheets, yet the writer of popular fiction; as personally tasteful and stylish, yet down to earth in her writing, along with her own skilled manoeuvering of media – has allowed her to gain some legitimacy. It remains to be seen whether she is a unique phenomenon or whether she is starting a trend for a new literature of the new middle classes.

Dé's novels, like Yash Chopra's films and the film magazines, depict the aspirations and fantasies of the new middle classes. While the financial capital to sustain these actual lifestyles lies beyond the means of most of the readers and viewers, they can enjoy them vicariously in the pleasures of consuming these texts. While lifestyle possibilities afforded by this wealth form the surface of these texts, the deeper concerns are to do with loving relationships, sex and romance. Women are central to these texts, no longer as upholders of the feudal concept of *izzat* ('honour') as in *Mother India*, but as emotionally literate and mature, bourgeois figures. They often have to choose between love and money, the wise always preferring the former. The attractions and pleasures of wealth are only part of, not substitutes for, romantic, erotic and familial love, which is depicted as the major source of happiness. As Aziz Mirza put it so nicely in his film *Yes Boss!* (1997): 'All you want is money, all you need is love.'

Notes

1. *Socialite Evenings* (1988), *Starry Nights* (1991), *Sisters* (1992), *Strange Obsession* (1992), *Sultry Days* (1994), *Snapshots* (1995) and *Second Thoughts* (1996). She has also published a collection of short stories, *Small Betrayals*.
2. *Society*, *Celebrity* and *Stardust*.
3. *Swaabhimaan*.
4. A selection of her newspaper columns was published in Dé, 1994b.
5. Only speculative articles are available, such as Sunil Shetty 'De in, De out.' *Seminar 384: New Writing in English*, August 1991: 40–2.
6. *Socialite Evenings* had sold 35,000 by 1992 whereas most fiction in India is thought to sell fewer than a thousand copies. These huge sales are reputed to allow her publisher Penguin India to publish more so-called 'serious' writing.
7. Quoted in W. Dalrymple, 'India's empress of erotica', *The Sunday Times*, 12 April 1992: 30–7.
8. Dé dedicated her collection of short stories to her critics.
9. *Sultry Days* and *Socialite Evenings* were published by Simon & Schuster, New York, in 1995, but Dé's major market is India.
10. Subhash K. Jha, 'Starry nights with Shobha De', *The Times of India* (Patna),

7 July 1991.
11. Although ancient India's erotic arts are well documented, no study of Indian pornography has yet been published.
12. Sugita Katyal, 'Collins clone', *India Today*, 15 April 1992: 163.
13. Simran Bhargava, *The Pioneer*, 9 January 1993.
14. Krishna Menon, 'More of the hot, steamy stuff', *South Asian*, July 1992: 63–4.
15. As in Katyal's title, see n. 12.
16. Nirmal Mitra, 'Big, bad world of Hindi films', *India Abroad*, 3 January 1992: 30.
17. Shubra Mazumdar, Review of *Starry Nights*, *Sunday Mail*, 7 July 1991: 34–5.
18. Farzana Versey, 'A vapid assembly-line product', *Weekend Observer*, 11 September 1992.
19. Mazumdar, see n. 17.
20. Of course, the boundaries between 'classic' and 'popular' novel are not clear-cut. See, for example, Hawkins, 1990.
21. There are clear parallels to the outcry that was heard in the UK when Penguin published the writing of Shirley Conran.
22. Radway, 1987.
23. *Pyaasa*, dir. Guru Dutt, 1957.
24. Dé, 1991: 20–1.
25. S. Krishan, 'Heroine in a whirl', *The Hindu*, Tuesday, 2 July 1991.

26. Notably in the work of Thomas, Vasudevan, Nandy, *et al.* See bibliography.
27. See Thomas, 1989, and Dissanayake and Sahai, 1992, for an analysis of the construction of evil among viewers of *Sholay*, one of the all-time hit films in India.
28. *Stardust,* see Chapter 6.
29. *Starry Nights*: 46.
30. *Starry Nights*: 31.
31. See Chapter 4 above, also Dyer, 1979, on the life of the star as text. For a study of Indian stars, see Gandhy and Thomas, 1991.
32. E.g. *Bombay Chat*, Channel 4, 1993/4, *Clive James' Postcard from Bombay*, BBC, 1995.
33. Amita Malik, 'Starry nights', *Sunday Observer*, 9 June 1991: 22.
34. Versey (n. 18).
35. Subhash K. Jha, 'Starry nights with Shobha De', *The Times of India* (Patna), 7 July 1991.
36. Prema Nandakumar, 'Naked nonsense', *Deccan Herald*, 20 September 1992.
37. See Chapters 2 and 6, above. For a summary of the language situation in India, see Fasold, 1984: 20–30. See also Brass, 1990, in particular chapter 5, 'Language problems': 129–34.
38. *Starry Nights*: 76.
39. Shubra Mazumdar, Review of *Starry Nights, Sunday Mail*, 7 July 1991: 34–5.
40. Katyal (n. 12).
41. Madhu Jain, *India Today*, 15 April 1992: 163.
42. Katyal (n. 12).
43. Jain (n. 41).
44. Rachel Dwyer and Keith Fernandes, 'A De in the life of popular culture', *Sunday Times of India*, 9 April 1995.
45. As have a number of other writers, notably Rushdie. Rushdie draws on the Bombay film extensively for his work. See a summary of this in Chakravarty, 1993: 1–4. Jennings, 1993, uses the world of the Hindi cinema as a backdrop but does not engage with it in depth. Tharoor, 1994, is a send-up of the whole industry which is often amusing and accurate but fails to analyse or understand its cultural significance. See also Meer, 1995.
46. Sunder Rajan, 1992.
47. An interesting reappropriation of terms 'high' and 'low' is made by audiences who view western art films as pornography. For example, Peter Greenaway's *The Cook, the Thief, the Wife and Her Lover* was advertised in Bombay in 1991 as a pornographic film.
48. Ranjit Hoskote, 'The dawning of a new De', *The Times of India*, 2 April 1995.

Appendix

Film Synopses

Kabhi Kabhie ('Sometimes') 1976

Starring: Waheeda Rehman, Amitabh Bachchan, Shashi Kapoor, Raakhee Gulzar, Neetu Singh, Rishi Kapoor, Naseem, Simi Garewal, Parikshit Sahni
Story: Pamela Chopra; Director of photography: Kay Gee; Written by Sagar Sarhadi; Lyrics: Sahir Ludhianvi; Music: Khayyam
Directed and produced by Yash Chopra

Amit Malhotra (Amitabh Bachchan) woos Pooja (Raakhee) with his poetry. Although they fall in love they agree that they should not transgress their parents' wishes so she marries an architect Vijay Khanna (Shashi Kapoor) and Amit abandons poetry to take over the family business, a quarry. Amit's parting gift is a book of his poetry, which she has inspired: *Kabhi Kabhie*. Vijay, while no poet, loves poetry and presents her with this book on their wedding night. Pooja sings the poem to her husband as he undresses her. She falls in love with him and they form a happy family with their son, Vicki (Rishi Kapoor), sharing close and loving relationships. Vicki becomes a jockey, falls in love with Pinky (Neetu Singh), the daughter of Dr and Mrs Kapoor (Simi Garewal and Parikshit Sahni). Kapoor is the Khannas' doctor and both families readily agree to the marriage when the children tell them of their love. Meanwhile Amit is interviewed on television by Pooja; he recites a revised version of *Kabhi Kabhie* where hope has been replaced by loss and misery. On visiting the Khannas, he leaves abruptly. The Kapoors and the Khannas discuss the dilemma they face in telling Pinky she is adopted. Although the Khannas advise against it, they decide to do so and give her the name of her natural mother. Vicki tries to dissuade Pinky, but when she goes to find her mother, Vicki follows her on his father's advice. Pinky's mother, Anjali (Waheeda Rehman), invites her to stay, pretending to her husband, Amit, and her daughter, Sweetie (Naseem) that she is her niece. Her excessive affection is noted with anger by Amit, whose love is entirely centred on Sweetie. Vicki arrives but hides his connection with Pinky; Sweetie falls in love with him and persuades Amit to employ him in the quarry. Vijay brings Pooja with him on a business trip to build a hotel. When Amit comes to collect them for dinner, Vijay overhears him and Pooja talking of their previous affair, and, although he realizes the awful irony of his giving Pooja the book on their wedding night, he bears no grudge against either of them for their past affair. In contrast, when Amit finds out that Pinky is the illegitimate child of Anjali and an airforce pilot who died before their marriage, he rejects Anjali, branding her a sinner. Events come to a head when Sweetie, on discovering that Vicki and Pinky are lovers, tries to commit suicide by heading for the part of the quarry where blasting is to occur. She is saved by the concerted efforts of all. Amit suddenly remembers Anjali and rushes back to the house to find her about to leave. He expresses his regret for his lack of understanding. The film ends with the marriage of Vicki and Pinky; the three sets of parents performing the rites, with Sweetie as the bridesmaid.

Mother India, 1957

Starring: Nargis, Sunil Dutt, Raaj Kumar, Rajendra Kumar, Kanhaiyalal
Screenplay: Wajahat Mirza, S. Ali Raza; Lyrics: Shakeel Badayuni; Music: Naushad; Camera: Faredoon Irani
Directed and produced by Mehboob Khan

Radha (Nargis) is honoured by being asked to open a dam. She recalls her life, beginning with her arrival in the village as a young bride. Her beauty and hard work win her universal approval, but her mother-in-law has mortgaged the family land to pay for the wedding, leaving Radha and Shyam (Raaj Kumar) and their children in debt to the village money-lender, Sukhilal (Kanhaiyalal). Encouraged by Radha to plough uncultivated land, Shyam loses his arms in an accident and fearing he is just a burden, abandons his family. Radha believes he will return, and continues to try to pay Sukhilal while avoiding his sexual advances. Floods destroy the village, and one of Radha's sons is lost in the flood. The other two sons are polar opposites: Ram (Rajendra Kumar) is the good, law-abiding son, while Birju (Sunil Dutt) is a rebel, who attempts to take the law into his own hands. Birju falls in love with the schoolteacher, but his major goal is restoring his mother's honour, symbolized by the wedding bangles she has mortgaged to Sukhilal. Birju kidnaps Sukhilal's daughter, and Radha, forced to choose between her love for Birju and the honour of the village, kills her beloved son.

Pakeezah ('The pure one') 1971

Starring: Meena Kumari, Raaj Kumar, Ashok Kumar
Screenplay: Kamal Amrohi; Lyrics: Kamal Amrohi, Kaif Bhopali, Majrooh Sultanpuri, Kaifi Azmi; Music: Ghulam Mohammed, Naushad; Camera: Josef Wirsching
Directed and produced by Kamal Amrohi

The courtesan Nargis (Meena Kumari) hopes to marry her lover Shahabuddin (Ashok Kumar), but is rejected by his family. She goes to a cemetery, where she dies giving birth to a daughter, Sahibjaan, who in turn grows up to become a courtesan (Meena Kumari). She is looked after by her aunt, Nawabjaan, who keeps Sahibjaan's lineage secret. Sahibjaan falls in love with Salim (Raaj Kumar), who wishes to marry her but is forbidden by his uncle, Shahabuddin. Sahibjaan is invited to dance at Salim's wedding, where she dances on glass, lacerating her feet. Shahabuddin is reconciled with his daughter, and Sahibjaan and Salim are married.

Silsila ('The affair') 1981

Starring: Shashi Kapoor, Amitabh Bachchan, Jaya Bachchan, Rekha, Sanjeev Kumar
Story: Mrs Preeti Bedi; Screenplay: Sagar Sarhadi and Yash Chopra; Lyrics: Javed Akhtar, Rajendra Krishan, Hasan Kamal, Nida Fazli, Harivanshrai Bachchan; Music: Shiv-Hari (Shivkumar Sharma and Hariprasad Chaurasia)
Directed and produced by Yash Chopra

Shekhar (Shashi Kapoor), an airforce pilot, and Shobha (Jaya Bachchan) are lovers who are about to be married. He invites his younger brother Amit (Amitabh Bachchan) to meet her and they discuss the marriage with her mother. Amit meets Chandni (Rekha) at a wedding and falls in love. An aspiring playwright, he invites her to a performance, after which romance follows. He tells his brother he intends to marry her but when Shekhar is killed in the (1971?) war, leaving Shobha pregnant, Amit agrees to marry her to save everyone's honour. Amit is involved in a car accident in which Shobha loses the baby. Her physician, Dr Anand (Sanjeev Kumar), turns out to be Chandni's husband. Chandni visits Amit, they meet subsequently when he explains why he had to leave her and their affair recommences. Shobha meanwhile begins to fall in love with Amit. His friend, Vidyarthi, and Shobha become suspicious of his relationship with Chandni but nothing is said. Chandni knocks a boy down when she is out with Amit at night. They go to the police station and narrowly avoid meeting Dr Anand. However, the policeman turns out to be Shobha's cousin, and, recognizing Amit, reproaches him. At Dr Anand's Holi party, Amit consumes too much *bhaang* (marijuana paste), and sings a traditional song about a cuckold. As he sings, his relationship with Chandni becomes clear to the other spouses, who later discuss this in parables. A scene (dream sequence?) is shown where Shobha and Jaya agree to fight for Amit. Meanwhile Amit and Chandni decide to set up a new life together. While Chandni leaves while her husband is out of town, Amit tells Shobha he is leaving her. Shobha declares her resolve to win him back. Amit and Chandni meet Amit's friend and go to his parents' Golden Wedding. The ceremony reminds them of the sanctity of marriage. Suddenly the phone rings: Shobha tells Amit Dr Anand has been in a plane crash. Amit and Chandni rush to the site: as Amit rushes to help Dr Anand, Shobha reveals she is pregnant. Amit promises to return to her. Amit saves Dr Anand, who leaves on a stretcher, accompanied by Chandni. Shobha and Amit are reunited.

Films Discussed

Aan, dir. Mehboob Khan, 1952
Admi aur Insaan, dir. Yash Chopra, 1969
Agneepath, dir. Mukul Anand, 1990
Alam Ara, dir. Ardeshir Irani, 1931
An Evening in Paris, dir. S. Samanta, 1967
Anand, dir. Hrishkesh Mukherjee, 1970
Andaz, dir. Mehboob Khan, 1949
Aradhana, dir. Shakti Samanta, 1969
Arth, dir. Mahesh Bhatt, 1982
Aurat, dir. Mehboob Khan, 1940
Awāra, dir. Raj Kapoor, 1951
Bandit Queen, dir. Shekhar Kapur, 1994
Bobby, dir. Raj Kapoor, 1973
Bombay, dir. Mani Rathnam, 1995
Chandni, dir. Yash Chopra, 1989
Daag, dir. Yash Chopra, 1973
Dar, dir. Yash Chopra, 1993
Deewaar, dir. Yash Chopra, 1975
Devdas, dir. P.C. Barua, 1935

Devdas, dir. Bimal Roy, 1955
Dharmaputra, dir. Yash Chopra, 1961
Dhool ka phool, dir. Yash Chopra, 1959
Dil To Pagal Hai, dir. Yash Chopra, 1997
Dilwale Dulhaniya Le Jayenge, dir. Aditya Chopra, 1995
Faasle, dir. Yash Chopra, 1985
Fire, dir. Deepa Mehta, 1996
Ganga Jumna, dir. Nitin Bose, 1961
Ghare Baire, dir. Satyajit Ray, 1984
Guide, dir. Vijay Anand, 1965
Hazaar Chaurasi ki maa, dir. Govind Nihalani, 1998
Ittefaq, dir. Yash Chopra, 1969
Kaagaz ke phool, dir. Guru Dutt, 1959
Kabhi Kabhie, dir. Yash Chopra, 1976
Kala Pathar, dir. Yash Chopra, 1979
Kaliya mardan, dir. D.G. Phalke, 1919
Kamasutra, dir. Mira Nair, 1997
Khalnayak, dir. Subhash Ghai, 1993
Khuddar, dir. Iqbal Durrani, 1994
Kuch kuch hota hai, dir. Karan Johar, 1998
Lamhe, dir. Yash Chopra, 1991
Lanka dahan, dir. D.G. Phalke, 1917
Lawaaris, dir. Prakash Mehra, 1981
Madhumati, dir. Bimal Roy, 1958
Main khiladi tu anari, dir. Sameer Malkan, 1994
Maine pyar kiya, dir. Sooraj Barjatya, 1989
Mashaal, dir. Yash Chopra, 1984
Mother India, dir. Mehboob Khan, 1957
Muqaddar ka Sikander, dir. Prakash Mehra, 1978
Namak haram, dir. Hrishikesh Mukherjee, 1973
Naseeb, dir. Manmohan Desai, 1981
Pakeezah, dir. Kamal Amrohi, 1971
Parampara, dir. Yash Chopra, 1992
Pardes, dir. Subhash Ghai, 1997
Pather Panchali, dir. Satyajit Ray, 1955
Pukar, dir. Sohrab Modi, 1939
Qayamat se qayamat tak, dir. Mansoor Khan, 1988
Raja Babu, dir. David Dhawan, 1994
Raja Harischandra, dir. D.G. Phalke, 1913
Razia Sultan, dir. Kamal Amrohi, 1983
Rudaali, dir. Kalpana Lajmi, 1992

Sahib, bibi aur ghulam, dir. Abrar Alvi, 1962
Sangam, dir. Raj Kapoor, 1964
Sholay, dir. Ramesh Sippy, 1975
Shree 420, dir. Raj Kapoor, 1955
Shri Krishna janma, dir. D.G. Phalke, 1919
Silsila, dir. Yash Chopra, 1981
Trishul, dir. Yash Chopra, 1978
Umrao Jaan, dir. Muzaffar Ali, 1981
Ustav, dir. Girish Karnad, 1984
Vijay, dir. Yash Chopra, 1988
Waqt, dir. Yash Chopra, 1965
Yes boss! dir. Aziz Mirza, 1997
Zanjeer, dir. Prakash Mehra, 1973

Filmography of Yash Chopra

Films directed by Yash Chopra

		Producer:
1959	*Dhool ka phool*	BR Films
1961	*Dharmaputra*	BR Films
1965	*Waqt*	BR Films
1969	*Admi aur Insaan*	BR Films
	Ittefaq	BR Films
1973	*Joshila*	Trimurti Films
	Daag	Yash Raj Films
1975	*Deewaar*	Trimurti Films
1976	*Kabhi Kabhie*	Yash Raj Films
1978	*Trishul*	Trimurti Films
1979	*Kala Pathar*	Yash Raj Films
1981	*Silsila*	Yash Raj Films
1984	*Mashaal*	Yash Raj Films
1985	*Faasle*	Yash Raj Films
1988	*Vijay*	Yash Raj Films
1989	*Chandni*	Yash Raj Films
1991	*Lamhe*	Yash Raj Films
1992	*Parampara*	Nadiadwala
1993	*Darr*	Yash Raj Films
1997	*Dil to pagal hai*	Yash Raj Films

Films produced and presented by Yash Chopra

		Director:
1977	*Doosra Aadmi*	Ramesh Talwar
1979	*Noorie*	Manmohan Krishna
1981	*Nakhuda*	Dilip Naik
1989	*Sawaal*	Ramesh Talwar
1993	*Aaina*	Deepak Sarin
1994	*Yeh Dillagi*	Naresh Malhotra
1995	*Dilwale Dulhania Le Jayenge*	Aditya Chopra

Awards

Filmfare

1965	*Waqt*	Best Director
1969	*Ittefaq*	Best Director
1973	*Daag*	Best Director
1975	*Deewaar*	Best Director
1995	*Dilwale Dulhania Le Jayenge*	Best Producer
1997	*Dil To Pagal Hai*	Best Film

Other

1962	*Dharamputra*	President's Gold Medal
1989	*Chandni*	National Award for best film providing popular and wholesome entertainment
1994	*Darr*	National Award for best film providing popular and wholesome entertainment

The films have won many other awards for music, songs, best actors, etc. *Deewaar*, *Dilwale Dulhania Le Jayenge* and *Dil To Pagal Hai* took nearly all the *Filmfare* awards in 1975, 1995 and 1997.

Glossary

babu	Indian clerk (derogatory)
bhadralok	gentlefolk
bhaiyya	brother; man from north India
bhajan	Hindu devotional song
bhakti	loving devotion
bhava	emotion
crore (Rs)	10 million rupees
Dalit	oppressed person; formerly called 'Untouchable'
darshan	sight, vision, act of seeing as part of worship
desi	indigenous
dhvani	voice; theory of literature
Doordarshan	Indian state television
dost	friend
garbi	form of Gujarati lyric
ghazal	form of lyric poem
Holi	spring festival associated with Krishna
kama	love
kavya	poetry, literature
lakh	one hundred thousand
Mahabharata	title of epic poem
mujra	style of dance associated with courtesans
pativrata	faithful wife
puja	act of worship
Ramayana	title of epic poem
rasa	sentiment
shakti	female power
shastra	authoritative text
Shiv Sena	Maharashtrian political party
shringara-rasa	sentiment of love
swadeshi	from one's own country
zenana	women's quarters, harem

Bibliography

Abramson, Paul and Steven D. Pinkerton (eds) (1995) *Sexual Nature, Sexual Culture*. Chicago: University of Chicago Press.

Ali, Daud (1996) 'Regimes of Pleasure in Early India: A Genealogy of Practice at the Chola Court.' Unpublished PhD, University of Chicago.

Alter, Joseph S. (1996) 'The celibate wrestler: sexual chaos, embodied balance and competitive politics in north India', in Patricia Uberoi (ed.), *Social Reform, Sexuality and the State*. New Delhi: Sage, pp. 108–31.

Alter, Joseph S. (1997) *The Wrestler's Body: Identity and Ideology in North India*. New Delhi: Munshiram Manoharlal.

Amin, Shahid (1984) 'Gandhi as Mahatma: Gorakhpur district, Eastern U. P., 1921–2', in Ranajt Guha (ed.), *Subaltern Studies III*.

Anderson, Benedict (1991) *Imagined Communities: Reflections on the Origin and Spread of Nationalism*, 2nd edn. London: Verso.

Anderson, Digby and Peter Mullen (eds) (1998) *Faking It: The Sentimentalisation of Modern Society*. London: Penguin.

Ang, Ien (1985) *Watching Dallas: Soap Opera and the Melodramatic Imagination*. London: Routledge.

Appadurai, Arjun (1988) 'How to make a national cuisine: cookbooks in contemporary India', *Comparative Studies in Society and History*, 30 (January): 3–24.

Appadurai, Arjun (1995) 'Playing with modernity: the decolonization of Indian cricket', in Carol Breckenridge (ed.), *Consuming Modernity: Public Culture in a South Asian World*. Minneapolis and London: University of Minnesota Press, pp. 23–48.

Appadurai, Arjun (1997) *Modernity at Large: Cultural Dimensions of Globalization*. Delhi: Oxford University Press.

Appadurai, Arjun and Carol Breckenridge (1995) 'Public modernity in India', in Carol Breckenridge (ed.), *Consuming Modernity: Public Culture in a South Asian World*. Minneapolis and London: University of Minnesota Press, pp. 1–22.

Appadurai, Arjun, Frank J. Korom and Margaret A. Mills (eds) (1991) *Gender, Genre and Power in South Asian Expressive Traditions*. Philadelphia: University of Pennsylvania Press.

Babb, Lawrence A. (1975) *The Divine Hierarchy: Popular Hinduism in Central India*. New York: Columbia University Press.

Babb, Lawrence A. (1981) 'Glancing: visual interaction in Hinduism', *Journal of Anthropological Research*, 37(4): 387–401.

Babb, Lawrence and Susan Wadley (eds) (1995) *Media and the Transformation of Religion in South Asia*. Philadelphia: University of Pennsylvania Press.

Bagchi, Amiya Kumar (1970) 'European and Indian entrepreneurship in India, 1900–30', in

E. Leach and S. N. Mukherjee (eds), *Elites in South Asia*. Cambridge: Cambridge University Press, pp. 79–94.

Bagchi, Jashodhara (1995) *Indian Women: Myth and Reality*. Hyderabad: Sangam Books.

Bakhtin, Mikhail M. (1981) *The Dialogic Imagination: Four Essays by M. M. Bakhtin*, trans. C. Emerson and M. Holquist. Austin: University of Texas Press. [Essays of 1934–41. Orig. pub. 1975.]

Ballard, Roger (ed.) (1994) *Desh Pardesh: The South Asian Experience in Britain*. London: Hurst & Company.

Banerjee, Sumanta (1989) *The Parlour and the Streets: Elite and Popular Culture in Nineteenth Century Calcutta*. Calcutta: Seagull Books.

Banerjee, Sumanta (1998) *Dangerous Outcast: The Prostitute in Nineteenth Century Bengal*. Calcutta: Seagull Books.

Banerjee-Guha, Swapna (1995) 'Urban development process in Bombay: planning for whom?', in Sujata Patel and Alice Thorner (eds), *Bombay: Metaphor for Modern India*. Bombay: Oxford University Press, pp. 100–12.

Banks, Marcus (1992) *Organizing Jainism in India and England*. Oxford: Clarendon Press.

Bardhan, Pranab (1985) *The Political Economy of Development in India*. Delhi: Oxford University Press.

Bardhan, Pranab (1988) 'Dominant proprietary classes and India's democracy', in Atul Kohli (ed.), *India's Democracy: An Analysis of Changing State–Society Relations*. Princeton: Princeton University Press, pp. 214–24.

Barnouw, Erik and S. Krishnaswamy (1980) *Indian Film*, 2nd edn. New York: Oxford University Press.

Barthes, Roland (1973) *Mythologies*. Selected and translated from the French *Mythologies* (1957) by Annette Lavers. London: Paladin Books.

Barthes, Roland (1975) *The Pleasure of the Text*. Introduction by Richard Howard. New York: Hill and Wang.

Barthes, Roland (1977) *Image, Music, Text*. Essays selected and translated by Stephen Heath. London: Fontana.

Barthes, Roland (1990) *Fragments: A Lover's Discourse*, trans. Richard Howard. London: Penguin.

Baskaran, Sundararaj Theodore (1981) *The Message Bearers: The Nationalist Politics and the Entertainment Media in South India*. With an introduction by Dr Christopher Baker. Madras: Cre-A.

Basu, Amrita (1992) *Two Faces of Protest: Contrasting Modes of Women's Activism in India*. Berkeley: University of California Press.

Baxi, Upendra and Bhikhu Parekh (eds) (1995) *Crisis and Change in Contemporary India*. New Delhi: Sage.

Bayly, Christopher (1983) *Rulers, Townsmen and Bazaars: North Indian Society in the Age of British Expansion, 1770–1870*. Cambridge: Cambridge University Press.

Beck, Brenda E. F. (1989) 'Core triangles in the folk epics of India', in Stuart Blackburn *et al.* (eds), *Oral Epics in India*. Berkeley: University of California Press, pp. 155–75.

Bennett, Lynn (1983) *Dangerous Wives and Sacred Sisters: Social and Symbolic Roles of High-Caste Women in Nepal*. New York: Columbia University Press.

Bhaduri, Amit and Deepak Nayyar (1996) *The Intelligent Person's Guide to Liberalisation*. New Delhi: Penguin.

Bhagvat, Vidyut (1995) 'Bombay in Dalit literature', in Sujata Patel and Alice Thorner (eds), *Bombay: Mosaic of Modern Culture*. Bombay: Oxford University Press, pp. 113–25.

Bharucha, Rustom (1995) 'Dismantling men: crisis of male identity in *Father, Son and Holy War*', *Third Text*, 3–16.

Bhatia, Gautam (1994) *Punjabi Baroque and Other Memories of Architecture*. New Delhi: Penguin.

Bhattacharyya, Narendra Nath (1975) *History of Indian Erotic Literature*. New Delhi: Munshiram Manoharlal.

Blackburn, Stuart H. (1989) 'Patterns of development for Indian oral epics', in Stuart H. Blackburn *et al.* (eds), *Oral Epics in India*. Berkeley: University of California Press, pp. 15–32.

Blackburn, Stuart H. and Joyce B. Flueckiger (1989) 'Introduction', in Blackburn *et al.* (eds), *Oral Epics in India*. Berkeley: University of California Press, pp. 1–14.

Blackburn, Stuart H. *et al.* (eds) (1989) *Oral Epics in India*. Berkeley: University of California Press.

Bordwell, David and Kristin Thompson (1990) *Film Art: An Introduction*. London: McGraw Hill.

Bose, Pradip Kumar (1995) 'Sons of the nation: child rearing in the new family', in Partha Chatterjee (ed.), *Texts of Power: Emerging Disciplines in Colonial Bengal*. Minneapolis: University of Minnesota Press, pp. 118–44.

Bose, Sugata and Ayesha Jalal (eds) (1997) *Nationalism, Democracy and Development: State and Politics in India*. Delhi: Oxford University Press.

Bourdieu, Pierre (1977) *Outline of a Theory of Practice*. Cambridge: Cambridge University Press.

Bourdieu, Pierre (1984) *Distinction: A Social Critique of the Judgement of Taste*, trans. Richard Nice. Cambridge, Mass.: Harvard University Press.

Bourdieu, Pierre (1993) *The Field of Cultural Production: Essays on Art and Literature*, ed. Randal Johnson. London: Polity Press.

Brass, Paul (1990) *The Politics of India since Independence (The New Cambridge History of India, IV.1)*. Cambridge: Cambridge University Press.

Breckenridge, Carol (ed.) (1995) *Consuming Modernity: Public Culture in a South Asian World*. Minneapolis and London: University of Minnesota Press.

Breckenridge, Carol A. and Peter van der Veer (eds) (1993) *Orientalism and the Postcolonial Predicament: Perspectives on South Asia*. Philadelphia: University of Pennsylvania Press.

Brockington, John L. (1981) *The Sacred Thread: Hinduism in Its Continuity and Diversity*. Edinburgh: Edinburgh University Press.

Brooks, Peter (1995) *The Melodramatic Imagination: Balzac, Henry James, Melodrama and the Mode of Excess*. New Haven: Yale University Press. [1976]

Brosius, Christiane and Melissa Butcher (eds) (1999) *Image Journeys: Audio-visual Media and Cultural Change in India*. New Delhi: Sage.

Brough, John (1968) *Poems from the Sanskrit*. Harmondsworth: Penguin.

Brown, Judith (1989) *Gandhi*. New Haven: Yale University Press.

Brown, Robert (1987) *Analyzing Love*. Cambridge: Cambridge University Press.

Bruzzi, Stella (1997) *Undressing Cinema: Clothing and Identity in the Movies*. London: Routledge.

Cannadine, David (1998) *Class in Britain*. New Haven: Yale University Press.

Carstairs, G. Morris (1958) *The Twice-Born: A Study of a Community of High-Caste Hindus*. Bloomington: Indiana University Press.

Chakravarti, Uma (1990) 'Whatever happened to the Vedic *dasi*? Orientalism, nationalism, and a script for the past', in Kumkum Sangari and Sudesh Vaid (eds), *Recasting*

Women: Essays in Indian Colonial History. New Brunswick, NJ: Rutgers University Press, pp. 27–87.

Chakravarti, Uma (1998) 'Inventing saffron history: a celibate hero rescues an emasculated nation', in Mary E. John and Janaki Nair (eds), *A Question of Silence? The Sexual Economies of Modern India.* New Delhi: Kali for Women, pp. 243–68.

Chakravarty, Sumita S. (1989) 'National identity and the realist aesthetic: Indian cinema of the Fifties', *Quarterly Review of Film and Video,* 11: 31–48.

Chakravarty, Sumita S. (1993) *National Identity in Indian Popular Cinema, 1947–1987.* Austin: University of Texas Press.

Chandavarkar, Raj (1994) *The Origins of Industrial Capitalism in India: Business Strategies and the Working Classes in Bombay, 1900–1940.* Cambridge: Cambridge University Press.

Chandra, Sudhir (1994) *The Oppressive Present: Literature and Social Consciousness in Colonial India.* Delhi: Oxford University Press.

Chandra, Vikram (1997) *Love and Longing in Bombay.* London: Faber.

Chatterjee, P. (1986) *Nationalist Thought and the Colonial World: A Derivative Discourse?* London: Zed Books for the United Nations University.

Chatterjee, Partha (1993) *The Nation and Its Fragments: Colonial and Postcolonial Histories.* Delhi: Oxford University Press.

Chatterjee, Partha (ed.) (1995) *Texts of Power: Emerging Disciplines in Colonial Bengal.* Minneapolis: University of Minnesota Press.

Chaudhuri, Sukanta (ed.) (1990) *Calcutta: The Living City,* vols 1 and 2. Calcutta: Oxford University Press.

Cohen, Lawrence (1995) 'The pleasures of castration: the postoperative status of hijras, jankhas and academics', in Paul Abramson and Steven D. Pinkerton (eds), *Sexual Nature, Sexual Culture.* Chicago: University of Chicago Press, pp. 276–304.

Conlon, Frank F. (1995) 'Dining out in Bombay,' in Carol Breckenridge (ed.), *Consuming Modernity: Public Culture in a South Asian World.* Minneapolis and London: University of Minnesota Press, pp. 90–127.

Coulson, Michael (1981) *Three Sanskrit Plays.* London: Penguin.

Dalmia, Vasudha (1997) *The Nationalization of Hindu Traditions: Bharatendu Harischandra and Nineteenth-Century Banaras.* Delhi: Oxford University Press.

Dalmia, Vasudha and Theo Damsteegt (eds) (1998) *Narrative Strategies: Essays on South Asian Literature and Film.* Leiden: Research School CNWS.

Das Gupta, Chidananda (1991) *The Painted Face.* New Delhi: Roli Books.

Dasi, Binodini (1998) *My Story* and *My Life as an Actress,* ed. and trans. Rimli Bhattacharya. New Delhi: Kali for Women.

Davis, Richard H. (1991) *Ritual in an Oscillating Universe: Worshipping Śiva in Medieval India.* Princeton: Princeton University Press.

Dé, Shobha (1988) *Socialite Evenings.* New Delhi: Penguin.

Dé, Shobha (1991) *Starry Nights.* New Delhi: Penguin.

Dé, Shobha (1992a) *Sisters.* New Delhi: Penguin.

Dé, Shobha (1992b) *Strange Obsession.* New Delhi: Penguin.

Dé, Shobha (1994a) *Sultry Days.* New Delhi: Penguin.

Dé, Shobha (1994b) *Shooting from the Hip: Selected Writings.* New Delhi: UBS.

Dé, Shobha (1995a) *Small Betrayals.* New Delhi: UBS.

Dé, Shobha (1995b) *Snapshots.* New Delhi: Penguin.

Dé, Shobha (1996) *Second Thoughts.* New Delhi: Penguin.

Dé, Shobha (1998) *Selective Memory: Stories from My Life.* New Delhi: Penguin.

De, Sushil Kumar (1959) *Ancient Indian Erotics and Erotic Literature*. Calcutta: Firma K. L. Mukhopadhyay.

Deep, Mohan (1998) *Simply Scandalous: Meena Kumari*. Bombay: Magna.

Derné, Steve (1995a) *Culture in Action: Family Life, Emotion, and Male Dominance in Banaras, India*. New York: State University of New York Press.

Derné, Steve (1995b) 'Market forces at work: religious themes in commercial Hindi films', in Lawrence Babb and Susan Wadley (eds), *Media and the Transformation of Religion in South Asia*. Philadelphia: University of Pennsylvania Press, pp. 191–216.

Desani, G. V. (1972) *All about H. Hatterr*. London: Penguin. [1948]

Devi, M. (1988) 'Draupadi', trans. with a foreword by G. C. Spivak, in G. C. Spivak (ed.), *In Other Worlds: Essays in Cultural Politics*. London: Routledge, pp. 179–96.

D'haen, Theo (ed.) (1998) *(Un)writing Empire*, Cross/cultures: Readings in the Post/colonial Literatures in English, number 30. Amsterdam and Atlanta: Rodopi.

Dharwadkar, Vinay (1993) 'Orientalism and the study of Indian literatures', in Carol A. Breckenridge and Peter van der Veer (eds), *Orientalism and the Postcolonial Predicament: Perspectives on South Asia*. Philadelphia: University of Pennsylvania Press, pp. 158–85.

Dickey, Sara (1993a) *Cinema and the Urban Poor in South India*. Cambridge: Cambridge University Press.

Dickey, Sara (1993b) 'The politics of adulation: cinema and the production of politicians in South India', *Journal of Asian Studies*, **52**(2), May: 340–72.

Dimock, Edward C. *et al.* (eds) (1974) *The Literatures of India: An Introduction*. Chicago: University of Chicago Press.

Dirks, N. B. (1995) '*The Home and the World*: the invention of modernity in colonial India', in R. Rosenstone (ed.), *Revisioning History: Film and the Construction of a New Past*. Princeton: Princeton University Press, pp. 44–63.

Dissanayake, Wimal and Malti Sahai (1992) *Sholay: A Cultural Reading*. New Delhi: Wiley Eastern.

Dobbin, Christine (1970) 'Competing elites in Bombay city politics in the mid-nineteenth century (1852–83)', in E. Leach and S. N. Mukherjee (eds), *Elites in South Asia*. Cambridge: Cambridge University Press, pp. 79–94.

Dobbin, Christine (1972) *Urban Leadership in Western India: Politics and Communities in Bombay City 1840–1885*. London: Oxford University Press.

Dundas, Paul (1992) *The Jains*. London: Routledge.

Dwivedi, Sharada and Rahul Mehrotra (1995) *Bombay: The Cities Within*. Bombay: Eminence Designs for IBHP.

Dwyer, Rachel (1991) 'Jalaram', in John Hinnells *et al.* (eds), *Who's Who in World Religion*. New York: Simon & Schuster, pp. 184–5.

Dwyer, Rachel (1994) 'Caste, religion and sect in Gujarat: followers of Vallabhacharya and Swaminarayan', in Roger Ballard (ed.), *Desh Pardesh: The South Asian Experience in Britain*. London: Hurst, pp. 165–90.

Dwyer, Rachel (1998a) ' "Starry nights": the novels of Shobha Dé', in Theo D'haen (ed.), *(Un)writing Empire*, Cross/cultures: Readings in the Post/colonial Literatures in English, number 30. Amsterdam and Atlanta: Rodopi, pp. 117–33.

Dwyer, Rachel (1998b) 'Hindi romantic cinema: Yash Chopra's *Kabhi Kabhie* and *Silsila*', *South Asia* **21**(1), June (Special volume: 'Translatings: images from India's half century): 181–212.

Dwyer, Rachel (1999) *The Poetics of Devotion: The Gujarati Lyrics of Dayaram*. London: Curzon.

Dwyer, Rachel [2000a] 'Shooting stars: the Indian film magazine *Stardust*', in Rachel

Dwyer and Christopher Pinney (eds), *Pleasure and the Nation: The Politics and Consumption of Popular Culture in India*. Delhi: Oxford University Press.

Dwyer, Rachel [2000b] '*Lamhe* and *Indian Summer*: the romantic cinema of Yash Chopra and the diaspora', in Philip Lutgendorf and Cory Creekmuir (eds), *Bollywood (Un)limited: Global Responses to Indian Cinema*.

Dwyer, Rachel and Christopher Pinney [2000] (eds) *Pleasure and the Nation: The Politics and Consumption of Popular Culture in India*. Delhi: Oxford University Press.

Dyer, Richard (1977) 'Entertainment and utopia', *Movie* 24, Spring: 2–13.

Dyer, Richard (1979) *Stars*. London: British Film Institute.

Dyer, Richard (1982) 'Don't look now: the male pin-up', *Screen* 23(3–4), Sept.–Oct.: 61–73.

Dyer, Richard (1986) *Heavenly Bodies: Film Stars and Society*. London: British Film Institute.

Dyer, Richard (1993) *The Matter of Images: Essays on Representations*. London: Routledge.

Dyer, Richard (1997) *White*. London: Routledge.

Earle, Peter (1989) *The Making of the English Middle Class: Business, Society and Family Life in London, 1660–1730*. London: Methuen.

Eck, Diana L. (1985) *Darsan: Seeing the Divine Image in India*, 2nd edn. Chambersburg, PA: Anima.

Eck, Diana L. and Françoise Mallison (eds) (1991) *Devotion Divine: Bhakti Traditions from the Regions of India. Studies in Honour of Charlotte Vaudeville*. Paris: EFEO.

Ellis, John (1992) *Visible Fictions: Cinema, Television, Video*. London: Routledge. [First edition 1982.]

Elsaesser, Thomas (1985) 'Tales of sound and fury: observations on the family melodrama', reprinted in Bill Nichols (ed.), *Movies and Methods*, vol. 2. Berkeley: University of California Press, pp. 165–89. [1972]

Engineer, Asghar Ali (1980) *The Bohras*. Ghaziabad: Vikas.

Erndl, Kathleen (1991) 'The mutilation of Surpanakha', in Paula Richman (ed.), *Many Ramayanas: The Diversity of a Narrative Tradition in South Asia*. Berkeley: University of California Press, pp. 67–113.

Evenson, Norma (1989) *The Indian Metropolis: A View Towards the West*. New Haven: Yale University Press.

Evenson, Norma (1995) 'An architectural hybrid', in Sujata Patel and Alice Thorner (eds), *Bombay: Mosaic of Modern Culture*. Bombay: Oxford University Press, pp. 165–81.

Ezekiel, Nissim (1989) 'From Very Indian poems in Indian English', in his *Collected Poems, 1952–88*. With an introduction by Gieve Patel. Delhi: Oxford University Press.

Fasold, Ralph (1984) *The Sociolinguistics of Society*. Oxford: Basil Blackwell.

Feldhaus, Anne (ed.) (1998) *Images of Women in Maharashtrian Society*. New York: State University of New York Press.

Ferguson, Harvie (1990) *The Science of Pleasure: Cosmos and Psyche in the Bourgeois World View*. London: Routledge.

Forbes, Geraldine (1996) *Women in Modern India*, The New Cambridge History of India, Volume IV.2. Cambridge: Cambridge University Press.

Foucault, Michel (1981) *A History of Sexuality*, vol. 1: *An Introduction*, trans. Robert Hurley. Harmondsworth: Penguin. [1976]

Foucault, Michel (1985) *A History of Sexuality*, vol. 2: *The Use of Pleasure*, trans. Robert Hurley. Harmondsworth: Penguin. [1984]

Foucault, Michel (1986) *A History of Sexuality*, vol. 3: *The Care of the Self*, trans. Robert Hurley. Harmondsworth: Penguin. [1984]

Fox, Richard G. (1985) *Lions of the Punjab: Culture in the Making*. Berkeley: University of California Press.

Freud, Sigmund (1953) 'Three essays on the theory of sexuality', in *The Standard Edition of the Complete Psychological Works of Sigmund Freud*, vol. 7. London: Hogarth Press and the Institute of Psycho-analysis. [1905]

Gandhi, M. K. (1982) *An Autobiography*, trans. M. Desai. Harmondsworth: Penguin.

Gandhi, Ramchandra (1992) *Sita's Kitchen: A Testimony of Faith and Enquiry*. New Delhi: Penguin.

Gandhy, Behroze and Rosie Thomas (1991) 'Three Indian film stars', in Christine Gledhill (ed.), *Stardom: Industry of Desire*. London: Routledge, pp. 107–31.

Gay, Peter (1986) *The Bourgeois Experience, Victoria to Freud*, vol. 2: *The Tender Passion*. Oxford: Oxford University Press.

Geetha, V. (1998) 'On bodily love and hurt', in Mary E. John and Janaki Nair (eds), *A Question of Silence? The Sexual Economies of Modern India*. New Delhi: Kali for Women, pp. 304–31.

Gerow, Edwin (1974) 'The *rasa* theory of Abhinavagupta and its application', in Edward Dimock *et al*. (eds), *The Literature of India: An Introduction*. Chicago: University of Chicago Press, pp. 216–27.

Giddens, Anthony (1992) *The Transformation of Intimacy: Sexuality, Love and Eroticism in Modern Societies*. Cambridge: Polity.

Gillion, K. L. (1968) *Ahmedabad: A Study in Indian Urban History*. Berkeley and Los Angeles: University of California Press.

Gledhill, Christine (ed.) (1987) *Home Is Where the Heart Is: Studies in Melodrama and the Woman's Film*. London: BFI Books.

Gledhill, Christine (1988) 'Pleasurable negotiations', in E. D. Pribram (ed.), *Female Spectators: Looking at Film and Television*. London: Verso, pp. 64–89.

Gledhill, Christine (ed.) (1991a) *Stardom: Industry of Desire*. London: Routledge.

Gledhill, Christine (1991b) 'Signs of melodrama', in *Stardom: Industry of Desire*. London: Routledge, pp. 207–32.

Gokhale, Shanta (1995) 'Rich theatre, poor theatre', in Sujata Patel and Alice Thorner (eds), *Bombay: Mosaic of Modern Culture*. Bombay: Oxford University Press, pp. 194–209.

Gopal, Priyamvada (1999) 'Of victims and vigilantes: the "Bandit Queen" controversy', in Rajeshwari Sunder Rajan (ed.), *Signposts: Gender Issues in Post-Independence India*. New Delhi: Kali for Women, pp. 292–330.

Gopalan, Lalitha (1997) 'Avenging women in Indian cinema', *Screen* 38(1), Spring: 42–59.

Guha-Thakurta, Tapti (1992a) 'The ideology of the "aesthetic": the purging of visual tastes and the campaign for a new Indian art in late nineteenth/early twentieth century Bengal', *Studies in History*, 8(2) n.s.: 237–81.

Guha-Thakurta, Tapti (1992b) *The Making of a New 'Indian' Art: Artists, Aesthetics and Nationalism in Bengal, c.1850–1920*. Cambridge: Cambridge University Press.

Haggard, Stephen (1988) 'Mass media and the visual arts in twentieth-century South Asia: Indian film posters, 1947–present', *South Asia Research*, 8(2), May: 78–88.

Hansen, Kathryn (1988) 'The Virangana in north Indian history, myth and popular culture', *Economic and Political Weekly*, 25(18) (April 30), WS: 25–33.

Hansen, Kathryn (1992) *Grounds for Play: The Nautanki Theatre of North India*. Berkeley: University of California Press.

Hansen, Kathryn [2000] 'The *Inder sabha* phenomenon: public theatre and consumption in Greater India (1853–1956)', in Rachel Dwyer and Christopher Pinney (eds), *Pleasure and the Nation: The Politics and Consumption of Popular Culture in India*. Delhi: Oxford University Press.

Hansen, Thomas Blom (1998) 'BJP and the politics of Hindutva in Maharashtra', in Thomas Blom Hansen and Christophe Jaffrelot, *The BJP and the Compulsions of Politics in India*. Delhi: Oxford University Press, pp. 121–62.

Hansen, Thomas Blom and Christophe Jaffrelot (1998) *The BJP and the Compulsions of Politics in India*. Delhi: Oxford University Press.

Hardiman, David (1987) *The Coming of the Devi: Adivasi Assertion in Western India*. Delhi: Oxford University Press.

Harris, Nigel (1995) 'Bombay in the global economy', in Sujata Patel and Alice Thorner (eds), *Bombay: Metaphor for Modern India*. Bombay: Oxford University Press, pp. 47–63.

Hawkins, Harriet (1990) *Classics and Trash: Traditions and Taboos in High Literature and Popular Modern Genres*. London: Harvester Wheatsheaf.

Hawley, J. S. (1981) *At Play with Krishna: Pilgrimage Dramas from Brindavan*. In association with Shrivatsa Goswami. Princeton: Princeton University Press.

Hawley, John S. (1983) *Krishna, the Butter Thief*. Princeton: Princeton University Press.

Hawley, J. S. (1991) 'A feast for Mount Govardhan', in Diana L. Eck and Françoise Mallison (eds), *Devotion Divine: Bhakti Traditions from the Regions of India. Studies in Honour of Charlotte Vaudeville*. Paris: EFEO, pp. 155–79.

Hawley, J. S. and M. Juergensmayer (eds and trans.) (1988) *Songs of the Saints of India*. New York: Oxford University Press.

Haynes, Douglas (1991) *Rhetoric and Ritual in Colonial India: The Shaping of a Public Culture in Surat City, 1852–1928*. Berkeley: University of California Press.

Haynes, Douglas and Gyan Prakash (eds) (1991) *Contesting Power: Resistance and Everyday Social Relations in South Asia*. Delhi: Oxford University Press.

Heifetz, Hank (1985) *The Origin of the Young God: Kalidasa's Kumarasambhava*. Translated, with annotation and an introduction. Berkeley: University of California Press.

Hein, N. (1972) *The Miracle Plays of Mathurā*. New Haven: Yale University Press.

Hermes, Joke (1995) *Reading Women's Magazines: An Analysis of Everyday Media*. Cambridge: Polity Press.

Heuzé, Gérard (1995) 'Cultural populism: the appeal of the Shiv Sena', in Sujata Patel and Alice Thorner (eds), *Bombay: Metaphor for Modern India*. Bombay: Oxford University Press, pp. 213–47.

Hiltebeitel, Alf (1988) *The Cult of Draupadi*, Volume I: *From Gingee to Kurukṣetra*. Chicago: University of Chicago Press.

Hiltebeitel, Alf (1991) 'The folklore of Draupadī: saris and hair', in Arjun Appadurai, Frank Korom and Margaret A. Mills (eds), *Gender, Genre and Power in South Asian Expressive Traditions*. Philadelphia: University of Pennsylvania Press, pp. 395–427.

Hinnells, John *et al.* (eds) (1991) *Who's Who in World Religion*. New York: Simon & Schuster.

Illouz, Eva (1997) *Consuming the Romantic Utopia: Love and the Cultural Contradictions of Capitalism*. Berkeley: University of California Press.

Inden, R. B. (1999) 'Transnational class, erotic arcadia and commercial utopia in Hindi films', in Christine Brosius and Melissa Butcher (eds), *Image Journeys: Audio-visual Media and Cultural Change in India*. New Delhi: Sage, pp. 41–66.

Inden, R. B. (2000) 'Entertainment, repeat viewers and the Hindi film *Jeet*'. Unpublished paper.

Jaffrelot, Christophe (1996) *The Hindu Nationalist Movement and Indian Politics, 1925 to the 1990s*. London: Hurst & Co.

Jaffrelot, Christophe [2000] *India's Silent Revolution: The Rise of the Lower Castes*. London: Hurst & Co.

James, Clive (1996) *The Silver Castle*. London: Jonathan Cape.

Jameson, Fredric (1989) 'Nostalgia for the present', *South Atlantic Quarterly*, **88**(2), Spring: 517–37.

Jameson, Fredric (1981) *The Political Unconscious*. London: Methuen.

Jayawardena, K. (1986) *Feminism and Nationalism in the Third World*. London: Zed Books. See esp. Chapter 6, 'Women, social reform and nationalism in India', pp. 73–108.

Jeffrey, Robin (1996) 'Ad-men of India', *Asia-Pacific Magazine*, 3, June: no page numbers.

Jeffrey, Robin [1999] *India's Newspaper Revolution: Capitalism, Technology and the Indian-Language Press, 1977–1997*. London: Hurst & Co.

Jennings, Luke (1993) *Breach Candy*. London: Hutchinson.

John, Mary E. (1998) 'Globalisation, sexuality and the visual field: issues and non-issues for cultural critique', in Mary E. John and Janaki Nair (eds), *A Question of Silence? The Sexual Economies of Modern India*. New Delhi: Kali for Women, pp. 368–96.

John, Mary E. and Janaki Nair (eds) (1998) *A Question of Silence? The Sexual Economies of Modern India*. New Delhi: Kali for Women.

Johnson, Gordon (1970) 'Chitpavan Brahmins and politics in western India in the late nineteenth and early twentieth centuries', in Edmund Leach and S. N. Mukherjee (eds), *Elites in South Asia*. Cambridge: Cambridge University Press, pp. 95–118.

Johnson, Gordon (1973) *Provincial Politics and Indian Nationalism: Bombay and the Indian National Congress, 1880–1915*. Cambridge: Cambridge University Press.

Jordens, J. T. F. (1997) *Dayananda Sarasvati: His Life and Ideas*. Delhi: Oxford University Press.

Joshi, V. C. (ed.) (1975) *Rammohun Roy and the Process of Modernization in India*. Delhi: Vikas Publishing House.

Kabir, Nasreen (ed.) (1985) *Les Stars du cinéma indien*. Paris: Centre Georges Pompidou/ Centre Nationale de la Cinematographie.

Kakar, Sudhir (1981a) *The Inner World: A Psycho-analytic Study of Childhood and Society in India*, 2nd edn. Delhi: Oxford University Press.

Kakar, Sudhir (1981b) 'The ties that bind: family relationships in the mythology of Indian cinema', *India International Quarterly*, Special Issue: 'Indian popular cinema: myth, meaning and metaphor', ed. Pradip Krishen, 8(1): 11–21.

Kakar, Sudhir (1989a) *Intimate Relations: Exploring Indian Sexuality*. New Delhi: Viking.

Kakar, Sudhir (1989b) 'The maternal-feminine in Indian psychoanalysis', *International Review of Psycho-analysis*, **16**. Reprinted in his (1997) *Culture and Psyche: Selected Essays*. Delhi: Oxford University Press, pp. 60–73.

Kakar, Sudhir (1990) *Shamans, Mystics, Doctors: A Psychological Inquiry into India and Its Healing Traditions*. Delhi: Oxford University Press.

Kakar, Sudhir (1997) *Culture and Psyche: Selected Essays*. Delhi: Oxford University Press.

Kakar, Sudhir and John M. Ross (1986) *Tales of Love, Sex and Danger*. Delhi: Oxford University Press.

Kale, M. R. (1934) *The Uttararamacharita of Bhavabhuti*. Edited with the commentary of Viraraghava, various readings, introduction, a literal English translation, exhaustive notes and appendices. Reprinted Delhi: Motilal Banarsidass.

Kannan, Lakshmi (1993) 'Draupadi', in A. Zide (ed.), *In Their Own Voice: The Penguin Anthology of Contemporary Indian Women Poets*. New Delhi: Penguin, pp. 97–8.

Kapur, Anuradha (1993) 'Deity to crusader: the changing iconography of Ram', in

Gyanendra Pandey (ed.), *Hindus and Others: The Question of Identity in India Today*. New Delhi: Penguin, pp. 79–109.

Karanjia, B. K. (1984) 'Le star-système', in Aruna Vasudeva and Philippe Lenglet (eds), *Les Cinémas indiens*, CinémAction, 30. Paris: Editions du Cerf, pp. 150–7.

Karlekar, Malavika (1991) *Voices from Within: Early Personal Narratives of Bengali Women*. Delhi: Oxford University Press.

Kasbekar, Asha [2000] 'Hidden pleasures: negotiating the myth of the female ideal in popular Hindi cinema', in Rachel Dwyer and Christopher Pinney (eds), *Pleasure and the Nation: The Politics and Consumption of Popular Culture in India*. Delhi: Oxford University Press.

Kautilya (1992) *The Arthashastra*. With an introduction and notes, trans. L. V. Rangarajan. New Delhi: Penguin.

Kaviraj, Sudipta (1995) *The Unhappy Consciousness: Bankimchandra Chattopadhyay and the Formation of Nationalist Discourse in India*. Delhi: Oxford University Press.

Khilnani, Sunil (1997) *The Idea of India*. London: Hamish Hamilton.

Khoroche, Peter (1992) 'The story of Śakuntalā from the *Mahābhārata*' (translation), in William Radice (ed.), *Śakuntalā*. London: The Folio Society, pp. 105–23.

Kinsley, David (1986) *Hindu Goddesses: Visions of the Divine Feminine in the Hindu Religious Tradition*. Delhi: Motilal Banarsidass.

Kirkham, P. and J. Thumim (eds) (1993) *You Tarzan: Masculinity, Movies and Men*. London: Lawrence and Wishart.

Kishwar, Madhu and Ruth Vanita (eds) (1984) *In Search of Answers: Indian Women's Voices from* Manushi. London: Zed Books.

Knox, T. M. (1952) *Hegel's Philosophy of Right*, trans. with notes by T. M. Knox. Oxford: Clarendon Press.

Kopf, David (1969) *British Orientalism and the Bengal Renaissance: The Dynamics of Indian Modernization 1773–1835*. Berkeley: University of California Press.

Kosambi, Meera (1995) 'British Bombay and Marathi Mumbai: some nineteenth century perceptions', in Sujata Patel and Alice Thorner (eds), *Bombay: Mosaic of Modern Culture*. Bombay: Oxford University Press, pp. 2–24.

Kosambi, Meera (1998) 'Child brides and child mothers: the age of consent controversy in Maharashtra as a conflict of perspectives on women', in Anne Feldhaus (ed.), *Images of Women in Maharashtrian Society*. New York: State University of New York Press, pp. 135–62.

Kothari, Komal (1989) 'Performers, gods, and heroes in the oral epics of Rajasthan', in Stuart H. Blackburn *et al.* (eds), *Oral Epics in India*. Berkeley: University of California Press, pp. 102–17.

Kristeva, Julia (1984) *Revolution in Poetic Language*, trans. Margaret Waller. New York: Columbia University Press. [1974]

Kristeva, Julia (1987) *Tales of Love*, translated by L. S. Roudiez. New York: Columbia University Press. (First published in French 1983)

Kumar, Radha (1993) *The History of Doing: An Illustrated Account of Movements for Women's Rights and Feminism in India, 1800–1990*. New Delhi: Kali for Women.

Kurtz, Stanley N. (1992) *All the Mothers Are One: Hindu India and the Reshaping of Psychoanalysis*. New York: Columbia University Press.

Laplace, Maria (1987) 'Producing and consuming the woman's film: discursive struggle in *Now, Voyager*', in Christine Gledhill (ed.), *Home Is Where the Heart Is: Studies in Melodrama and the Woman's Film*. London: BFI Books, pp. 138–66.

Leach, Edmund and S N. Mukherjee (eds) (1970) *Elites in South Asia*. Cambridge: Cambridge University Press.

Lebra-Chapman, Joyce (1986) *The Rani of Jhansi: A Study in Female Heroism in India*. Honolulu: University of Hawaii Press.

Leslie, I. Julia (1989) *The Perfect Wife: The Orthodox Hindu Woman According to the Stridharmapaddhati of Tryambakayajvan*. Delhi: Oxford University Press.

Lintas Media Guide India, 1995.

Luhrmann, Tanya M. (1996) *The Good Parsi: The Fate of a Colonial Elite in a Postcolonial Society*. Cambridge, Mass., and London: Harvard University Press.

Lukacs, George (1972) *Studies in European Realism: Balzac, Stendhal, Zola*. London: Merlin Press. [1935–9]

Lukacs, George (1978) 'Tagore's Gandhi novel: review of Rabindranath Tagore, *The Home and the World*', in his *Reviews and Articles*, trans. Peter Palmer. London: Merlin Press, pp. 8–11. [1922]

Lutgendorf, Philip (1991a) *The Life of a Text: Performing the* Ramcaritmanas *of Tulsidas*. Berkeley: University of California Press.

Lutgendorf, Philip (1991b) 'The secret life of Ramcandra of Ayodhya', in Paula Richman (ed.), *Many Ramayanas: The Diversity of a Narrative Tradition in South Asia*. Berkeley: University of California Press, pp. 217–34.

Lutgendorf, Philip (1995) 'All in the (Raghu) family: a video epic in cultural context', in Lawrence Babb and Susan Wadley (eds), *Media and the Transformation of Religion in South Asia*. Philadelphia: University of Pennsylvania Press, pp. 217–53.

Lutgendorf, Philip and Cory Creekmuir (eds) (forthcoming) *Bollywood (Un)limited: Global Responses to Indian Cinema*.

MacCabe, Colin (1985) *Theoretical Essays: Film, Linguistics, Literature*. Manchester: Manchester University Press.

MacCabe, Colin (ed.) (1986) *High Theory/Low Culture: Analysing Popular Television and Film*. Manchester: Manchester University Press.

McCracken, Ellen (1993) *Decoding Women's Magazines: From* Mademoiselle *to* Ms. New York: St Martin's Press.

McDonald, Ellen E. and Craig M. Stark (1969) *English Education, Nationalist Politics and Elite Groups in Maharashtra, 1885–1915*. Berkeley: University of California Press.

McRobbie, Angela (1991) *Feminism and Youth Culture: From 'Jackie' to 'Just Seventeen'*. London: Macmillan.

Mallison, Françoise (1995) 'Bombay as the intellectual capital of the Gujaratis', in Sujata Patel and Alice Thorner (eds), *Bombay: Mosaic of Modern Culture*. Bombay: Oxford University Press, pp. 76–87.

Mani, Lata (1998) *Contentious Traditions: The Debate on Sati in Colonial India*. Berkeley: University of California Press.

Mankekar, Purnima (1993a) 'Television tales and a woman's rage: a nationalist recasting of Draupadi's disrobing', *Public Culture*, 5: 469–92.

Mankekar, Purnima (1993b) 'National texts and gendered lives: an ethnography of television viewers in a north Indian city', *American Ethnologist*, 20(3): 543–63.

Manu (1991) *The Laws of Manu*. With an introduction and notes, trans. Wendy Doniger with Brian K. Smith. New Delhi: Penguin.

Manuel, Peter (1991) 'The popularization and transformation of the light-classical Urdu *ghazal*-song', in Arjun Appadurai *et al.* (eds), *Gender, Genre and Power in South Asian Expressive Traditions*. Philadelphia: University of Pennsylvania Press, pp. 347–61.

Manuel, Peter (1993) *Cassette Culture: Popular Music and Technology in North India.* Chicago: University of Chicago Press.

MARG and IRMB market research 'Where is the middle-class market?' Document.

Markovits, Claude (1995) 'Bombay as a business centre in the colonial period: a comparison with Calcutta', in Sujata Patel and Alice Thorner (eds), *Bombay: Metaphor for Modern India.* Bombay: Oxford University Press, pp. 26–46.

Masud, Iqbal (1986) 'Calcutta, romanticism and Guru Dutt', *Sunday Telegraph*, 13 July, pp. 5–9.

Matthews, David J., Christopher Shackle and Shahrukh Husain (1985) *Urdu Literature.* London: Third World Foundation for Social and Economic Studies.

Mayo, Katherine (1998) *Selections from* Mother India. Edited and with an introduction by Mrinalini Sinha. New Delhi: Kali for Women.

Meer, Amina (1995) *Bombay Talkie.* London: Serpent's Tail.

Mehrotra, Arvind Krishna (1991) *The Absent Traveller: Prakrit Love Poetry from the Gathasaptasati of Satavahana Hala.* Delhi: Ravi Dayal.

Merchant, Khozem (1996) *The Television Revolution: India's New Information Order.* Green College, Oxford, Reuter Foundation Paper 42.

Metcalf, Barbara Daly (1990) *Perfecting Women: Maulana Ashraf 'Ali Thanawi's* Bihishti Zewar*: A Partial Translation with Commentary.* Berkeley: University of California Press.

Miller, Barbara Stoler (1978) *The Hermit and the Love-Thief.* New York: Columbia University Press.

Miller, Barbara Stoler (1984) *Gītagovinda of Jayadeva. Love Song of the Dark Lord.* Delhi: Motilal Banarsidass. (First published 1977)

Miller, Daniel (ed.) (1995) *Acknowledging Consumption: A Review of New Studies.* London: Routledge.

Mines, Mattison (1994) *Public Faces, Private Voices: Community and Individuality in South Asia.* Berkeley: University of California Press.

Mishra, Pankaj (1995) *Butter Chicken in Ludhiana: Travels in Small Town India.* New Delhi: Penguin India.

Mishra, Vijay (1985) 'Towards a theoretical critique of Bombay cinema', *Screen*, 26(3–4): 133–46.

Mishra, Vijay, Peter Jeffery and Brian Shoesmith (1989) 'The actor as parallel text in Bombay cinema', *Quarterly Review of Film and Video*, 11: 49–68.

Misra, B. B. (1961) *The Indian Middle Classes: Their Growth in Modern Times.* Delhi: Oxford University Press.

Mitra, Ananda (1993) *Television and Popular Culture in India: A Study of the Mahabharat.* New Delhi: Sage.

Mitter, Sara S. (1991) *Dharma's Daughters: Contemporary Indian Women and Hindu Culture.* New Brunswick, NJ: Rutgers University Press.

Modleski, Tania (1982) *Loving with a Vengeance: Mass-produced Fantasies for Women.* London: Routledge.

Mohamed, Khalid (1985) 'Introduction', in Nasreen Kabir (ed.), *Les Stars du cinéma indien.* Paris: Centre Georges Pompidou/Centre Nationale de la Cinematographie, pp. 14–51.

Mohamed, Khalid (1993) 'In another limelight', in Dileep Padgaonkar (ed.), *When Bombay Burned: Reportage and Comments on the Riots and Blasts from 'The Times of India'.* New Delhi: UBSPD, pp. 276–90.

Monteiro, Anjali (1998) 'Official television and unofficial fabrications of the self: the spectator as subject', in Ashis Nandy (ed.), *The Secret Politics of Our Desires: Innocence, Culpability and Popular Cinema.* London: Zed Books, pp. 157–207.

Muhammad Hadi (Mirza Mohammad Hadi Ruswa) (1993) *Umrao Jan Ada: Courtesan of Lucknow*, trans. Khushwant Singh and M. A. Husaini. Hyderabad: Disha Books by arrangement with Sangam Books. [1899]

Mukerji, C. and M. Schudson (eds) (1991) *Rethinking Popular Culture: Contemporary Perspectives in Cultural Studies*. Berkeley: University of California Press.

Mukherjee, M. (1985) *Realism and Reality: The Novel and Society in India*. Delhi: Oxford University Press.

Mukta, Parita (1997) *Upholding the Common Life: The Community of Mirabai*. Delhi: Oxford University Press.

Mulvey, Laura (1975) 'Visual pleasure and narrative cinema', *Screen*, **16**(3): 6–18.

Mulvey, Laura (1981) 'Afterthoughts on "Visual pleasure and narrative cinema" inspired by King Vidor's *Duel in the Sun* (1946)', *Framework*, **15/16/17**: 12–15.

Naik, J. V. (1995) 'The seed period of Bombay's intellectual life: 1822–1857', in Sujata Patel and Alice Thorner (eds), *Bombay: Mosaic of Modern Culture*. Bombay: Oxford University Press, pp. 61–75.

Naipaul, V. S. (1977) *India: A Wounded Civilization*. London: Penguin.

Naipaul, V. S. (1990) *India: A Million Mutinies Now!* London: Heinemann.

Nandy, A. (1988) *The Intimate Enemy: Loss and Recovery of Self under Colonialism*. Delhi: Oxford University Press. [1983]

Nandy, Ashis (1989) *The Tao of Cricket: On Games of Destiny and the Destiny of Games*. New York: Viking.

Nandy, Ashis (1990a) 'Satyajit Ray's secret guide to exquisite murders', *East–West Film Journal*, **4**(2): 14–37.

Nandy, Ashis (1990b) 'Woman versus womanliness in India: an essay in cultural and political psychology', in *At the Edge of Psychology*. Delhi: Oxford University Press, pp. 32–46.

Nandy, Ashis (1993) 'How "Indian" is Ray?' *Cinemaya*, **20**: 40–5.

Nandy, Ashis (1994) *The Illegitimacy of Nationalism: Rabindranath Tagore and the Politics of Self*. Delhi: Oxford University Press.

Nandy, Ashis (1995a) 'An intelligent critic's guide to the Indian cinema', in *The Savage Freud and Other Essays on Possible and Retrievable Selves*. Delhi: Oxford University Press, pp. 196–236.

Nandy, Ashis (1995b) 'The discreet charms of Indian terrorism', in *The Savage Freud and Other Essays on Possible and Retrievable Selves*. Delhi: Oxford University Press, pp. 1–31.

Nandy, Ashis (ed.) (1998) *The Secret Politics of Our Desires: Innocence, Culpability and Popular Cinema*. London: Zed Books.

Nandy, Ashis [2000] 'Invitation to an antique death: the journey of Pramathesh Barua as the origin of the terribly effeminate, maudlin, self-destructive heroes of Indian cinema', in Rachel Dwyer and Christopher Pinney (eds), *Pleasure and the Nation: The Politics and Consumption of Popular Culture in India*. Delhi: Oxford University Press.

Narayana Rao (1991) 'A Ramayana of their own: women's oral tradition in Telugu', in Paula Richman (ed.), *Many Ramayanas: The Diversity of a Narrative Tradition in South Asia*. Berkeley: University of California Press, pp. 114–36.

Neale, Steve (1986) 'Melodrama and tears', *Screen*, **27**(6): 6–22.

Nehru, J. (1989) *The Discovery of India*. New Delhi: Jawaharlal Nehru Memorial Fund/ Oxford University Press. [1946]

Nelson, Cary and Lawrence Grossberg (eds) (1988) *Marxism and the Interpretation of Culture*. Basingstoke: Macmillan Education.

Nichols, Bill (1985) *Movies and Methods*, vol. 2. Berkeley: University of California Press.

Niranjana, Tejaswini, P. Sudhir and Vivek Dhareshwar (eds) (1993) *Interrogating Modernity: Culture and Colonialism in India*. Calcutta: Seagull.

Nowell-Smith, G. (ed.) (1996) *The Oxford History of World Cinema*. Oxford: Oxford University Press.

O'Flaherty, Wendy Doniger (1973) *Asceticism and Eroticism in the Mythology of Śiva*. London: Oxford University Press.

O'Flaherty, Wendy Doniger (1980) *Women, Androgynes, and Other Mythical Beasts*. Chicago: University of Chicago Press.

O'Flaherty, Wendy Doniger (trans. and ed.) (1981) *The Rig Veda: An Anthology*. One hundred and eight hymns, selected, translated and annotated by Wendy Doniger O'Flaherty. London: Penguin.

O'Hanlon, Rosalind (1985) *Caste, Conflict and Ideology: Mahatma Jotirao Phule and Low Caste Protest in Nineteenth-Century Western India*. Cambridge: Cambridge University Press.

O'Hanlon, Rosalind (1994) *A Comparison between Women and Men: Tarabai Shinde and the Critique of Gender Relations in Colonial India*. Madras: Oxford University Press.

Oldenburg, Veena Talwar (1989) *The Making of Colonial Lucknow 1856–1877*. Delhi: Oxford University Press.

Oldenburg, Veena Talwar (1991) 'Lifestyle as resistance: the case of the courtesans of Lucknow', in Douglas Haynes and Gyan Prakash (eds), *Contesting Power: Resistance and Everyday Social Relations in South Asia*. Delhi: Oxford University Press, pp. 26–31.

Orsini, Francesca (1996) 'The Hindi Public Sphere, 1920–1940'. Unpublished PhD thesis, University of London.

Orsini, Francesca (1998) 'Reading a social romance: *Cand hasīm ke khutūt*', in Vasudha Dalmia and Theo Damsteegt (eds), *Narrative Strategies: Essays on South Asian Literature and Film*. Leiden: Research School CNWS, pp. 185–210.

Orsini, Francesca (2000) *The Hindi Public Sphere: Language, Literature and Nationalism*. Delhi: Oxford University Press.

Ortega y Gasset, José (1959) *On Love ... Aspects of a Single Theme*. Translated from the Spanish by Toby Talbot. London: Jonathan Cape.

Padgaonkar, Dileep (ed.) (1993) *When Bombay Burned: Reportage and Comments on the Riots and Blasts from 'The Times of India'*. New Delhi: UBSPD.

Pandey, Gyanendra (ed.) (1993) *Hindus and Others: The Question of Identity in India Today*. New Delhi: Penguin.

Pandian, M. S. S. (1992) *The Image Trap*. Delhi: Sage.

Parekh, Bhikhu (1989a) *Gandhi's Political Philosophy: A Critical Examination*. Basingstoke: Macmillan.

Parekh, Bhikhu (1989b) *Colonialism, Tradition and Reform: An Analysis of Gandhi's Political Discourse*. New Delhi: Sage.

Patel, Sujata (1995) 'Bombay's urban predicament', in Sujata Patel and Alice Thorner (eds), *Bombay: Metaphor for Modern India*. Bombay: Oxford University Press, pp. xi–xxxiii.

Patel, Sujata and Alice Thorner (eds) (1995a) *Bombay: Metaphor for Modern India*. Bombay: Oxford University Press.

Patel, Sujata and Alice Thorner (eds) (1995b) *Bombay: Mosaic of Modern Culture*. Bombay: Oxford University Press.

Paz, Octavio (1996) *The Double Flame: Essays on Love and Eroticism*. London: Harvill Press.

Pfleiderer, Beatrix and Lothar Lutze (1985) *The Hindi Film: Agent and Re-agent of Cultural Change*. New Delhi: Manohar.

Phillips, Adam (1993) *On Kissing, Tickling and Being Bored*. London: Faber and Faber.

Phillips, Adam (1994) *On Flirtation*. London: Faber and Faber.

Pinney, Christopher (1997) *Camera Indica: The Social Life of Indian Photographs*. London: Reaktion Books.

Pinney, Christopher [2000] 'Public, popular and other cultures', in Rachel Dwyer and Christopher Pinney (eds), *Pleasure and the Nation: The Politics and Consumption of Popular Culture in India*. Delhi: Oxford University Press.

Prasad, M. Madhava (1996) 'Formal into real subsumption? Signs of ideological re-form in two recent films', *Journal of Arts and Ideas*, **29** (January 1996): 27–43.

Prasad, M. Madhava (1998) *Ideology of the Hindi Film: A Historical Construction*. Delhi: Oxford University Press.

Pribram, E. D. (ed.) (1988) *Female Spectators: Looking at Film and Television*. London: Verso.

Pritchett, Frances (1991) *The Romance Tradition in Urdu: Adventures from the Dastan of Amir Hamzah*. New York: Columbia University Press.

Pritchett, Frances (1994) *Nets of Awareness: Urdu Poetry and Its Critics*. Berkeley: University of California Press.

Purushottam, Agarwal (1995) 'Savarkar, Surat and Draupadi: legitimising rape as a political weapon', in Tanika Sarkar and Urvashi Butalia (eds), *Women and the Hindu Right: A Collection of Essays*. New Delhi: Kali for Women, pp. 29–57.

Qureshi, Omar (1996) 'Twentieth-century Urdu literature', in Nalini Natarajan (ed.), *Handbook of Twentieth-Century Literatures of India*. Westport, Connecticut: Greenwood Press, pp. 329–62.

Radice, William (ed.) (1992) *Śakuntalā*. London: The Folio Society.

Radway, Janice (1987) *Reading the Romance: Women, Patriarchy and Popular Literature*. London: Verso.

Radway, Janice (1991) 'Interpretive communities and variable literacies: the functions of romance reading', in C. Mukerji and M. Schudson (eds), *Rethinking Popular Culture: Contemporary Perspectives in Cultural Studies*. Berkeley: University of California Press, pp. 465–86.

Raheja, Gloria Goodwin and Ann Grodzins Gold (1994) *Listen to the Heron's Words: Reimagining Gender and Kinship in a North Indian Village*. Berkeley: University of California Press.

Rajadhyaksha, Ashish (1987) 'The Phalke era', *Journal of Arts and Ideas*, **14–15**: 47–75. Reprinted in Tejaswini Niranjana, P. Sudhir and Vivek Dhareshwar (eds) (1993), *Interrogating Modernity: Culture and Colonialism in India*. Calcutta: Seagull, pp. 47–82.

Rajadhyaksha, Ashish (1996a) 'Indian cinema: origins to independence', in G. Nowell-Smith (ed.), *The Oxford History of World Cinema*. Oxford: Oxford University Press, pp. 398–409.

Rajadhyaksha, Ashish (1996b) 'India: filming the nation', in G. Nowell-Smith (ed.), *The Oxford History of World Cinema*. Oxford: Oxford University Press, pp. 678–89.

Rajadhyaksha, Ashish (1996c) 'Strange attractions', *Sight and Sound*, **6**(8): 28–31.

Rajadhyaksha, Ashish and Paul Willemen (1994) *An Encyclopaedia of Indian Cinema*. London: British Film Institute.

Rajgopal, Arvind (1999) 'Thinking about the new Indian middle class: gender advertising and politics in an age of globalization', in R. Sunder Rajan (ed.), *Signposts*. New Delhi: Kali for Women, pp. 57–100.

Ramanujan, A. K. (1994) *The Interior Landscape: Love Poems from a Classical Tamil Anthology*. Delhi: Oxford University Press (first published 1967).

Ramasubban, Radhika and Crook, Nigel (1995) 'Spatial patterns of health and mortality', in Sujata Patel and Alice Thorner (eds), *Bombay: Metaphor for Modern India*. Bombay: Oxford University Press, pp. 143–69.

Rao, Anupama (1999) 'Understanding Sirasgaon: notes towards conceptualising the role of law, caste and gender in a case of "atrocity" ', in Rajeshwar Sunder Rajan (ed.), *Signposts: Gender Issues in Post-Independence India*. New Delhi: Kali for Women, pp. 204–47.

Rao, Raja (1989) *Kanthapura*, 2nd edn. Delhi: Oxford University Press. [1938]

Raval, S. C. (ed.) (1953) *Dayārām-rassudhā (rās-garbī-garbo and gīto)*. Bombay: N. M. Tripathi.

Ray, Rajat (1975) 'Introduction', in V. C. Joshi (ed.), *Rammohun Roy and the Process of Modernization in India*. Delhi: Vikas Publishing House, pp. 1–20.

Ray, Satyajit (1976) *Our Films, Their Films*. Hyderabad: Orient Longman.

Richman, Paula (ed.) (1991a) *Many Ramayanas: The Diversity of a Narrative Tradition in South Asia*. Berkeley: University of California Press.

Richman, Paula (1991b) 'E. V. Ramasami's reading of the Ramayana', in *Many Ramayanas: The Diversity of a Narrative Tradition in South Asia*. Berkeley: University of California Press.

Robinson, Andrew (1989) *Satyajit Ray: The Inner Eye*. London: André Deutsch.

Robison, Richard and David S. G. Goodman (eds) (1996) *The New Rich in Asia: Mobile Phones, McDonald's and Middle-Class Revolution*. London: Routledge.

Rosenstone, R. (ed.) (1995) *Revisioning History: Film and the Construction of a New Past*. Princeton: Princeton University Press.

Roy, Kumkum (1998) 'Unravelling the *Kamasutra*', in Mary E. John and Janaki Nair (eds), *A Question of Silence? The Sexual Economies of Modern India*. New Delhi: Kali for Women, pp. 52–76.

Roy, Tapti (1995) 'Disciplining the printed text: colonial and nationalist surveillance of Bengali literature', in Partha Chatterjee (ed.), *Texts of Power: Emerging Disciplines in Colonial Bengal*. Minneapolis: University of Minnesota Press, pp. 30–62.

Rubin, David (1998) *The Return of Sarasvati: Four Hindi Poets*. Delhi: Oxford University Press.

Rushdie, Salman (1982) *Midnight's Children*. London: Picador. [1981]

Rushdie, Salman (1995) *The Moor's Last Sigh*. London: Cape.

Rushdie, Salman (1999) *The Ground Beneath Her Feet*. London: Jonathan Cape.

Sadiq, Muhammad (1995) *A History of Urdu Literature*, 2nd edn. Delhi: Oxford University Press. [1964]

Sangari, Kumkum (1990) 'Mirabai and the spiritual economy of *bhakti*', parts 1 and 2, *Economic and Political Weekly*, 25(27) (July 7): 1464–75; 25(28) (July 14): 1537–52.

Sangari, Kumkum and Sudesh Vaid (1990) *Recasting Women: Essays in Indian Colonial History*. New Brunswick, NJ: Rutgers University Press.

Sardesai, Rajdeep (ed.) (1993) 'The great betrayal', in Dileep Padgaonkar (ed.), *When Bombay Burned: Reportage and Comments on the Riots and Blasts from 'The Times of India'*. New Delhi: UBSPD, pp. 179–210.

Sarkar, Sumit (1983) *Modern India: 1885–1947*. Basingstoke: Macmillan.

Sarkar, Tanika and Urvashi Butalia (eds) (1995) *Women and the Hindu Right: A Collection of Essays*. New Delhi: Kali for Women.

Seabrook, Jeremy (1999) *Love in a Different Climate: Men Who Have Sex with Men in India*. London: Verso.

Seiler, Lars-Winfried (1993) 'The image of the female body in commercial Indian films', *Internationales Asienforum*, **24**(3–4): 229–50.

Sen, Mala (1991) *India's Bandit Queen: The True Story of Phoolan Devi*. London: Harvill.

Seth, Vikram (1993) *A Suitable Boy*. London: Orion.

Shackle, Christopher and Zawahir Moir (1992) *Ismaili Hymns from South Asia: An Introduction to the Ginans*. SOAS South Asian Texts No. 3. London: School of Oriental and African Studies.

Shackle, Christopher and Rupert Snell (1990) *Hindi and Urdu since 1800: A Common Reader*. London: School of Oriental and African Studies, pp. 1–20.

Sharma, Ashwini (1993) 'Blood, sweat and tears: Amitabh Bachchan, urban demi-god', in P. Kirkham and J. Thumim (eds), *You Tarzan: Masculinity, Movies and Men*. London: Lawrence and Wishart, pp. 167–80.

Sharma, Kalpana (1995) 'Chronicle of a riot foretold', in Sujata Patel and Alice Thorner (eds), *Bombay: Metaphor for Modern India*. Bombay: Oxford University Press, pp. 268–86.

Sheth, D. L. (1995) 'The great language debate: politics of metropolitan versus vernacular India', in Upendra Baxi and Bhikhu Parekh (eds), *Crisis and Change in Contemporary India*. New Delhi: Sage, pp. 187–215.

Shukla, Sonal (1995) 'Gujarati cultural revivalism', in Sujata Patel and Alice Thorner (eds), *Bombay: Mosaic of Modern Culture*. Bombay: Oxford University Press, pp. 88–98.

Siegel, L. (1978, 1990) *Sacred and Profane Dimensions of Love in Indian Traditions as Exemplified in the* Gītagovinda *of Jayadeva*. Delhi: Oxford University Press.

Siegel, Lee (1983) *Fires of Love: Waters of Peace: Passion and Renunciation in Indian Culture*. Honolulu: University of Hawaii Press.

Singer, Irving (1984a) *The Nature of Love*, vol. 1: *From Plato to Luther*. Chicago: University of Chicago Press.

Singer, Irving (1984b) *The Nature of Love*, vol. 2: *Courtly and Romantic*. Chicago: University of Chicago Press.

Singer, Irving (1987) *The Nature of Love*, vol. 3: *The Modern World*. Chicago: University of Chicago Press.

Singer, Irving (1994) *The Pursuit of Love*. Baltimore: Johns Hopkins University Press.

Singh, Amita Tyagi and Patricia Uberoi (1994) 'Learning to "adjust": conjugal relations in Indian popular fiction', *Indian Journal of Gender Studies*, 1(1): 91–120.

Sinha, Mrinalini (1995) *Colonial Masculinity: The 'Manly Englishman' and the 'Effeminate Bengali' in the Late Nineteenth Century*. Manchester: Manchester University Press.

Smith, Murray (1995) *Engaging Characters: Fiction, Emotion, and the Cinema*. Oxford: Clarendon Press.

Sontag, Susan (1983) 'Notes on camp', reprinted in *A Susan Sontag Reader*. London: Penguin, pp. 105–19. [1964]

Spacks, Patricia Meyer (1985) *Gossip*. New York: Alfred A. Knopf.

Spivak, G. C. (ed.) (1988a) *In Other Worlds: Essays in Cultural Politics*. London: Routledge.

Spivak, Gayatri C. (1988b) 'Can the subaltern speak?', in Cary Nelson and Lawrence Grossberg (eds), *Marxism and the Interpretation of Culture*. Basingstoke: Macmillan Education, pp. 271–313.

Srivatsan, R. (1991) 'Looking at films hoardings: labour, gender, subjectivity and everyday life in India', *Public Culture*, **4**(1)(Fall): 1–23.

Stacey, Jackie (1993) *Star Gazing: Hollywood Cinema and Female Spectatorship*. London: Routledge.

Stern, Robert W. (1993) *Changing India: Bourgeois Revolution on the Subcontinent.* Cambridge: Cambridge University Press.

Sunder Rajan, Rajeshwari (1992) *The Lie of the Land.* Delhi: Oxford University Press.

Sunder Rajan, Rajeshwari (1993) *Real and Imagined Women: Gender, Culture and Postcolonialism.* London: Routledge.

Sunder Rajan, Rajeshwari (ed.) (1999) *Signposts: Gender Issues in Post-Independence India.* New Delhi: Kali for Women.

Tagore, Rabindranath (1985) *Home and the World*, trans. Surendranath Tagore. London: Penguin. [1916]

Tarlo, Emma (1996) *Clothing Matters: Dress and Identity in India.* London: Hurst & Co.

Thadani, Giti (1996) *Sakhiyani: Lesbian Desire in Ancient and Modern India.* London: Cassell.

Thapar, Meenakshi (ed.) (1997) *Embodiment: Essays on Gender and Identity.* Delhi: Oxford University Press.

Tharoor, Shashi (1994) *Showbusiness.* London: Picador.

Tharu, Susie and K. Lalita (eds) (1995a) *Women Writing in India: 600 BC to the Present*, vol. 1: *600 BC to the Early 20th Century.* Delhi: Oxford University Press.

Tharu, Susie and K. Lalita (eds) (1995b) *Women Writing in India: 600 BC to the Present*, vol. 2: *The 20th Century.* Delhi: Oxford University Press.

Thomas, Rosie (1985) 'Indian cinema: pleasures and popularity: an introduction', *Screen*, 26(3–4): 61–131.

Thomas, Rosie (1989) 'Sanctity and scandal: the mythologization of Mother India', *Quarterly Review of Film and Video*, 11: 11–30.

Thomas, Rosie (1995) 'Melodrama and the negotiation of morality in mainstream Hindi film', in Carol Breckenridge (ed.), *Consuming Modernity: Public Culture in a South Asian World.* Minneapolis and London: University of Minnesota Press, pp. 157–82.

Tilak, Lashmibai (1998) *I Follow After: An Autobiography*, trans. E. Josephine Inkster (written in Marathi 1934–7). Delhi: Oxford University Press.

Timberg, Thomas (1978) *The Marwaris: From Traders to Industrialists.* New Delhi: Vikas.

Tindall, Gillian (1982) *City of Gold: The Biography of Bombay.* London: Temple Smith.

Toomey, P. M. (1990) 'Krishna's consuming passions: food as metaphor and metonym for emotion at Mount Govardhan', in O. M. Lynch (ed.), *Divine Passions: The Social Construction of Emotion in India.* Delhi: Oxford University Press, pp. 157–81.

Toomey, P. M. (1992) 'Mountain of food, mountain of love: ritual inversion in the *annakūta* feast at Mount Govardhan', in R. Skhare (ed.), *The Eternal Food: Gastronomic Ideas and Experiences of Hindus and Buddhists.* New York: State University of New York Press, pp. 117–45.

Turner, Bryan S. (1996) *The Body and Society: Explorations in Social Theory*, 2nd edn. London: Sage.

Uberoi, Patricia (ed.) (1993) *Family, Kinship and Marriage in India.* Delhi: Oxford University Press.

Uberoi, Patricia (ed.) (1996) *Social Reform, Sexuality and the State.* New Delhi: Sage.

Uberoi, Patricia (1997) 'Dharma and desire, freedom and destiny: rescripting the man–woman relationship in popular Hindi cinema', in Meenakshi Thapar (ed.), *Embodiment: Essays on Gender and Identity.* Delhi: Oxford University Press, pp. 145–71.

Uberoi, Patricia (1998) 'The diaspora comes home: disciplining desire in *DDLJ*', *Contributions to Indian Sociology*, n.s. 32(2): 305–36.

Uberoi, Patricia [2000] 'Imagining the family: an ethnography of viewing "Hum aapke hain koun ...!"', in Rachel Dwyer and Christopher Pinney (eds), *Pleasure and the Nation: The Politics and Consumption of Popular Culture in India*. Delhi: Oxford University Press.

Vaidehi (Janaki Srinivas Murthy) (1995) 'Shakuntale yondige kaleda aparahna [An afternoon with Shakuntala]', trans. from Kannada by Jaswant Jadav, in Susie Tharu and K. Lalita (eds), *Women Writing in India: 600 BC to the Present*, vol. 2: *The 20th Century*. Delhi: Oxford University Press, pp. 535–47.

Valicha, Kishore (1988) *The Moving Image: A Study of Indian Cinema*. London: Sangam.

van der Vate, J. (1981) *Romantic Love: A Philosophical Inquiry*. London: Pennsylvania State University Press.

van der Veer, Peter (1994) *Religious Nationalism: Hindus and Muslims in India*. Berkeley: University of California Press.

Vanaik, Achin (1990) *The Painful Transition: Bourgeois Democracy in India*. London: Verso.

Varia, Kush (1999) 'Celebrating Sexualities in Indian Cinema'. Programme notes for Bombay Exposé, special event at 13th London lesbian and gay film festival. London: British Film Institute.

Varma, Pavan K. (1998) *The Great Indian Middle Class*. New Delhi: Viking.

Vasudeva, Aruna and Philipe Lenglet (eds) (1984) *Les Cinémas indiens*, CinémAction 30. Paris: Editions du Cerf.

Vasudevan, Ravi (1989) 'The melodramatic mode and commercial Hindi cinema', *Screen*, 30(3): 29–50.

Vasudevan, Ravi (1993) 'Shifting codes, dissolving identities: the Hindi social film of the 1950s as popular culture', *Journal of Arts and Ideas*: 23–4, 51–79 (plus appendix).

Vasudevan, Ravi (1998) 'Sexuality and the film apparatus: continuity, non-continuity and discontinuity in Bombay cinema', in Mary E. John and Janaki Nair (eds), *A Question of Silence? The Sexual Economies of Modern India*. New Delhi: Kali for Women, pp. 192–215.

Viswanathan, G. (1989) *Masks of Conquest: Literary Study and British Rule in India*. London: Faber and Faber.

Weeks, Jeffrey (1980) *Sexuality*. London: Routledge.

Whitehead, Judy (1996) 'Modernising the motherhood archetype: public health models and the Child Marriage Restraint Act of 1929', in Patricia Uberoi (ed.), *Social Reform, Sexuality and the State*. New Delhi: Sage, pp. 187–209.

Windsor, David A. (1998) 'Nargis, Ray, Rushdie and the real', *South Asia*, 21(1), June (Special volume: 'Translatings: Images from India's Half Century'): 229–42.

Winship, Janice (1987) *Inside Women's Magazines*. London: Pandora.

Wujastyk, Dominic (1998) *The Roots of Ayurveda*. New Delhi: Penguin.

Young, Robert J. C. (1995) *Colonial Desire: Hybridity in Theory, Culture and Race*. London: Routledge.

Zide, A. (ed.) (1993) *In Their Own Voice: The Penguin Anthology of Contemporary Indian Women Poets*. New Delhi: Penguin.

Index